States of Injury

States of Injury

POWER AND FREEDOM IN
LATE MODERNITY

Wendy Brown

PRINCETON UNIVERSITY PRESS
PRINCETON, NEW JERSEY

Copyright © 1995 by Princeton University Press
Published by Princeton University Press, 41 William Street,
Princeton, New Jersey 08540
In the United Kingdom: Princeton University Press,
Chichester, West Sussex

All Rights Reserved

Library of Congress Cataloging-in-Publication Data

Brown, Wendy.
States of injury : power and freedom in late modernity /
Wendy Brown.
p.   cm.
Includes index.
ISBN 0-691-02990-3 (cloth : acid-free paper). — ISBN 0-691-02989-X
(pbk. : acid-free paper)
1. Political science—Philosophy.   2. Power (Social sciences).
3. Culture.   4. Feminist theory.   5. Liberty.   I. Title.
JA74.B724   1995   303.3—dc20   94-24068

This book has been composed in Bembo

Princeton University Press books are printed on acid-free paper
and meet the guidelines for permanence and durability of the
Committee on Production Guidelines for Book Longevity of the
Council on Library Resources

Printed in the United States of America
10 9 8 7 6 5 4 3 2 1
10 9 8 7 6 5 4 3 2 1
(Pbk.)

For Sheldon S. Wolin

Contents

Preface

THESE STUDIES consider how certain well-intentioned contemporary political projects and theoretical postures inadvertently redraw the very configurations and effects of power that they seek to vanquish. The topics explored in the course of this consideration include the liberal, capitalist, and disciplinary origins of the force of *ressentiment* in late modern political and theoretical discourse; the gendered characteristics of late modern state power and the paradoxical nature of appeals to the state for gender justice; the convergences of juridical and disciplinary power in contemporary efforts to procure rights along lines of politicized identity; and the gendered sexuality of liberal political discourse.

If the immediate provocation for each essay is a specific problem in contemporary political thought or activity, taken together these provocations provide an occasion of another sort: reflection on the present-day value of some of the last two centuries' most compelling theoretical critiques of modern political life. Thus, the chapters on identity and morality in contemporary intellectual and political formations critically engage Nietzsche; the chapters on rights and liberalism reconsider Marx's critique of liberalism and Foucault's critique of regulation through individuation; the chapters concerned with state power are in dialogue with Weber, Foucault, and liberal thought; and the early Baudrillard is engaged to reflect on Catharine MacKinnon's adaptation of Marx for a theory of gender.

Such a schema of the book's objectives, however, involves a trick of retrospection that lends coherence to contingency when, in fact, like many works written in the dizzying intellectual and political pace of the late twentieth century, this one started and finished as quite different projects. Conceived in the mid-1980s as a critical feminist theory of late modern state power (now chapter 7), it quickly outgrew the confines established both by gender as a governing political concern and by the state as a delimitable domain of political power. From the outset, my interest in developing a feminist critique of the state was animated less by intrinsic fascination with the state than by concern over the potential dilution of emancipatory political aims entailed in feminism's turn to the state to adjudicate or redress practices of male dominance. Nor was my worry about such dilution limited to the politics of gender but rather engaged a larger question: What are the perils of pursuing emancipatory political aims within largely repressive, regulatory, and depoliticizing institutions that themselves carry elements of the regime (e.g., masculine dominance) whose subversion is being sought? Discerning "the man in the state" was thus a way to concentrate such a query on the problem of feminist political reform.

There was a certain disingenuousness, however, even to this formulation. Theorizing the state as a largely negative domain for democratic political transformation was not circumscribed by the state's expressly gendered features, by its history and genealogy as mirror and accomplice of male dominance. Nor was the state the only domain of antidemocratic powers about which I thought feminists ought to be wary. Indeed, my own effort to "deconstruct" the state, to avoid the kind of reifications of that potent fiction to which theories of the state are so vulnerable, revealed an ensemble of familiar powers: the state's "gender" could be traced in its mediations of capitalism, welfarism, and militarism, as well as in the specific liberal and bureaucratic discourses through which legislation, adjudication, policy execution, and administration transpire. But to argue that each of these dimensions of state power was problematic for feminist aims not only because it was inscribed with gender but because it carried generically antidemocratic tendencies betrayed both "feminism" and "the state" as having something of a metaphorical operation in my own political *Weltanschauung*. Feminism was being freighted with a strong democratic ambition, with aspirations for radical political freedom and equality, while the state was carrying the weight of all the discourses of power against which I imagined radically democratizing possibilities to be arrayed. While some feminists may be radical democrats, no ground exists for marking such a political posture as either indigenous or consequent to the diverse attachments traveling under feminism's name. Similarly, although the state may be an important site of convergence of antidemocratic discourses, it is hardly the only place where they make their appearance, nor always the best lens through which to study them. Discourses of sovereign individuality, or of bureaucratic depoliticization of gendered class relations, for example, can be discerned in the state but are not limited to operations there. Indeed, one of the richer sites of radical democratic agitation in the last decade, practices gathered under the rubric of "cultural politics," is premised precisely on the notion that neither domination nor democratic resistance are limited to the venue of the state.

The confining qualities of gender and the state as categories of political analysis did not exhaust the sources undoing the "feminist theory of the state" project. The point of mapping the configurations of power in which contemporary democratic political opposition took shape was to understand where and how such opposition might do other than participate in contemporary orders of regulation, discipline, exploitation, and domination—in short, in existing regimes of unfreedom. But to pose the problem as one of negotiating these orders was to leave uninterrogated the question of the subject doing the negotiating; indeed, it was to assume that the politically committed subject sufficiently cognizant of the map of power would plot appropriate strategies and tactics given its aim of democratizing political life. What such an assumption eschews was the problem of subject formation by and through the very discourses being charted as sites and zones of unfreedom.

Nor was such neglect a minor matter: the viability of a radical democratic alternative to various political discourses of domination in the present is not determined only by the organization of institutional forces opposing that alternative but is shaped as well by political subjects' *desire* for such an alternative. Even if, for example, feminists could be persuaded of the antidemocratic character of certain state-centered reforms, would they count this as an objection to such reforms? Even if the inscription of gendered, racial, or sexual identity in legal discourse could be shown to have the effect of reaffirming the historical injuries constitutive of those identities, thus installing injury as identity in the ahistorical discourse of the law, would proponents of such actions necessarily despair over this effect? To what extent have the particular antidemocratic powers of our time produced subjects, often working under the banner of "progressive politics," whose taste for substantive political freedom is attenuated by a historically unique form of political powerlessness amid historically unprecedented discourses of individual liberty? And if this peculiar form of powerlessness is sometimes worn rather straightforwardly as the conservative raiment of despair, misanthropy, narrow pursuit of interest, or bargains of autonomy for state protection, when does it twist into a more dissimulated political discourse of paralyzing recriminations and toxic resentments parading as radical critique?

To pursue these questions was to shift attention from the conditions framing and facing contemporary political opposition to the constitutive material of the opposition itself. Insofar as this moved the analysis into a more psychological and less institutional line of inquiry, for some the appropriate theoretical consultants at this point might have been Freud or Lacan bent toward history, insedimented with culture, and tethered by economic and political context. In my own theoretical lexicon, however, this shift entailed moving from the register of Marx and Weber to that of Nietzsche and Foucault. While Marx and Weber trace power as a problem of macrophysical social processes, whether those of capital or of instrumental rationality institutionalized as bureaucracy, Nietzsche and Foucault concern themselves with the psychic, social, and moral economies imbricated with such processes. Put slightly differently, if Marx and Weber delineate forces—capital and rationalization—that can be said to shape the contours of modern "history" (even as their more teleological versions of history have been exposed as fictions), Nietzsche and Foucault discern the atomic powers of history in microphysical particles, in "descriptive" languages, in moral systems, and in thwarted aggression and ideals—in short, in the very making of bodily subjects and socio-political desire.

Methodologically, discerning contemporary inhibitions of radical democratic aims in the very material of contemporary subject formation confounds a "subject/world" distinction in political science that takes the disciplinary form of infelicitous distinctions between studies of "political psychology" and "political institutions," as well as between "political behavior" and "political theory." Politically, this inquiry into the making of contemporary political desire interrupts a tendency to externalize political disappointment by blaming failures on the character of power "out there," being bound instead to the more sober practice of searching for political disappointment's "cause" in our own psychic and social ranks. What kind of attachments to unfreedom can be discerned in contemporary political formations ostensibly concerned with emancipation? What kinds of injuries enacted by late modern democracies are recapitulated in the very oppositional projects of its subjects? What conservative political impulses result from a lost sense of futurity attendant upon the breakdown of progressive narratives of history?

This effort to understand the contemporary preemption of liberatory politics in the liberators themselves turned still further from the study of political institutions as it turned toward the politics of contemporary theory. Could Nietzschean themes of *ressentiment,* revenge, and a thwarted will to power be found in some of the more troubling stalemates and furious debates occupying those on the academic Left, including academic feminism? How might certain wounded attachments and profound historical disorientations form the basis for ungrounded persistence in ontological essentialism and epistemological foundationalism, for infelicitous formulations of identity rooted in injury, for litigiousness as a way of political life, and for a resurgence of rights discourse among left academics? Could the rhetorical force, the theoretical incoherence, and the politically invidious effects of Catharine MacKinnon's social theory of gender be understood in terms of broken progressive theoretical and social narratives that leave immediate suffering without a redemptive place in history and without guarantees of political redress? Could Patricia Williams's seemingly paradoxical enthusiasm for rights be read not only as reaction to white radical discourses blithely dismissive of them but also as a desire to resuscitate the fictions of sovereign accountability (despite their depoliticizing effects) as a weapon against public irresponsibility on the one side and late-twentieth-century deracinations of personhood on the other? And might the effort to establish such individual accountability and boundaries through discourses of rights and responsibility conveniently cast the powers of economy and state as relatively benign at a historical moment when both seem nearly unassailable anyway?

Insofar as academic and popular political discourses are neither identical nor distinct, this concern with the politics of theory does not constitute a turn away from "the world"; nor, however, is it a direct study of whatever we mean by this bold term. Rather, perhaps these seemingly academic quandaries, in addition to their intrinsic interest, can operate diagnostically. Perhaps they can serve as a rich text for reading aspects of our historically and culturally configured fears, anxieties, disorientation, and loss of faith about the future. And while there are no guarantees about the use to which such a reading might be put, one possibility is this: that these afflictions not metamorphose unchecked into political expression, not have their own indirect way in political life, but be actively contested with rejuvenated self-consciousness, irony, and passion in the difficult labor of the collective self-fashioning that is democratic politics.

Acknowledgments

ALTHOUGH I work largely in isolation, I am thankful for those who disrupted such habits over the years these essays were composed: Norman O. Brown, Judith Butler, William Connolly, Drucilla Cornell, J. Peter Euben, Carla Freccero, Susan Harding, Valerie Hartouni, Gail Hershatter, George Kateb, Robert Meister, Helene Moglen, Joan W. Scott. I was also fortunate to have in William Connolly, Kathy Ferguson, and Judith Butler three superb readers of the entire manuscript; my refusal to respond to all of their suggestions for improvement is consequent to my own stubbornness, not their lack of perspicacity. I am grateful as well to the many audiences who engaged with spoken versions of these thoughts and to several anonymous readers who substantially enriched the written accounts. Two research assistants, Ashley Smith and Maile Pickett, pursued bibliographic details with aplomb. The manuscript was beautifully handled by Ann Himmelberger Wald, political theory editor at Princeton University Press, and much improved by the artful copyediting of Alice Falk.

I am deeply appreciative of two extraordinary institutions: At the University of California, Santa Cruz, my work was supported by the Academic Senate Committee on Research, the Division of Humanities, and the Women's Studies Program. And the School of Social Science of the Institute for Advanced Study at Princeton harbored me in its graceful way while I sought to bring this manuscript to completion.

Once in a lifetime or less, one encounters a teacher without whom, it seems, one would not read or think as one does. It is to such a teacher that this volume is dedicated, however insufficient a tribute it may be to his own intellectual offerings.

. . .

Permission to reprint material published elsewhere has been granted as follows:

"Postmodern Exposures, Feminist Hesitations," *differences* 3.1 (Spring 1991), revised as chapter 2.

"Wounded Attachments: Oppositional Political Formations in Late Modern Democracy," *Political Theory* 21.3 (August 1993), for a portion of chapter 3.

"Finding the Man in the State," *Feminist Studies* 18.1 (Spring 1992), revised as chapter 7.

States of Injury

CHAPTER ONE

Introduction: Freedom and the Plastic Cage

> The political, ethical, social, philosophical problem of our days is not to try to liberate the individual from the state . . . but to liberate us both from the state and from the type of individualization which is linked to the state.
>
> —Michel Foucault, "The Subject and Power"
>
> If men wish to be free, it is precisely sovereignty they must renounce.　　—Hannah Arendt, "What Is Freedom?"
>
> The road to freedom for gays and lesbians is paved with lawsuits.
>
> —Spokesperson, National Center for Lesbian Rights

THESE ESSAYS investigate dimensions of late modern modalities of political power and opposition by engaging, in various combinations, the thinking of Marx, Nietzsche, Weber, Foucault, and selected contemporary feminist and cultural theorists. They serve in part to reflect upon the present-day value of such thinkers, to measure the capacity of their thought to apprehend contemporary formations of power and contribute to strategies for democratizing those formations. But these essays have another purpose as well. Working heuristically from Foucault's relatively simple insight that political "resistance" is figured by and within rather than externally to the regimes of power it contests, these essays examine ostensibly emancipatory or democratic political projects for the ways they problematically mirror the mechanisms and configurations of power of which they are an effect and which they purport to oppose. The point of such exploration is not the small-minded one of revealing hypocrisy or internal contradictions, nor the strictly practical one of exposing limited political efficacy. While these studies are not exercises in what today traffics under the sign of "normative political theory" and they develop no political or even theoretical program, they make no pretense at being free of normative impulses. Rather, they work in the slightly old-fashioned genre of political theoretical critique, a genre neither directly accountable to political practicalities on the one hand nor bound to a fixed set of political principles on the other. Structured by a set of cares and passions making up an amorphous but insistent vision of an alternative way of political life, this vision is itself shaped and textured by the activity of criticizing the present; in this regard, the critique and the alternative it figures never feign independence of one another.

The question animating these explorations is bound to a remnant of Hegelian-Marxist historiography almost embarrassing to name, given its tattered ontological, epistemological, and historical premises. Can something of a persistent desire for human freedom be discerned even in the twisted projects of this aim, even in its failure to realize itself, its failure to have the courage, or the knowledge, of its own requisites? Such a question need not assume, with Arendt, that freedom is "the *raison d'être* of politics"[1] nor, with Marx, that "history" is tethered to the project of freedom, that "history" has a project at all, or that "freedom" is the telos of "human" (species) being. Certainly politics, the place where our propensity to traffic in power is most explicit, is saturated with countless aims and motivations other than freedom—from "managing populations," negotiating conflicting interests, or providing for human welfare, to the expression of open revenge, aggression spurred by injury, pleasure in domination, or the prestige of power.

The question, then, is not whether freedom can be discerned as *the* aim of politics or of history in the political projects of the present but a more modest, albeit still tendentious one, which borrows as much from the devolutionary outlook of Rousseau as from the teleological thinking of Marx: Might the desire for some degree of collective self-legislation, the desire to participate in shaping the conditions and terms of life, remain a vital element—if also an evidently ambivalent and anxious one—of much agitation under the sign of progressive politics? Equally important, might the realization of substantive democracy continue to require a desire for political freedom, a longing to share in power rather than be protected from its excesses, to generate futures together rather than navigate or survive them? And have we, at the close of the twentieth century, lost our way in pursuing this desire? With what consequences?

.   .   .

In the context of recent "democratizing" developments in the former eastern bloc and Soviet Union, in South Africa, in parts of Latin America, and in the Middle East, it may seem perverse if not decadent to suggest that Western intellectuals and political activists have grown disoriented about the meaning and practice of political freedom. Freedom,

---

[1] "What Is Freedom?" in *Between Past and Future: Eight Exercises in Political Thought* (New York: Viking, 1954), p. 144.

of course, is an eternally nettlesome political value as well as a matter of endless theoretical dispute, and it is not my purpose to reflect here upon its genealogy or its history as a concept. Rather, freedom's recent predicament might be captured schematically thus: Historically, semiotically, and culturally protean, as well as politically elusive, "freedom" has shown itself to be easily appropriated in liberal regimes for the most cynical and unemancipatory political ends. Philosophically vexing throughout modernity for the formulations of will and agency it appears to invoke, it has been rendered utterly paradoxical by poststructuralist formulations of the subject as not simply oppressed but brought into being by—that is, an effect of—subjection.[2] Yet despite these assaults on its premises, freedom persists as our most compelling way of marking differences between lives whose terms are *relatively* controlled by their inhabitants and those that are less so, between conditions of coercion and conditions of action, between domination by history and participation in history, between the space for action and its relative absence. If, politically, freedom is a sign—and an effect—of "democracy," where democracy signifies not merely elections, rights, or free enterprise but a way of constituting and thus distributing political power, then to the extent that Western intellectuals have grown disoriented about the project of freedom, we must be equally bewildered about the meaning and tasks of democratic political life.[3] Indeed, much of the progressive political agenda in recent years has been concerned not with democratizing power but with distributing goods, and especially with pressuring the state to buttress the rights and increase the entitlements of the socially vulnerable or disadvantaged: people of color, homosexuals, women, endangered animal species, threatened wetlands, ancient forests, the sick, and the homeless. Without disputing the importance of such projects, especially in a political economy fundamentally impervious to human, ecological, and aesthetic life, the dream of democracy—that humans might govern themselves by governing together—is difficult to discern in the proliferation of such claims of rights, protections, regulations, and entitlements.

"[W]hat the Left needs is a postindividualist concept of freedom, for it is still over questions of freedom and equality that the decisive ideological battles are being waged."[4] So argues Chantal Mouffe in response to two

---

[2] See Michel Foucault, *History of Sexuality*, vol. 1, *An Introduction*, trans. R. Hurley (New York: Vintage, 1980); Judith Butler, *Gender Trouble: Feminism and the Subversion of Identity* (New York: Routledge, 1989); and Butler's forthcoming work on "subjection."

[3] On democracy as a problem of distribution of power, see Sheldon Wolin, *The Presence of the Past: Essays on the State and the Constitution* (Baltimore: Johns Hopkins University Press, 1989), chaps. 9–11.

[4] "Hegemony and New Political Subjects: Toward a New Concept of Democracy," in *Marxism and the Interpretation of Culture*, ed. Cary Nelson and Lawrence Grossberg (Chicago: University of Illinois Press, 1988), p. 100.

decades of conservative political and theoretical efforts to define and practice freedom in an individualist, libertarian mode, a phenomenon Stuart Hall calls "the great moving right show."[5] Yet as Hall keenly appreciates, "concepts" of freedom, posited independently of specific analyses of contemporary modalities of domination, revisit us with the most troubling kind of idealism insofar as they deflect from the local, historical, and contextual character of freedom. Even for philosopher Jean-Luc Nancy, "freedom is everything except an 'Idea.' "[6] Freedom is neither a philosophical absolute nor a tangible entity but a relational and contextual practice that takes shape in opposition to whatever is locally and ideologically conceived as unfreedom. Thus in slaveholding and male dominant fifth-century Athenian "democracy," Arendt argues, freedom was conceived as escape from an order of "necessity" inhabited by women and by slaves; what was called Athenian freedom thus entailed a metaphysics of domination and a necessary practice of imperialism. Liberal freedom, fitted to an economic order in which property and personhood for some entails poverty and deracination for others, is conveyed by rights against arbitrary state power on one side and against anarchic civil society or property theft on the other. As freedom from encroachment by others and from collective institutions, it entails an atomistic ontology, a metaphysics of separation, an ethos of defensiveness, and an abstract equality. Rendering either the ancient or liberal formations of freedom as "concepts" abstracts them from the historical practices in which they are rooted, the institutions against which they are oriented, the domination they are designed to contest, the privileges they are designed to protect. Treating them as concepts not only prevents appreciation of their local and historical character but preempts perception of what is denied and suppressed by them, of what kinds of domination are enacted by particular practices of freedom.

It would also appear that the effort to develop a new "postindividualist" *concept* of freedom responds less to the antidemocratic forces of our time than to a ghostly philosophical standoff between historically abstracted formulations of Marxism and liberalism. In other words, this effort seeks to resolve a problem in (a certain) history of ideas rather than a problem in history. Like a bat flying around the owl of Minerva at dusk, it would attempt to formulate a philosophy of freedom on the grave of selected philosophical traditions rather than to consider freedom in existing configurations of power—economic, social, psychological, political. This is not to say that the contemporary disorientation about

[5] Stuart Hall, *The Hard Road to Renewal: Thatcherism and the Crisis of the Left* (London: Verso, 1988).

[6] *The Experience of Freedom,* trans. B. MacDonald (Stanford: Stanford University Press, 1993), p. 11.

freedom is without theoretical dimensions nor is it to suggest that freedom's philosophical crisis, about which more shortly, is merely consequent to a historical or "material" one. I want only to register the extent to which the problematic of political freedom as it relates to democratizing power, while of profound philosophical interest, cannot be resolved at a purely philosophical level if it is to be responsive to the particular social forces and institutions—the sites and sources of domination—of a particular age.

But this opens rather than settles the problem of how to formulate a discourse of freedom appropriate to contesting contemporary antidemocratic configurations of power. One of the ironies of what Nietzsche boldly termed the "instinct for freedom" lies in its inceptive self-cancellation, its crossing of itself in its very first impulse. Initial figurations of freedom are inevitably reactionary in the sense of emerging in reaction to perceived injuries or constraints of a regime from within its own terms. Ideals of freedom ordinarily emerge to vanquish their imagined immediate enemies, but in this move they frequently recycle and reinstate rather than transform the terms of domination that generated them. Consider exploited workers who dream of a world in which work has been abolished, blacks who imagine a world without whites, feminists who conjure a world either without men or without sex, or teenagers who fantasize a world without parents. Such images of freedom perform mirror reversals of suffering without transforming the *organization of the activity through which the suffering is produced* and without addressing the *subject constitution that domination effects,* that is, the constitution of the social categories, "workers," "blacks," "women," or "teenagers."

It would thus appear that it is freedom's relationship to identity—its promise to address a social injury or marking that is itself constitutive of identity—that yields the paradox in which the first imaginings of freedom are always constrained by and potentially even require the very structure of oppression that freedom emerges to oppose. This, I think, is not only a patently Foucaultian point but is contained as well in Marx's argument that "political emancipation" within liberalism conceived formal political indifference to civil particularity as liberation because political privilege according to civil particularity appeared as the immediate nature of the domination perpetrated by feudal and Christian monarchy. "True human emancipation" was Marx's formula for escaping the innately contextual and historically specific, hence limited, forms of freedom. True human emancipation, achieved at the end of history, conjured for Marx not simply liberation from particular constraints but freedom that was both thoroughgoing and permanent, freedom that was neither partial nor evasive but temporally and spatially absolute. However, since true human emancipation eventually acquired for Marx a negative referent (capitalism) and positive content (abolition of capitalism), in time it too would reveal its profoundly historicized and thus limited character.

Invoking Marx recalls a second dimension of this paradox in which freedom responds to a particular practice of domination whose terms are then often reinstalled in its practice. When institutionalized, freedom premised upon an already vanquished enemy keeps alive, in the manner of a melancholic logic, a threat that works as domination in the form of an absorbing ghostly battle with the past.[7] Institutionalized, freedom arrayed against a particular image of unfreedom sustains that image, which dominates political life with its specter long after it has been vanquished and preempts appreciation of new dangers to freedom posed by institutions designed to hold the past in check. Yet the very institutions that are erected to vanquish the historical threat also recuperate it as a form of political anxiety; so, for example, functions the "state of nature" or the "arbitrary sovereign" in the liberal political imagination.

It may be the extent to which freedom institutionalized transmogrifies into its opposite that led Foucault to insist upon understanding liberty as a *practice* rather than a state, as that which can "never [be] assured by . . . institutions and laws" but "must be exercised."[8] Sheldon Wolin presses a similar point in his provocation that "a constitution, in setting limits to politics, set limits as well to democracy. . . . Democracy thus seems destined to be a moment rather than a form."[9] In Jean-Luc Nancy's account, "freedom . . . is the very thing that prevents itself from being founded."[10] And a similar concern can be discerned in Hannah Arendt's insistence on the perniciousness of equating freedom with sovereignty, along with her counterproposition that freedom as "virtuosity" is defined by the *contingency* of action, as the place where "the I-will and the I-can coincide" as power.[11]

Recognition of the tension, if not the antinomy, between freedom and institutionalization compounds the difficulties of formulating a politics of freedom in the late twentieth century, the age of institutions. Not only do we require a historically and institutionally specific reading of contemporary modes of domination, but freedom's "actualization" would appear to be a frustratingly indeterminate matter of ethos, of bearing toward institutions, of the *style* of political practices, rather than a matter

[7] This logic is drawn from Freud's *The Ego and the Id,* trans. J. Rivière, ed. J. Strachey (New York: Norton, 1960), pp. 18–19, although transformed as it is allegorized for political purposes unintended by Freud.

[8] "Space, Knowledge, and Power," interview by Paul Rabinow, in *The Foucault Reader,* ed. Rabinow (New York: Pantheon, 1984), p. 245.

[9] "Fugitive Democracy" (paper presented at the Foundations of Political Thought conference Democracy and Difference, New Haven, April 1993), pp. 9, 23.

[10] *Experience of Freedom,* p. 12.

[11] "What Is Freedom?" pp. 153–54, 160, 164–65, 168–69.

of policies, laws, procedures, or organization of political orders. This is not to say that freedom becomes aesthetic, but rather that it depends upon a formulation of the political that is richer, more complicated, and also perhaps more fragile than that circumscribed by institutions, procedures, and political representation.

. . .

These reflections on the inherently difficult, paradoxical, even delusional features of freedom frame but do not exhaust freedom's contemporary predicament in North America. Why, today, do we not only confront the limited or paradoxical qualities of freedom but appear disoriented with regard to freedom's very value? Why, as versions of freedom burst out around the globe, are critical theorists and progressive political activists in established liberal regimes disinclined to place freedom on their own political agenda, other than to endorse and extend the type of "freedom" the regime itself proffers?

Certainly this disorientation is partly consequent to the conservative political culture ascendant in the United States in the 1980s, a culture that further narrowed the meaning of freedom within liberalism's already narrow account. Throughout that decade, "freedom" was deployed by the Right to justify thuggish mercenaries in Central America, the expenditure of billions on cold war defense, the deregulation of toxic enterprise, the destruction of unions with "right to work" protection, the importance of saluting—and the blasphemy of burning—the flag. Meanwhile, liberal or radical formulations of freedom were smeared by charges of selfishness and irresponsibility—as in women who put their own desires and ambitions on a par with family obligations—or charges of infantilism and death—as in repudiations of juvenile past involvements with liberation struggles, or narratives of the AIDS epidemic in which the "sexually emancipated" 1970s were placed in a direct causal relation to the plague of death in the 1980s.[12] In the contemporary popular refrain, freedom other than free enterprise was cast as selfish, infantile, or killing, and placed in ignominious counterpoise to commitment, maturity, discipline, sacrifice, and sobriety.[13] This discourse, in which

[12] See Randy Shilts, *And the Band Played On* (New York: St. Martin's, 1987); and Jon Pareles, "The '60s: Only the Beat Goes On," *New York Times,* February 5, 1989, H-1, 21.

[13] Of course, freedom *as* free enterprise also began to emerge as infantile and irresponsible during these years: such were the scandals concerning junk bonds, insider trading, and S&L real estate deals. But the point is that as liberal, let alone radical, commitments to freedom came into severe disrepute, numerous progressive political operations dropped it from their agenda. Even those political identities most recently forged from liberation movements—black, feminist, gay—pursued relatively unremarkable agendas concerned with rights and minimalist economic redistribution during the 1980s. And so also did the

"good freedom" was imperialist, individualist, and entrepreneurial, while "bad freedom" was decadent if not deadly, was not an easy one for the Left to counter. But if it was easier to drop freedom from its own political lexicon, what was the price of such a disavowal?

Contemporary disorientation about freedom also appears consequent to the Right's programmatic attack on the welfare state since the mid-1970s. This attack incited liberal and left protectiveness toward the state and, for many, rendered critiques of the state tantamount to luxury goods in bad times. This disorientation appears consequent as well to the discredited critique of liberalism contained in the communist ideal; it was abetted too by the stark abandonment of freedom as an element of the communist project long before its 1989 "fall." The cumulative effect of these tendencies is that as the powers constituting late modern configurations of capitalism and the state have grown more complex, more pervasive, and simultaneously more diffuse and difficult to track, both critical analyses of their power and a politics rooted in such critique have tended to recede. Indeed, Western leftists have largely forsaken analyses of the liberal state and capitalism as sites of *domination* and have focused instead on their implication in political and economic *inequalities*. At the same time, progressives have implicitly assumed the relatively unproblematic instrumental value of the state and capitalism in redressing such inequalities.

Thus, as the Right promulgated an increasingly narrow and predominantly economic formulation of freedom and claimed freedom's ground as its own, liberals and leftists lined up behind an equally narrow and predominantly economic formulation of equality. In this regard, leftists ceded important ground to liberal doctrine, which generally places equality and freedom on perpendicular axes in inverse relation to each other, casting their relationship as something of political philosophy's Phillip's curve. While Marxism promised to escape this trade-off by divesting both freedom and equality of their economic scarcity and reconciling them through collective ownership, and thinkers such as Arendt sought to reformulate the problematic of political freedom on fully noneconomic ground, most late-twentieth-century progressives have shied from these alternative formulations of freedom and equality to embrace a vision involving state-administered "economic justice" combined with a

---

"radical" wings of these movements direct most of their appeals to the state: threats by black organizers in Chicago and Detroit to revive the Black Panther Party including its tactics of violence were based on the failure to get a share of the economic pie; ACT UP largely targeted government (in)attention to AIDS and AIDS research. The other "radical" wing of each of these movements largely eschewed the project of freedom in favor of various kinds of culturalisms and nationalisms—queer, Afrocentric, Islamic, feminist, and so forth.

panoply of private liberties. This would seem to characterize Chantal Mouffe's call for "postindividualist liberalism," or "radical, plural, and libertarian democracy" to "rearticulate ideas of equality and justice," as well as the argument of Samuel Bowles and Herbert Gintis for "post-liberal democracy" in which, oddly, the primary instrument of struggle is "personal rights."[14] Significantly, neither Mouffe nor Bowles and Gintis regard their positions as a retrenchment of their commitment to radical democracy but rather, through renewed appreciation of individual rights and liberties combined with state administered economic redistribution, as the fulfillment of that commitment.[15]

Yet for all the admirable effort to blend commitments of economic equality with liberal civil goods, as well as to enfranchise—theoretically and politically—a diverse range of identity-based struggles, what is difficult to discern in the work of those who have appropriated the name "radical democrats" in recent years is precisely where the radicalism lies. What constitutes the ostensible departure from liberal democracy and from the forms of domination liberalism both perpetrates and obscures? Such differentiation is especially faint in their formulation of liberty, which rather faithfully replicates that of the sovereign subject of liberalism whose need for rights is born out of subjection by the state, out of an economy not necessarily bound to human needs or capacities, and out of stratifications within civil society (renamed "social antagonisms" by Ernesto Laclau and Chantal Mouffe), all of which may be attenuated but are at the same time codified by the rights advocated by the "radical democrats."

It is interesting as well that the optimism of the radical (social) democratic vision is fueled by that dimension of liberalism which presumes social and political forms to have relative autonomy from economic ones, to be that which can be tinkered with independently of developments in the forces of capitalism.[16] Indeed, it is here that the radical democrats

---

[14] "Hegemony and New Political Subjects," pp. 102, 103; Bowles and Gintis, *Democracy and Capitalism: Property, Community, and the Contradictions of Modern Social Thought* (New York: Basic Books, 1986).

[15] Both works seek to address as well the recent proliferation of politicized identities other than class. Mouffe actually measures "democratization" by the extent of acknowledgment and connection between these identity-based struggles: "The longer the chain of equivalences set up between the defense of the rights of one group and those of other groups, the deeper will be the democratization process" ("Hegemony and New Political Subjects," p. 100). Democratization here presumably refers to a nonliberal form of recognition and criteria for participation: "In addition to . . . traditional social subjects [citizens and workers], we must recognize the existence of others and their political characters: women and the various minorities also have a right to equality and to self-determination."

[16] In *Hegemony and Socialist Strategy* (London: Verso, 1985), Ernesto Laclau and Chantal Mouffe do offer a historical reading of "new social antagonisms" rooted in the permeation

become vulnerable to the charge of "idealism," where idealism marks the promulgation of select political ideals de-linked from historical configurations of social powers and institutions, much as calling for a "politics of meaning" without addressing the sources of meaning's evisceration from politics is an idealist response to the problem of vacuity.[17] This is not to say, in a fashion that mistakes positivism for historical materialism, that capitalist economies require liberal political orders nor that collective economic ownership is incompatible with individual rights. Rather, it is to ask: When do certain political solutions actually codify and entrench existing social relations, when do they mask such relations, and when do they directly contest or transform them? Against what backdrop of economic and political power, for example, are rights claimed to health care, housing, privacy, or autonomy? What abrogation of these needs is presumed to inhere in the political economy against which such rights are asserted? If rights are, however useful, a paradoxical form of power insofar as they signify something like the permanent presence of an endangering power or violation, if rights thus codify even as they may slightly mitigate certain modalities of subordination or exclusion, it behooves radical democrats not simply to proliferate rights but to explore the historically and culturally specific ground of the demand for them.

This lack of attention to the historical relationship between economic and political formations may be understood somewhat differently by considering the place of capitalism as such in contemporary theoretical discourses, a place that has been diminished both by Foucault and by other post-Marxist tendencies. Foucault's salutary critique of a model of power as an expropriable and transferable commodity, combined with his concern to confound a materialist/idealist antinomy with the notion of discourse—in sum, his quarrels with Marx—resulted in analytically reducing the importance of capitalism itself, and not only disputing economistic formulations of capital's power.[18] In fact, by ascribing a for-

---

of capitalism into both the domain of consumption and into more "subjective" reaches of social life. Yet there is a profound difference between this kind of historical reading and one that emphasizes the relationship between particular political forms and particular "modes of production." Mouffe, citing C. B. MacPherson, notes that "democracy" was rendered "liberal" not without "struggle" and notes as well, citing Stuart Hall, that the Right struggled through the 1980s to pull liberalism away from democracy. From this she concludes that if the new social antagonisms are rendered as struggles, democracy can be wrested away from liberalism and be made "radical" and "plural." If democracy can indeed be radicalized without capitalism being substantially augmented, one can only wonder about the significance of democracy in this formulation. See "Hegemony and New Political Subjects," especially pp. 96, 102.

[17] "Hegemony and New Political Subjects," p. 104.

[18] Thus, for example, Foucault inclines toward reversals where complex rethinking might have better suited his aims: "In the last analysis, we must produce truth as we must

mulation of power as a commodity to Marxism, Foucault deprives Marxism of its analysis of the diffusion of domination throughout the production process, where it inheres not only in the extraction of surplus value but in the *discourses* enabling commodity fetishism, reification, and ideologies of free and equal exchange. Certainly the notion that labor power is expropriable or that surplus value is extracted from labor casts power in the image of a commodity. Yet it is Marx's appreciation of the very perversity and singularity of this achievement within capitalism that constitutes the basis of his theory of the social activity of labor as power. Indeed, Marx is at pains to explain the process whereby the human activity of labor becomes a commodity wielded over and against its site of generation, how it is both produced and circulated by capitalist relations such that it is transformed into something alien to itself. In other words, for Marx, unlike Foucault perhaps, a commodity is never just a commodity but, as the effect of the complex and dissimulating activity of *commodification*, always remains itself a social force as well as the condensed site of social forces. Interestingly enough, this is precisely the way Foucault himself speaks of individuals—as "an effect of power, and at the same time . . . the element of its articulation," as both constituted by power and "at the same time its vehicle."19

Foucault's de-emphasis on capital as a domain of power and source of domination issues from a substantially different source than that of contemporary post-Marxists, neo-Marxists, and "radical democrats." While thinkers such as Bowles and Gintis, Laclau and Mouffe, and the analytical Marxism school are certainly critical of capitalism's inequities, they are less concerned with capitalism as a political economy of domination, exploitation, or alienation, precisely those terms by which the problem of freedom is foregrounded as a problem of social and economic power and not only a matter of political or legal statutes. It is as if the terrible unfreedom and indignities attendant upon "actually existing socialisms" of the last half century persuaded such thinkers that free enterprise really is freer than the alternatives, that alienation is inherent in all labor, and that freedom, finally, is a matter of consumption, choice, and expression: an individual good rather than a social and political practice. Ironically, it is this conceptual move—and not the historical practices it claims to describe or decry—that succeeds in finally rendering Marxism as economism. Indeed, such apparent imperviousness to domination by capital—its mode of constructing and organizing social life and its specific form of

---

produce wealth, indeed we must produce truth in order to produce wealth in the first place" ("Two Lectures," in *Power/Knowledge: Selected Interviews and Other Writings, 1972–1977*, ed. C. Gordon [New York: Pantheon, 1980], pp. 93–94).

19 Ibid., p. 98.

subject production, combined with a preoccupation with goods and with private "liberty"—was precisely the nightmare forecast a quarter century ago by Herbert Marcuse in *One-Dimensional Man*. Marcuse's anxieties, however, were addressed to the consciousness he associated with "mass society"; did he ever imagine that such indifference to freedom would infect left thinking itself?[20]

In equating the positive dimensions of socialism with a method for distributive economic justice and equating liberalism with a system of individual liberties and satisfactions, socialism is reduced to the status of a (nonpolitical) economic practice while liberalism is treated as a (noneconomic) political practice. This rendering, in addition to eclipsing the social power that Marx argued was generated in modes of production and constitutive of a specific political and social architecture, in addition to resuscitating the very division between civil life and political life that he criticized as an ideological split within liberalism, *mirrors rather than criticizes* recent histories of socialism. As Marxism was contorted into bleak and repressive modalities of state ownership and distribution in places such as Eastern Europe, liberalism phantasmically figured the dream of sunny pleasures and liberty, whether conceived as freedom of expression, as consumer choice, or freedom of expression *as* consumer choice.[21] Yet if Marxism had any analytical value for *political* theory, was it not in the insistence that the problem of freedom was contained in the social relations implicitly declared "unpolitical"—that is, naturalized—in liberal discourse? Was not Marx's very quarrel with the utopian socialists based on the insight that the problem of *domination* in capitalist relations cannot be solved at the level of distribution, no matter how egalitarian such distribution might be? Is not contemporary elision of this insight, in a "radical, plural democratic" vision, to jettison the dream of freedom in its social and economic—perhaps its most fundamental—dimensions?

Theoretical retreat from the problem of domination within capitalism is related to another noteworthy lost object of critique among those on the Left and among Foucaultians as well: the domination entailed in domestic

[20] As Marcuse remarks, "domination has its own aesthetics, and democratic domination has its democratic aesthetics" (*One-Dimensional Man* ([Boston: Beacon, 1964], p. 65). Not only does the domination inherent in capitalism and the state acquire little attention from most contemporary critical political theorists, few of them articulate a concern with the kind of bureaucratic domination first formulated by Max Weber and then developed into radical social theory by the Frankfurt School. Again, it is as if all the lack of freedom attendant upon bureaucratized societies was contained in the former socialist states, this notwithstanding Michel Foucault's own theorization of disciplinary power—the increasing organization of everything—as the pervasive mode of subjection in our age.

[21] On freedom of expression *as* consumer choice, see Slavenka Drakulic, *How We Survived Communism and Even Laughed* (New York: Norton, 1992).

state power.[22] As the Right attacked the state for sustaining welfare chis-elers and being larded with bureaucratic fat, liberals and leftists jettisoned two decades of "Marxist theories of the state" for a defense of the state as that which affords individuals "protection against the worst abuses of the market" and other structures of social inequality. In a 1987 essay, Frances Fox Piven and Richard Cloward argued that the welfare state empowers individuals by reducing their vulnerability to the impersonal social forces of capitalism and male dominance.[23] In the course of this defense, they decline to consider the state as a vehicle of domination or to reflect on "protection" as a technique of domination. This omission is equally striking in (former Marxist) Fred Block's discovery of the "caretaking state," as well as in many contemporary appeals to the state for protec-tion from injuries ranging from poverty to pornography to "hate speech."[24] But this response to the Right's attack on the state is perhaps nowhere more stark than in *The Mean Season: The Attack on the Welfare State,* authored by "democratic socialists" Fred Block, Richard Cloward, Barbara Ehrenreich, and Frances Fox Piven. According to the back cover blurb, "our boldest social thinkers . . . argue for [the welfare state's] real, hard-won accomplishments. More than a defense of the welfare state's economic efficiency and fairness, *The Mean Season* is a reaffirma-tion of those decent, humane values so much under attack in Reagan's America."[25] Such bold thinking hardly recalls the critical analyses of state paternalism and state management of capitalism's inequities authored by these same thinkers in an earlier era.

If the state has ceased to be a substantial object of criticism among left sociologists and political activists, so also has it been largely ignored by critical theorists as an object of study in the last decade.[26] Impugned by

[22] My characterization of Foucault as analytically eschewing the state and capital should be qualified by mention of his lectures on "governmentality" (in *The Foucault Effect: Studies in Governmentality,* ed. Graham Burchell, Colin Gordon, and Peter Miller [Chicago: University of Chicago Press, 1991]). Yet these lectures are also often used to mark Foucault's "liberal turn." It is noteworthy as well that notwithstanding the fine essays by Giovanna Procacci and Jacques Donzelot (in the volume cited above) that make use of these lectures, most contemporary appropriations of Foucault for political analysis continue to elide this work. See, for example, the volume *Foucault and the Critique of Institutions,* ed. John Caputo and Mark Yount (University Park: Pennsylvania State University Press, 1993), in which—the title notwithstanding—the state and capital barely make appearances.

[23] "The Contemporary Relief Debate," in Fred Block et al., *The Mean Season: The Attack on the Welfare State* (New York: Pantheon, 1987), especially pp. 95–98.

[24] *Revising State Theory: Essays in Politics and Postindustrialism* (Philadelphia: Temple University Press, 1987).

[25] *Mean Season,* back cover.

[26] There are obvious exceptions to this claim, including cultural theorists focusing on race in Britain and the United States, such as Wahneema Lubiano, Stuart Hall, and Paul Gilroy; and theorists analyzing conflicting state discourses of race, gender, religion, caste, and class in postcolonial states, such as M. Jacqui Alexander and Zakia Pathak.

poststructuralist critique for its tendency to reify and universalize rather than deconstruct and historically specify the state, the 1960s cottage industry in Marxist state theory was also derailed by Michel Foucault's historical-political argument that the distinctive feature of the post-monarchical nation-state is the decentered and decentralized character of political power.

> We should direct our researches on the nature of power not towards the juridical edifice of sovereignty, the State apparatuses and the ideologies which accompany them, but towards domination and the material operators of power, towards forms of subjection and the inflections and utilizations of their localized systems, and towards strategic apparatuses. We must eschew the model of Leviathan in the study of power. We must escape from the limited field of juridical sovereignty and State institutions, and instead base our analysis of power on the study of the techniques and tactics of domination.[27]

As with his summary dismissal of psychoanalysis and of the significance of capital in history, performed so that he might open a different kind of inquiry into sexuality and power, Foucault appears to steer hard away from the state in order to disrupt and displace an intellectual preoccupation with the state as *the* center or source of the power producing subjects. A formulation of power as productive rather than repressive, as discursive rather than commodity-like, as *irrigating* social life in a "capillary" mode rather than residing in particular sites or objects—all of these require a certain analytical diminution of the state in order to come into focus. However, as with his dismissal of psychoanalysis, Foucault is ultimately ensnared by this instrument of theoretical ground clearing: it triumphs over him as it transmogrifies from methodological strategy to political truth. The consequence is that two of the most significant contemporary domains of disciplinary power—the bureaucratic state and the organization of the social order by capital—are neither scrutinized by Foucault nor treated as significant sites of power by many of his disciples.

Foucault's injunction to "cut off the king's head in political theory" actually betrays an attachment to a formulation of political theory confined by liberalism's open preoccupation with sovereignty and its tendency to reduce the problem of the state to one of legitimacy.[28] But conceiving the state—and individual—as problems of sovereignty and legitimacy is quite a different matter from conceiving them as sites of convergence or "dense transfer points" of relations of power, conceiving them simultaneously as critical vehicle, effect, and legitimate administrators of power. Indeed, it is finally Foucault who, *by demanding its execu-*

---

[27] "Two Lectures," p. 102.
[28] "Truth and Power," in *Power/Knowledge,* p. 121.

tion, identifies king, state, and law: "I believe that the King remains the central personage in the whole legal edifice of the West."[29] This identification precludes Foucault from including the state as a critical site in the nonsovereign, nonrepressive or "productive," microphysical, and capillary workings of power to which he directs our attention. It is precisely when we set aside the problem of sovereignty that the state comes into view as a complex problem of power, as part of the "study of the techniques and tactics of domination" that Foucault defines as more crucial than the state for those interested in power.[30]

In the study of "governmentality" he undertook near the end of his life, this dichotomy between state and social power—including biopower, disciplinary power, and regulatory power of other sorts—appeared to loosen in Foucault's thought.[31] Indeed, here he seemed to be in at least partial accord with the argument that while the liberal state is necessarily *legitimated* through the language of sovereignty, its primary function has never been sovereignty—its own or that of the people. Rather, the state rises in importance with liberalism precisely through its provision of essential social repairs, economic problem solving, and the management of a mass population: in short, through those very functions that standard ideologies of liberalism and capitalism cast as self-generating in civil society and thus obscure as crucial state activities. As the social body is stressed and torn by the secularizing and atomizing effects of capitalism and its attendant political culture of individuating rights and liberties, economic, administrative, and legislative forms of repair are required. Through a variety of agencies and regulations, the liberal state provides webbing for the social body dismembered by liberal individualism and also administers the increasing number of subjects disenfranchised and deracinated by capital's destruction of social and geographic bonds.[32] If this kind of administration and regulation is not innocent of particular state interests, neither is it to one side of "techniques and tactics of domination."

From this perspective, the recent anti-statism of the Right appears as a late-breaking and dissimulating development as well as a departure from conservative precedents with regard to the state. Traditionally it has been left liberals, following in the tradition of Mill and Thoreau, who viewed the state as a danger to freedom (conceived as popular sovereignty); con-

---

[29] "Two Lectures," p. 94.

[30] Ibid., p. 102.

[31] See *Foucault Effect.*

[32] Although the Keynesianism of the 1930s moved this state function onto a more open stage as it became evident that neither a "hidden hand" nor "moral sentiments" could provide such social webbing, regulation, and economic problem solving, ideologies of the state preoccupied with sovereignty continue to obscure this function.

servative liberals such as Samuel Huntington or Henry Kissinger, following Hobbes and Hegel, tended to cast the state as a fount of freedom, protector against danger from without and domestic manager of our problematic particularity and atomistic energies. When freedom is equated with stability and order in this way, what is required is the containment rather than the enlargement of citizen powers, as the infamous 1973 Trilateral Commission Report decrying an "excess of democracy" made explicit. In this vein, Sheldon Wolin argues that the Right's 1980s rhetoric about "getting government off our backs" actually masked the steady expansion of state powers and retrenchment of citizen rights achieved through both foreign and domestic policy.[33] Stuart Hall reads Thatcherism in a similar way, citing the resuscitation of empire manifest in the Falklands War combined with the (heavily racialized) emphasis on law and order as evidence of expanded state domination shrouded in a discourse of anti-statism.[34]

If Wolin and Hall are right, it makes all the more troubling the phenomenon of recent progressive theoretical and political indifference to state domination, appeals to expand state benefits, and ever-increasing reliance on the state for adjudication of social injury. It means that critical theory turned its gaze away from the state at the moment when a distinctly late modern form of state domination was being consolidated: when expansion and extension of state power transpired not through centralization but through deregulation and privatization, through localizing and "contracting out" its activities—in short, through what some have identified as characteristically "postmodern" techniques of power.

． ． ．

Thus far, I have suggested that the retreat from a progressive politics of freedom responds to the Right's monopoly on positive discourses of freedom and to the consequent scorn recent decades have heaped upon the notion that freedom is a credible element of a socialist project. But I have hinted as well that developments in philosophy and in feminist, postcolonial, and cultural theory have eroded freedom's ground. For many toiling in these domains, "freedom" has been swept onto the dustheap of anachronistic, humanistic, androcentric, subject-centered, and "Western" shibboleths. Challenged politically as a token of the bourgeois-individualist modern West, freedom's valorization has been

---

[33] "Democracy and the Welfare State: The Political and Theoretical Connections between *Staatsräson* and *Wohlfahrtsstaatsräson*," in *Presence of the Past*, pp. 171–74.

[34] *Hard Road to Renewal*, chap. 4.

marked as ethnocentric and its pursuit as implicitly imperialistic. Challenged philosophically as a conceit of Enlightenment humanism, freedom has been cast by some as predicated upon a subject that does not exist, upon a fictional "will" that presumes such a subject, and upon a space emptied of power that turns out to be thoroughly cluttered. Moreover, Foucault's critique of the "repressive hypothesis"—the transcendent self and the world it hypostasizes—would appear to vitiate our capacity to mark either individuals or political orders as "free" or "unfree." The death of the essential subject appears to eliminate the possibility of the free subject, as the death of the essential world eliminates the possibility of a free world.

Recent political thought has also confounded a political theory and practice of freedom in its discovery of disciplinary power, which Foucault takes to be modernity's most pervasive mode of social power. The disciplinary institutions and discourses generative of obedient, disciplined subjects confound the premise of most emancipatory narratives: when discipline becomes the stuff of our desire, we cease to desire freedom. (And when psychoanalytic accounts are added to the picture, we may be seen not simply as lacking the desire for freedom, but as desiring our very subjection.) Moreover, Foucault and, under a different rubric, Weber and Marcuse have demonstrated that disciplinary power is extraordinarily effective in "colonizing" allegedly free subjects, for example, those highly individuated, self-interested subjects produced by liberal cultures and capitalist political economies. These turn out to be the subjects quintessentially susceptible to disciplinary power: their individuation and false autonomy is also their vulnerability. The proof lies in Bentham, who simultaneously and consistently developed a political theory of the self-interested liberal subject on the one hand, and techniques for administering the social whole through discipline and surveillance on the other.

In addition to generic posthumanist assaults upon a coherent politics of freedom, recent political thought has spawned several specifically feminist theoretical anxieties about such a politics. Most familiar is the claim that freedom of the bourgeois variety is male—premised upon and advancing the interests of an autonomous, self-interested, excessively individuated subject, a subject easily panicked by intimacy, averse to relationality, and obsessed with independence. According to objects relations theorists (Nancy Chodorow), feminist developmental psychologists (Carol Gilligan), feminist economists (Julie Nelson), some French feminists (Luce Irigaray), and some North American cultural feminists, women inhabit a different moral, psychological, cultural, or nascently political universe than men, with different sensibilities and concerns. Generally, the normative analogue of these accounts is that women seek

an intimate, connected, relational, nurturant human order, not necessarily an order suffused with freedom.[35] Feminist charges against the
masculinism of bourgeois freedom include its premise of a starkly autonomous subject, its abstract and alienated application, and its atomistic
social ontology.[36] Albeit issuing from a different epistemological and ontological site than the generic posthumanist critique of freedom, these
charges of masculinism achieve a convergent disintegration of the
"universalist" ground and context of Enlightenment formulations of
freedom.

A second feminist hesitation about a politics of freedom queries what
kind of freedom is possible or meaningful for women under conditions
of gender inequality, that is, under social relations of male dominance. A
liberal formulation of freedom, proffering liberty as individual license,
appears to aggravate the vulnerability of the socially weak to the socially
privileged, and thereby to facilitate as well as legitimize the exploitation
of wage labor by capital, the racially subordinate by the racially dominant, and the sexually vulnerable by the sexually exploitative. So, according to Catharine MacKinnon, "anyone with an ounce of political
analysis should know that freedom before equality, freedom before justice, will only further liberate the power of the powerful and will never
free what is most in need of expression."[37] It is in this vein she disdains as
"sexual liberals" those feminists who argue for expanding the domain of
sexual freedom in their defense of pornography, sadomasochism, and
other culturally stigmatized sexualities and sexual practices.

Albeit from concern with social inequality rather than regulatory subjection, MacKinnon thus joins Foucault in disputing the premises of conventional discourses of liberation: if, she argues, women are systematically and structurally positioned for exploitation by men, then the more
formally free the setting, the deeper this vulnerability *and* the more that

---

[35] Listen to Jessica Benjamin as she pejoratively contrasts freedom as autonomy to security, safety, and intimacy: "Both the assertion of women's absolute autonomy and the
shame at disclosing dependency . . . deny the initial thing that makes life worth living: that
sense of safety, of bodily intimacy and security, of familial and community cohesion which
many have experienced as the price of revolution" ("Shame and Sexual Politics," cited in
Pauline Johnson, "Feminism and Images of Autonomy," *Radical Philosophy,* Summer 1988,
p. 26).

[36] Certainly the essentialism, cultural narrowness, and reified femininity in this variant of
feminism has annoyed as many women as it has captured, but only a very few feminist
theorists have struggled to recast rather than sustain or reject the masculinist binary between intimacy and autonomy, relationality and independence. Joan Tronto's *Moral Boundaries* (New York: Routledge, 1993), and Kathy Ferguson's *The Feminist Case against
Bureaucracy* (Philadelphia: Temple University Press, 1984) are efforts at such recasting.

[37] *Feminism Unmodified: Discourses on Life and Law* (Cambridge: Harvard University
Press, 1987), p. 15.

male social power is masked. Here MacKinnon implies, and many feminists tacitly agree, that women are in greater need of social equality and political protection than of freedom. A similar critique of liberalism is implicit in other identity-based political arguments against freedom and for protection, such as those seeking legal or policy sanctions against "harassment" or "hate speech" targeted at socially marked groups—people of color, Jews, homosexuals, and women.[38] While the effort to replace liberalism's abstract formulation of equality with legal recognition of injurious social stratifications is understandable, what such arguments do not query is whether legal "protection" for a certain injury-forming identity discursively entrenches the injury–identity connection it denounces. Might such protection codify within the law the very powerlessness it aims to redress? Might it discursively collude with the conversion of attribute into identity, of a historical effect of power into a presumed cause of victimization?

. . .

For some, fueled by opprobrium toward regulatory norms or other modalities of domination, the language of "resistance" has taken up the ground vacated by a more expansive practice of freedom. For others, it is the discourse of "empowerment" that carries the ghost of freedom's val-

---

[38] Despite her avowed kinship with Marxism in proffering such an argument, MacKinnon's wariness about freedom struggles waged by structurally subordinate classes contrasts sharply with Marx's belief that such struggles almost always open progressive possibility. Marx speculated that the achievement of formal freedom and equality under substantively unfree and inegalitarian conditions can expose the inequities of such conditions, highlighting contradictions between ideas and practices, and thereby providing material for revolutionary consciousness. For Marx, every struggle for freedom generates human power and possibility, and thus releases a certain *force* into the social realm.

It is easy enough to criticize this perspective today. Marx bore little appreciation of the environmental limits of development, the psychological consequences of living in high-technology societies, or the colonizing power of extracapital forces. Still, Marx's insight into the relationship between power and even the most limited, contradictory forms of freedom retains a useful dimension for contemporary political thinking. Particularly for those whose identities have been shaped, *inter alia,* through dependence, shame, submissiveness, violation, helplessness, or inferiority, breaking these containing codes can spring loose latent capacities and generate powerful resistance to domination. In this formulation, *contra* Foucault, sometimes power really is repressed. Or, more subtly, perhaps Marx here offers a reminder that even the most limited freedom struggles can enhance the scarce political space needed by subordinated subjects seeking to alter their conditions. The early days of the Civil Rights movement and the Women's movement revealed that even partially unleashing subjects from subordinating codes of behavior and inciting them to action create a taste, space, and discourse for a politics of freedom. More recent history suggests that legally and politically codifying justice as matters of protection, prosecution, and regulation tends to turn us away from "practicing" freedom.

ence. Yet as many have noted, insofar as resistance is an effect of the regime it opposes on the one hand, and insofar as its practitioners often seek to void it of normativity to differentiate it from the (regulatory) nature of what it opposes on the other, it is at best politically rebellious; at worst, politically amorphous. Resistance stands against, not for; it is reaction to domination, rarely willing to admit to a desire for it, and it is neutral with regard to possible political direction. Resistance is in no way constrained to a radical or emancipatory aim, a fact that emerges clearly as soon as one analogizes Foucault's notion of resistance to its companion terms in Freud or Nietzsche. Yet in some ways this point is less a critique of Foucault, who especially in his later years made clear that his political commitments were not identical with his theoretical ones (and unapologetically revised the latter), than a sign of his misappropriation. For Foucault, resistance marks the presence of power and expands our understanding of its mechanics, but it is in this regard an analytical strategy rather than an expressly political one. "Where there is power, there is resistance, and yet, or rather consequently, this resistance is never in a position of exteriority to power. . . . [T]he strictly relational character of power relationships . . . depends upon a multiplicity of points of resistance: these play the role of *adversary, target, support, or handle* in power relations."[39] This appreciation of the extent to which resistance is by no means inherently subversive of power also reminds us that it is only by recourse to a very non-Foucaultian moral evaluation of power as bad or that which is to be overcome that it is possible to equate resistance with that which is good, progressive, or seeking an end to domination.

If popular and academic notions of resistance attach, however weakly at times, to a tradition of protest, the other contemporary substitute for a discourse of freedom—"empowerment"—would seem to correspond more closely to a tradition of idealist reconciliation. The language of resistance implicitly acknowledges the extent to which protest always transpires inside the regime; "empowerment," in contrast, registers the possibility of generating one's capacities, one's "self-esteem," one's life course, without capitulating to constraints by particular regimes of power. But in so doing, contemporary discourses of empowerment too often signal an oddly adaptive and harmonious relationship with domination insofar as they locate an individual's sense of worth and capacity in the register of individual feelings, a register implicitly located on something of an otherworldly plane vis-à-vis social and political power. In this regard, despite its apparent locution of resistance to subjection, contemporary discourses of empowerment partake strongly of liberal solipsism—the radical decontextualization of the subject characteristic of

---

[39] *History of Sexuality,* p. 95; emphasis added.

liberal discourse that is key to the fictional sovereign individualism of liberalism. Moreover, in its almost exclusive focus on subjects' emotional bearing and self-regard, empowerment is a formulation that converges with a regime's own legitimacy needs in masking the power of the regime.

This is not to suggest that talk of empowerment is always only illusion or delusion. It is to argue, rather, that while the notion of empowerment articulates that feature of freedom concerned with action, with being more than the consumer subject figured in discourses of rights and economic democracy, contemporary deployments of that notion also draw so heavily on an undeconstructed subjectivity that they risk establishing a wide chasm between the (experience of) empowerment and an actual capacity to shape the terms of political, social, or economic life. Indeed, the possibility that one can "feel empowered" without being so forms an important element of legitimacy for the antidemocratic dimensions of liberalism.

. . .

> Liberal institutions cease to be liberal as soon as they are attained: later on, there are no worse and no more thorough injurers of freedom than liberal institutions. Their effects are known well enough: they undermine the will to power; . . . they make men small, cowardly, and hedonistic.
>
> —Friedrich Nietzsche, *Twilight of the Idols*

In addition to the immediate political and philosophical reasons for which freedom has been jettisoned from contemporary progressive discourse, several persistent paradoxes appear to converge at the site of its evisceration. The first was confronted stoically by Weber as he traced how the desire for mastery animating instrumental rationality results in an iron cage of rationalization and enslavement to bureaucratic soullessness.[40] In this transmutation, freedom is simultaneously achieved and undone by the powers it fabricates and deploys to realize itself. Weber's "specialist without spirit" and "sensualist without heart" are not simply tragic figures of modern disenchantment but the unintended yet inevitable products of the quest for freedom conceived as mastery, or more precisely, conceived as maximizing predictability and rationality. These two figures are thus reminders that the will to institutionalize freedom, to resolve its contingent character and render it permanent, meta-

---

[40] See the final three pages of *The Protestant Ethic and the Spirit of Capitalism,* trans. T. Parsons (New York: Charles Scribner's Sons, 1958), and "Politics as a Vocation," in *From Max Weber: Essays in Sociology,* trans. and ed. H. H. Gerth and C. W. Mills (New York: Oxford University Press, 1946).

morphoses freedom into its opposite, into a system of constraints by norms of routinization and calculability, into unfreedom at the pinnacle of the project of rationality. For Gianni Vattimo, this constitutes "the discovery that the rationalization of the world turns against reason and its ends of perfection and emancipation, and does so not by error, accident, or a chance distortion, but precisely to the extent that it is more and more perfectly accomplished."[41] If this paradox confronts us especially sharply today, it is because the unprecedented "rationalization of the world" patently generates so little in the way of "perfection or emancipation." And we are haunted too by failed experiments in socialism in which the "rational" ordering of economy and society became a nightmare of bureaucratic dehumanization and soullessness.

A second paradox of freedom, about which Rousseau may have been most candid while Marx glossed it with dialectics and history, pertains to the dilemma that liberation from masters—god, king, history, or man—constrains us to an extraordinary responsibility for ourselves and for others. As we are emancipated from the tethers of history, we take up the weight of the future; "popular sovereignty" and "individual liberty" bequeath us the task to make something not only of ourselves but of the world whose making now lies in no hands but our own. Countless theorists and practitioners of freedom, of course, have sought to escape its paradoxical weight by defining freedom as license. But Plato's account of the seeds of tyranny inherent in licentious regimes, classical liberal descriptions of life as unhappy ("nasty, brutish, and short") in the politically free "state of nature," the Frankfurt School's theorization of liberal "choice" as an instrument of capitalist domination, and, more recently, Foucault's argument that sexual "liberation" transpires within rather than against regulatory discourses of sex—all of these serve as reminders that if liberty as license is ever freedom, it invariably transmutes into a form of domination.[42] This paradox, too, has a unique force in our time: as social mores become ever more obvious in their contingency, sovereignty and responsibility become increasingly difficult to inhabit, collectively and individually. Indeed, rarely have social "permissiveness" and social powerlessness coincided with the poignancy suggested by the current ungovernability of American cities.

These paradoxes incite a certain *ambivalence* and *anxiety* about freedom in which we dwell especially uncomfortably today. The pursuit of politi-

---

[41] *The Transparent Society,* trans. D. Webb (Baltimore: Johns Hopkins University Press, 1992), p. 78.

[42] Plato, *Republic* 564a; Hobbes, *Leviathan,* chap. 13; Marcuse, *One-Dimensional Man,* pp. 7–8. In Marcuse's account, domination refers not merely to overt subordination in a hierarchical relationship, but to that permeation of the social and individual body by the hegemonic powers—the needs and requirements—of a regime.

cal freedom is necessarily ambivalent because it is at odds with security, stability, protection, and irresponsibility; because it requires that we surrender the conservative pleasures of familiarity, insularity, and routine for investment in a more open horizon of possibility and sustained willingness to risk identity, both collective and individual. Freedom thus conceived is precisely at odds with the adolescent pleasures held out by liberal formulations of liberty as license. Indeed, the admonition to adolescents that "with freedom comes responsibilities" misses the point of this investment insofar as it isolates freedom from responsibility. The notion that there is a debt to pay for spending, a price to pay for indulgence, a weight to counter lightness already casts freedom as a matter of lightness, spending, indulgence—just the thing for adolescents or the relentlessly self-interested subject of liberalism. Freedom of the kind that seeks to set the terms of social existence requires inventive and careful use of power rather than rebellion against authority; it is sober, exhausting, and without parents. "For what is freedom," Nietzsche queries in *Twilight of the Idols,* but "that one has the will to assume responsibility for oneself."[43]

Freedom is a project suffused not just with ambivalence but with anxiety, because it is flanked by the problem of power on all sides: the powers against which it arrays itself as well as the power it must claim to enact itself. Against the liberal presumption that freedom transpires where power leaves off, I want to insist that freedom neither overcomes nor eludes power; rather, it requires for its sustenance that we take the full measure of power's range and appearances—the powers that situate, constrain, and produce subjects as well as the will to power entailed in practicing freedom. Here again, freedom emerges as that which is never achieved; instead, it is a permanent struggle against what will otherwise be done to and for us. "How is freedom measured in individuals and peoples?" Nietzsche asks, and answers, "according to the resistance which must be overcome, according to the exertion required, to remain on top . . . The free man is a warrior."[44]

If freedom is invariably accompanied by ambivalence and anxiety, these concomitants are magnified today both because of the kind of subjects we are and because of the particular figure of freedom required to counter contemporary forms of domination and regulation. The dimensions of responsibility for oneself and one's world that freedom demands often appear overwhelming and hopelessly unrealizable. They are overwhelming because history has become so fully secularized: there is

---

[43] *Twilight of the Idols,* in *The Portable Nietzsche,* ed. W. Kaufmann (New York: Viking, 1954), p. 542.
[44] Ibid.

nobody here but us—no "structures," no supervening agent, no cosmic force, no telos upon which we may count for assistance in realizing our aims or to which we may assign blame for failing to do so. Yet they are hopelessly unrealizable for an apparently opposite reason: the powers and histories by which the social, political, and economic world are knit together are so intricately globalized that it is difficult for defeatism not to preempt the desire to act. Moreover, bereft of the notion that history "progresses," or even that humans learn from history's most nightmarish episodes, we suffer a contemporary "disenchantment of the world" more vivid than Weber let alone Marx ever imagined. This is not so much nihilism—the oxymoronic belief in meaninglessness—as barely masked despair about the meanings and events that humans *have* generated. It is as if, notwithstanding the pervasiveness of nonteleological discourses of contingency, arbitrariness, and intervention, we were steeped in a consciousness of antiprogress. "What a ghastly century we have lived in," Cornel West ruminates, "there are misanthropic skeletons hanging in our closet. . . . [W]e have given up on the capacity of human beings to do *anything* right[,] . . . of human communities to solve any problem."[45]

If generic anxieties and ambivalence about freedom have intensified for reasons sketched in this chapter, they make still more understandable the tendency of late-twentieth-century "progressives" to turn back from substantive ambitions of a politics of freedom. But the consequences of such a retreat are traumatic for democratic thinking and projects, and they are not limited to the uncritical statism and attachments to redistributive justice characteristic of social democrats who call themselves radical. Rather, as chapters 2 and 3 of this work argue, the "instinct for freedom turned back on itself" surfaces in the form of a cultural ethos and politics of reproach, rancor, moralism, and guilt—the constellation detailed by Nietzsche's account of *ressentiment*. Nietzsche regarded our fundamental ambivalence about freedom—its demanding invocation of power and action—as capable of producing entire social formations, entire complexes of moral and political discourses, that denigrate the project of freedom rather than attempt it. For Nietzsche, when the negative moment in our ambivalence about freedom is ascendent, the will to power is redirected as a project of antifreedom; it takes the form of recrimination against action and power, and against those who affirm or embody the possibilities of action and power.

There is a second and related reason for taking up with Nietzsche in the ensuing reflections on contemporary forms of political life. His thought is useful in understanding the source and consequences of a contempo-

---

[45] *Prophetic Thought in Postmodern Times: Beyond Eurocentrism and Multiculturalism*, vol. 1 (Monroe, Maine: Common Courage Press, 1993), p. 6.

rary tendency to moralize in the place of political argument, and to understand the codification of injury and powerlessness—the marked turn away from freedom's pursuit—that this kind of moralizing politics entails. Examples of this tendency abound, but it is perhaps nowhere more evident than in the contemporary proliferation of efforts to pursue legal redress for injuries related to social subordination by marked attributes or behaviors: race, sexuality, and so forth.[46] This effort, which strives to establish racism, sexism, and homophobia as morally heinous in the law, and to prosecute its individual perpetrators there, has many of the attributes of what Nietzsche named the politics of *resentiment*: Developing a righteous critique of power from the perspective of the injured, it delimits a specific site of blame for suffering by constituting sovereign subjects and events as responsible for the "injury" of social subordination. It fixes the identities of the injured and the injuring as social positions, and codifies as well the meanings of their actions against all possibilities of indeterminacy, ambiguity, and struggle for resignification or repositioning. This effort also casts the law in particular and the state more generally as neutral arbiters of injury rather than as themselves invested with the power to injure. Thus, the effort to "outlaw" social injury powerfully legitimizes law and the state as appropriate protectors against injury and casts injured individuals as needing such protection by such protectors. Finally, in its economy of perpetrator and victim, this project seeks not power or emancipation for the injured or the subordinated, but the revenge of punishment, making the perpetrator hurt as the sufferer does.

It is important to be clear here. I am not impugning antidiscrimination law concerned with eliminating barriers to equal access to education, employment, and so forth. Nor am I suggesting that what currently travels under the sign of "harassment" is not hurtful, that "hate speech" is not hateful, or that harassment and hate speech are inappropriate for political contestation. Rather, precisely because they are hurtful, hateful, and political, because these phenomena are complex sites of political and historical deposits of discursive power, attempts to address them litigiously are worrisome. When social "hurt" is conveyed to the law for resolution, political ground is ceded to moral and juridical ground. Social injury such as that conveyed through derogatory speech becomes that which is "unacceptable" and "individually culpable" rather than that which symptomizes deep political distress in a culture; injury is thereby rendered intentional and individual, politics is reduced to punishment, and justice

---

[46] For the remarks that follow, I am indebted to Judith Butler's analysis of "hate speech" in "Burning Acts: On Injurious Speech," in *Performativity and Performance,* ed. Andrew Parker and Eve Sedgwick (New York: Routledge, 1994), and to conversations with her about that essay.

is equated with such punishment on the one hand and with protection by the courts on the other. It is in this vein that, throughout the ensuing chapters, I question the political *meaning* and *implications* of the turn toward law and other elements of the state for resolution of antidemocratic injury. In the course of such questioning, I worry about the transformation of the instrumental function of law into a political end, and about bartering political freedom for legal protection. I worry, too, about the recuperation of an anachronistic discourse of universal and particular that this turn seems to entail: if the range of political possibility today traffics between proliferating highly specified (identity-based) rights and entitlements and protecting general or universal rights, it is little wonder that tiresome debates about censorship, and about "identity politics" versus "universal justice," so preoccupy North American progressives in the late twentieth century.

When contemporary anxieties about the difficult imperatives of freedom are installed in the regulatory forces of the state in the form of increasingly specified codes of injury and protection, do we unwittingly increase the power of the state and its various regulatory discourses at the expense of political freedom? Are we fabricating something like a plastic cage that reproduces and further regulates the injured subjects it would protect? Unlike the "iron cage" of Weber's ascetics under capitalism, this cage would be quite transparent to the ordinary eye.[47] Yet it would be distressingly durable on the face of the earth: law and other state institutions are not known for their capacity to historicize themselves nor for their adaptation to cultural particulars. Nor is this cage fabricated only by those invested in social justice: Foucault's characterization of contemporary state power as a "tricky combination in the same political structures of individualization techniques, and of totalization procedures" suggests that progressive efforts to pursue justice along lines of legal recognition of identity corroborate and abet rather than contest the "political shape" of domination in our time.[48]

The danger here is that in the name of equality or justice for those historically excluded even from liberal forms of these goods, we may be erecting intricate ensembles of definitions and procedures that cast in the antihistorical rhetoric of the law and the positivist rhetoric of bureaucratic discourse highly specified identities and the injuries contingently constitutive of them. In this effort, notwithstanding its good intentions, will we not, as Foucault puts the matter, further "tie the individual to [it]self"? Is it not precisely this form of power that "applies itself to immediate everyday life [to] categorize the individual, mark him by his own

[47] *Protestant Ethic and the Spirit of Capitalism,* p. 181.
[48] "The Subject and Power," in *Michel Foucault: Beyond Structuralism and Hermeneutics,* ed. Herbert Dreyfus and Paul Rabinow (Chicago: University of Chicago Press, 1982), p. 213.

individuality, attach him to his own identity, impose a law of truth on him which he must recognize and which others have to recognize in him"?[49] Even as we seek to redress the pain and humiliation consequent to historical deprivation of freedom in a putatively "free" political order, might we thus sustain the psychic residues of these histories as the animus of political institutions constitutive of our future? It is against this grave possibility, and for alternatives, that these essays are written.

[49] Ibid., p. 212.

CHAPTER TWO

Postmodern Exposures, Feminist Hesitations

> The process of the emancipation of reason . . . has gone
> further than either idealism or positivism expected. Numerous
> peoples and cultures have taken to the world stage, and it has
> become impossible to believe that history is a unilinear process
> directed towards a telos. The realization of the universality of
> history has made universal history impossible.
> —Gianni Vattimo, *The Transparent Society*

> But the life that begins on earth after the last day is simply
> human life. —Georgio Agamben, *The Coming Community*

MANY THINKERS have hailed our times as "postmodern," yet there is little consensus among them about the configuration of this condition, its most striking markers, implications, and portents. Nor is there agreement about postmodernity's sites and sources of origin, current geo-demographic headquarters, or dynamic of production. Is postmodernity the issue of "advanced" capitalism; of late-twentieth-century technology, art, or architecture; of Europe's self-decentering or of a global intifada of the margins against the center; of postphilosophy's murder of truth, the subject, the solidity of the earth, and the promise of the heavens? The unresolved character of these questions themselves accord with late modern dissembling of origins, headquarters, engines of development, reason, coherence, and continuity in history. Refusal to self-define or write a single origins story also reflects a late modern or postmodern consciousness of the exclusions and violations accomplished by master narratives, the oppressiveness of closure on identity, and the vulnerability to colonization and regulation presented by definitive naming.[1]

---

[1] Although I prefer William Connolly's "late modern" appellation for our times, this chapter is concerned with mapping and responding to challenges to what its detractors have named "postmodernism" or "postmodern thought," and thus I have largely sought to work within the latter's locution throughout the essay. While the advantage of such a strategy is that it permits a more direct encounter with critics of "postmodernism," the disadvantage is that it concedes the existence of a doctrine or school of thought often more usefully called into question as such. For example: Is poststructuralism equivalent to postmodernism? What is the relationship of each to post-Marxism? And if Foucault, Lacan, Derrida, and

We may respect this refusal to speak definitively or consistently, this anxiety about closure and totality, and at the same time partially resist it. While what have come to be called postmodern epistemological and ontological insights commission political claims of a partial, situated, and local character, the development of an emancipatory or radically democratic politics within contemporary political conditions requires incessant theorization of these conditions and, at times at least, an accounting of their global movement. To do less, to abandon theory and accounts of global tendencies at this juncture, leaves us reeling in postmodernity rather than appropriating and navigating for radical political projects its peculiar (dis)organization of social, political, and economic life. Yet theory and global accounts today may also appear in a postmodernist parlance: self-consciously perspectival rather than Archimedean, temporally situated rather than floating above history, framed by and within a particular idiom rather than pretending to universal voice. Within the false purity of its etymological life, theory bears no inherent relation to the universalizing, colonizing, or ethnocentric tendencies with which it has lately been charged. The Greek *theoria* from which our term descends promises only the vision or perspective achieved by corporeal, cognitive, or spiritual traveling. Insofar as postmodernity's more treacherous attributes include disorientation resulting from boundary breakdowns, collapsed narratives, high object density, excessive speeds, and sensory bombardment, we are in no little need of the perspective theory promises. Confounded as well by the decertification of god, science, philosophy, and intuition as epistemological and normative authorities, theory's promise of vision—and especially of developing a postfoundational angle of (in)sight—also carries unparalleled contemporary importance.

. . .

With its affiliates—postindustrialism, postphilosophy, poststructuralism, post-Marxism, and *posthistoire*—postmodernity would seem to signify a pervasive condition and experience of "being after."[2] In political theory and practice, postmodernism is *after* Platonic forms, Hobbesian sovereignty, Hegelian totality, Millian liberty, Kantian reason and will, and Marxian dialectics and redemptive politics. In history, it is after

---

Donna Haraway are all poststructuralists, do *they* share a politics? What kinship does Vaclav Havel's "postmodernism" bear with Richard Rorty's? A more extended meditation on this problem appears in Judith Butler's "Contingent Foundations: Feminism and the Question of 'Postmodernism,' " in Seyla Benhabib et al., *Feminist Contentions: A Philosophical Exchange* (New York: Routledge, 1994).

[2] Ferenc Feher and Agnes Heller, *The Postmodern Political Condition* (Oxford: Polity Press, 1988), p. 4.

Hegelian and Marxian discernments of reason, purpose, and progress in time, human affairs, and human nature; it is also after periodicity, teleology, and facticity detached from discourse. In social life and sociology, postmodernity is marked by fragmentation without corresponding wholes, heterogeneity without the unity that converts difference to diversity, social surfaces without depths, and deracination of communities and peoples. In political economy, postmodernity registers postindustrial and increasingly decommodified capitalist production as well as capitalism's triumphant global reach in heretofore unimagined combination with substantial variety among regional capitalist cultures. Postmodern capitalism also features the reversal of a centuries-old process of economic concentration, although the shift from consolidated and hierarchical to dispersed and networked production is accompanied by increased privatization and monopoly of ownership. Postmodern capitalist power, like postmodern state power, is monopolized without being concentrated or centered: it is tentacular, roving, and penetrating, paradoxically advanced by diffusing and decentralizing itself.[3]

To speak of postmodernity as specific configurations and representations of social, economic, and political life is not (yet) to take a political position on it or within it, nor even to adopt, in Lyotard's intonation, a particular "sensibility."[4] It is simply to draw, in necessarily partial and contestable ways, some of the contours of the contemporary world within which there are as many political possibilities as there are political locations, attachments, and imaginations. Nietzsche, Rousseau, Hegel, and Marx were all theorists of modernity, were specifically produced by and preoccupied with modernity, but also adopted different positions *on* and *within* modernity. Similarly, while postmodern conditions produce certain historical, epistemological, and ontological ruptures in terms of which we are challenged to develop new political understandings and projects, these ruptures do not by themselves produce a particular politics; they have no necessary or inevitable political entailments.

From feminists who array themselves "against postmodernism," the rare acknowledgment of the distinction just drawn between postmodern conditions and theory, between epoch and politics, is a political move. The conflation of such registers by those steeped in materialist analysis and practiced at attending to fine gradations of modernist feminisms speaks a stubborn determination to vanquish evidence of historical devel-

---

[3] See Sheldon Wolin, "Democracy and the Welfare State: The Political and Theoretical Connections between *Staatsräson* and *Wohlfahrtsstaatsräson*," in *The Presence of the Past: Essays on the State and the Constitution* (Baltimore: Johns Hopkins University Press, 1989), pp. 173–79; and Wendy Brown, "Deregulating Women: The Trials of Freedom under a Thousand Points of Light," *sub/versions* 1 (1991), p. 4.

[4] "Rules and Paradoxes and Svelte Appendix," *Cultural Critique* 5 (1986–87), p. 209.

opments that its antagonists blame on thinking—the latter often portrayed as dangerously relativist, irresponsible, unpolitical, or unfeminist. In other words, the move to blur or collapse these critical distinctions bespeaks a desire to kill the messenger, and what I want to explore in this essay is the nature of this desire. If the "postmodern turn" in political/feminist theory is, at its best, an attempt to articulate and engage the characteristic powers of our age, what frightens feminism about this age and about developing a politics appropriate to it?

In casting postmodernity as a time, circumstance, and configuration rather than an intellectual tendency or political position, I do not mean to underestimate the troubling nature of some of its constituent qualities. For those desirous of alternatives to existing dominations, exploitations, and inequalities, our time carries abundant political perils, many of which are heightened by inadequate apprehension of specifically postmodern modes of power. Indeed, it is quite possible that our greatest impediments to developing cogent oppositional politics today arise not from the academically crumbled foundations of Truth, facticity, or the modernist subject, as those who array themselves against postmodern theory ordinarily contend, but rather from certain "material" features of our age: the expanding hegemony of technical reason, cultural-spatial disorientation, and a political tendency produced by this disorientation— "reactionary foundationalism." Each of these is briefly considered below.

Technical Reason.   Marcuse before Habermas, and Weber before Marcuse, identified as the most ominous feature of a fully "disenchanted age" not an immaculate nihilism but a form of nihilism in which "technical reason" (Marcuse), "means-end rationality" (Habermas), or "instrumental rationality" (Weber) becomes the dominant and unchallengeable discourse framing and ultimately suffusing all social practices. Technical reason is currently among the strongest contemporary forces erasing both the standing and significance of the subject; it is far more potent than the subject-disintegrating effects of postmodern theory. As Foucault makes clear in his analysis of the achieved partnership between jurisprudential and disciplinary discourse—the latter may be seen as one social face of the modernist hegemony of instrumental rationality— disciplinary or instrumental rationality easily absorbs both the modern subject and opposition from within liberal discourse.[5] Moreover, as even the most casual ethnographer of contemporary North American and European cultures may discern, technical reason extends its hegemony when other legitimating discourses of a culture—political, religious, or

---

[5] Michel Foucault, "Two Lectures," in *Power/Knowledge: Selected Interviews and Other Writings, 1972–1977*, ed. C. Gordon (New York: Pantheon, 1980), pp. 105–8.

scientific—are fractured or discredited, a process that is a defining feature of postmodernity.

Technical reason conjoins with postmodern fragmentations of political and social power to make the critical articulation of domination extraordinarily difficult, especially if this articulation is attempted in a modernist idiom. Postmodern power is often characterized as decentered and diffuse even while it incessantly violates, transgresses, and resituates social boundaries;[6] it flows on surfaces and irrigates through networks rather than consolidating in bosses and kings;[7] it is ubiquitous, liminal, potent in small and fluid doses.[8] In the absence of a critical discourse attuned to such configurations and conduits of power, we risk becoming unresisting vehicles of its objectionable contemporary functions, more eviscerated of soul than simulacra, more oblivious to our unfreedom than One-Dimensional Man. Here lies the serious threat of a thoroughly disintegrated subject, of false consciousness beyond what either Marx or radical feminism ever dreamed, of a total "system" that no longer requires a systematic form to operate as containment.[9]

Disorientation.   Another consequence of postmodernity's decentering and diffusion of power—its *centrifugation* of power—is that we are today very susceptible to simply getting lost. In Fredric Jameson's reading, insofar as being lost means being without (fixed) means of orientation, postmodernity renders this condition a normal feature of our world:

> What is striking about the new urban ensembles around Paris . . . is that there is *absolutely no perspective at all.* Not only has the street disappeared (that was already the task of modernism) but all profiles have disappeared as well. This is

---

[6] One clear example of this in the policy domain appears in the vicissitudes of welfare state policy over the last decade: the boundaries and relations between family, state, society, economy, workplace, and individual have been incessantly and contradictorily reworked. See Brown, "Deregulating Women"; Wolin, *Presence of the Past;* and Nancy Fraser, *Unruly Practices: Power, Discourse, and Gender in Contemporary Social Theory* (Minneapolis: University of Minnesota Press, 1989), chaps. 7, 8.

[7] Foucault, "Two Lectures," p. 98.

[8] Donna Haraway, "A Manifesto for Cyborgs: Science, Technology, and Socialist Feminism and the Privilege of Partial Perspective," in *Feminism/Postmodernism,* ed. Linda Nicholson (New York: Routledge, 1990), p. 195.

[9] Arguing that a good deal of this nightmare is already upon us, Sheldon Wolin names its expressly political face "democracy without the demos" or "managed democracies" that "make only rhetorical gestures toward egalitarianism [or] widespread participation in power" ("Democracy in the Discourse of Postmodernism," *Social Research* 57 [1990], p. 26). He also insists that postmodern theory, or the strand of it incarnated by Richard Rorty, accelerates and assists this phenomenon through celebrating the severance of truth from politics, adulating "difference" that is actually recycled liberal/repressive tolerance, and cultivating language games—"stories"—that mock the value of reportable, discussable, political reality (pp. 26–29).

bewildering, and I use existential bewilderment in this new postmodern space to make a final diagnosis of the loss of our ability to *position ourselves within this space and cognitively map it*. This is then projected back on the emergence of a global, multinational culture that is decentered and cannot be visualized, a culture in which one cannot position oneself.[10]

Stanley Aronowitz offers a similar reading of the effect of deterritorialization of production on the "patterns of everyday life. It means . . . that we have lost a sense of place."[11] In the absence of orienting instruments, to avert "existential bewilderment" inhabitants of postmodernity—substituting (poorly) for more comprehensive political analysis—resort to fierce assertions of "identities" in order to know/invent who, where, and what they are. Drawing upon the historically eclipsed meaning of disrupted and fragmented narratives of ethnicity, race, gender, sexuality, region, continent, or nation, identity politics permits a sense of situation—and often a sense of filiation or community—without requiring profound comprehension of the world in which one is situated. Identity politics permits positioning without temporal or spatial mapping, a feature that sharply distinguishes it from (Marxian) class analysis and reveals its proximity to (liberal) interest group politics. In this respect, identity politics, with its fierce assertion and production of subjects, appears less as a radical political response to postmodernity than a symptom of its ruptures and disorienting effects.[12] As much a symptom of a certain powerlessness as a redress of it, identity politics may also be read as a reaction to postmodernity's cross-cultural meldings and appropriations, as well as its boundless commodification of cultural practices and icons. Identity politics emerges partly as a reaction, in other words, to an ensemble of distinctly postmodern assaults upon the integrity of modernist communities producing collective identity.

Reactionary Foundationalism.   Along with identity politics, there has arisen a second coping strategy for our "lost" condition in postmodernity, one equally familiar to even the most casual reader of postmodern culture or the subset of it that is the knowledge industry. This is the strategy of political, religious, or epistemological fundamentalism, "foundationalism without a grand narrative," or reactionary founda-

---

[10] "Regarding Postmodernism—A Conversation with Fredric Jameson," in *Universal Abandon? The Politics of Postmodernism,* ed. Andrew Ross (Minneapolis: University of Minnesota Press, 1988), p. 7.

[11] "Postmodernism and Politics," in Ross, *Universal Abandon,* p. 48.

[12] See Ernesto Laclau and Chantal Mouffe, *Hegemony and Socialist Strategy* (London: Verso, 1985) for an alternate account of identity politics as a response to late modern capitalism.

tionalism.[13] What constitutes this strategy as reactionary rather than merely conservative is its truncated, instrumental link to a foundational narrative; it is rooted not in a coherent tradition but in a fetishized, decontextualized fragment or icon of such a narrative—"the American flag," "the great books," "the traditional family." Thus, "fundamentalists select one aspect of the dogma, one 'text of foundation' with regard to which they declare all attempts at hermeneutics politically subversive."[14] Importantly for our purposes, reactionary foundationalism is not limited to the political and intellectual Right, but emerges across the political spectrum from those hostile to what they take to be postmodern political decay and intellectual disarray. Like identity politics, it is both a symptom of and act of resistance against the epistemological, political, and social terrain postmodernity forces us to inhabit. Reactionary foundationalism, unlike its more coherent and dignified ancestor, rarely and barely postures as Truth. More often, it works in the idiom of moral utilitarianism, presenting and legitimating itself as the indispensable threads preserving some indisputable good, for example, Western civilization, the American way of life, feminism, or left politics.

Both the mien and the reasoning constitutive of Nancy Hartsock's principles for "revised and reconstructed [feminist] theory" exemplify the anxieties and strategies of reactionary foundationalism. In "Foucault on Power: A Theory for Women?" Hartsock writes: "[W]e need to . . . constitut[e] ourselves as subjects as well as objects of history. . . . [W]e need to be assured that some systematic knowledge about our world and ourselves is possible. . . . [W]e need a theory of power that recognizes that our practical daily activity contains an understanding of the world."[15] In her insistence that "we need" these (articles of faith? ontological assumptions? political principles?) if "we" are to have "feminist politics" at all—as other fundamentalists claim we need "the family" or taboos against homosexuality for "cultural survival"—Hartsock does not concern herself with the defensibility or persuasiveness of the narrative out of which these items are torn. She is concerned only with the (dubious) necessity of rescuing them from the discredited narratives, a

[13] Feher and Heller, *Postmodern Political Condition*, pp. 7–8.

[14] Ibid., p. 7. If one compares Allan Bloom's *Closing of the American Mind: How Higher Education Has Failed Democracy and Impoverished the Souls of Today's Students* (New York: Simon and Schuster, 1987), with earlier works in the Straussian tradition of interpreting political theory from which Bloom hails, one can see quite clearly the postmodern quality: the former operates as overt fundamentalism, is littered with icons of "truth," and opposes itself to "relativism" and hedonism, while the latter, however conservative, is foundationalism self-conscious of the indispensability of hermeneutics for its existence, intentionally and provocatively opposing itself to other interpretations in the political theory "canon."

[15] Nancy Hartsock, "Foucault on Power: A Theory for Women?" in Nicholson, ed., *Feminism/Postmodernism*, pp. 170–72.

rescue waged in order to "preserve" feminism from what she takes to be the disorienting, debilitating, and depoliticizing characteristics of post-modern intellectual maneuvers.

When these precepts "without which we cannot survive" issue from the intellectual or political Right, they are easy enough to identify as both reactionary and fundamentalist. It is fairly clear what they oppose and seek to foreclose: *inter alia,* democratic conversation about our collective condition and future. But when they issue from feminists or others on the "Left," they are more slippery, especially insofar as they are posed in the name of caring about political things, caring about "*actual* women" or about women's "*actual* condition in the world," and are lodged against those who presumably do not or cannot care, given their postmodern or poststructuralist entanglements.

The remainder of this essay turns this argument on its head. I will suggest that feminist wariness about postmodernism may ultimately be coterminous with a wariness about politics, when politics is grasped as a terrain of struggle without fixed or metaphysical referents and a terrain of power's irreducible and pervasive presence in human affairs. Contrary to its insistence that it speaks in the name of the political, much feminist anti-postmodernism betrays a preference for extrapolitical terms and practices: for Truth (unchanging, incontestable) over politics (flux, con-test, instability); for certainty and security (safety, immutability, privacy) over freedom (vulnerability, publicity); for discoveries (science) over de-cisions (judgments); for separable subjects armed with established rights and identities over unwieldy and shifting pluralities adjudicating for themselves and their future on the basis of nothing more than their own habits and arguments. This particular modernist reaction to postmoder-nism makes sense if we recall that the promise of the Enlightenment was a revision of the old Platonic promise to put an end to politics by sup-planting it with Truth. In its modern variant, this promise was tendered through the multiple technologies of nature's rationality in human affairs (Adam Smith); science, including the science of administration (Hobbes); and universal reason (Kant, Hegel, Marx). Modernity could not make good on this promise, of course, but modernists do not surrender the dream it instilled of a world governed by reason divested of power.[16] Avowed ambivalence about Western reason and rationality notwith-standing, feminist modernists are no exception, but the nature of our

[16] Jurgen Habermas remains the exemplar of this modernist impulse. See especially *Knowledge and Human Interests* (Boston: Beacon, 1971); *The Theory of Communicative Action,* vol. 1, *Reason and the Rationalization of Society,* trans. T. McCarthy (Boston: Beacon, 1984); "Modernity vs. Postmodernity," *New German Critique* 22 (1981), pp. 3–14; and "A Reply to My Critics," in *Habermas: Critical Debates,* ed. John B. Thompson and David Held (Cam-bridge: MIT Press, 1982).

attachment to this ironically antipolitical vision is distinctively colored by feminist projects. To the particulars of this attachment we now turn.

. . .

Contemporary Western nomenclature for politics emerges not only from *polis* but also from *politeia,* an ancient Greek term marking the singularly human practice of *constituting* a particular mode of collective life through the generation of multiple associations, institutions, boundaries, mores, habits, and laws. The rich connotative content of *politeia* suggests that politics refers always to a condition of plurality and difference, to the human capacity for *producing* a world of meanings, practices, and institutions, and to the constant implication of power among us—its generation, distribution, circulation, and effects.

The constitutive elements of politics suggested by *politeia* do not disappear in postmodernity but are starkly featured within it, at times exaggerated in topographical articulation and complexity. In the regional cultural diversification accompanying the relentless process of global integration, and in the discovery of difference's infinitude, the dimensions of human plurality productive of politics now appear as a permanent and irresolvable condition, no longer reducible to class society or interest-based politics, but also never innocent of power and stratification. The measure of our world-making capacity is paradoxically both amplified and diminished by postmodernity's disenchanting effects: without the crutch of progress, essences, god, teleologies, iron laws of development, or any other reasons in history, humans appear as the only fabricators of culture but simultaneously as so completely fabricated, so void of being of our own, that we do not exist, *we* create nothing. The subject is dissolved at the same time that postmodernity reveals us as all there is; there is no "maker" anywhere, only the constant effects of what has already been made, including ourselves.

Postmodernity produces a similar accentuation and diffusion of the political problematic of power. Bursting its modernist containment by the formal categories and boundaries of sovereignty and the public, power reveals itself everywhere: in gender, class, race, ethnicity, and sexuality; in speech, writing, discourse, representation, and reason; in families, curricula, bodies, and the arts. This ubiquity of power's appearance through postmodernity's incessant secularizations and boundary erosions both spurs and frustrates feminist epistemological and political work: on the one hand, it animates and legitimizes feminism's impulse to politicize all ideologically naturalized arrangements and practices; on the other, it threatens to dissipate us *and* our projects as it dissolves a relatively bounded formulation of the political and disintegrates the coherence of women as a collective subject.

While human plurality, human agency, and the problem of power are in these ways transmogrified in and by postmodernity, these elements of political life continue to constitute rich resources for feminist political imaginations. Yet it is significant that in the course of this brief itinerary of elements of *politeia* in postmodernity, there has been little mention of those three terms or practices without which some have argued that (feminist) politics cannot survive: the subject, truth, and normativity.[17] We may thus begin to wonder if it is not politics as such but politics of a particular, peculiarly modern and possibly problematic sort that depends so heavily upon this triad.

.   .   .

Despite Luce Irigaray's formulation of "the subject [as] always masculine," Judith Butler's exposure of the gendered subject as a "regulatory fiction," Denise Riley's account of the category "women" as "historically, discursively constructed, and always relative," and extensive feminist critiques of masculinist models and practices of the subject, deconstruction of the subject incites palpable feminist panic.[18] Insofar as the subject as self is a specific creation of modernity, and even more of liberalism, this panic would seem to rest in feminism's genealogically intelligible (albeit politically questionable) attachment to these overlapping political and cultural formations.[19] However, few feminist objections to postmodernism have been explicitly grounded in a valorization of liberalism, and few concerned with sustaining a strong notion of the

[17] In "Dilemmas of Difference," Christine Di Stefano characterizes "the feminist case against postmodernism" as consisting of "several related claims," including the following: "the postmodernist project, if seriously adopted by feminists, would make any semblance of a feminist politics impossible. To the extent that feminist politics is bound up with a specific constituency or subject, namely, women, the postmodernist prohibition against subject-centered inquiry and theory undermines the legitimacy of a broad-based organized movement dedicated to articulating and implementing the goals of such a constituency" (in Nicholson, ed., *Feminism/Postmodernism*, p. 76).

[18] Luce Irigaray, "Any Theory of the Subject Has Already Been Appropriated by the Masculine," *Speculum of the Other Woman*, trans. G. Gill (Ithaca: Cornell University Press, 1985); Judith Butler, *Gender Trouble: Feminism and the Subversion of Identity* (New York: Routledge, 1989); and Denise Riley, *"Am I that Name?": Feminism and the Category of "Women" in History* (Minneapolis: University of Minnesota Press, 1988).

[19] According to Di Stefano, "contemporary Western feminism is firmly, if ambivalently, located in the modernist ethos, which made possible the feminist identification and critique of gender" ("Dilemmas of Difference," p. 64).

subject express affection for the (masculine) liberal subject. Moreover, modes of political life transpiring prior to or beyond the boundaries of modern, Western cultures of liberalism have not been without promising feminist political formations. Indeed, insofar as the condition of politics as a problem of collective life is plurality rather than individuality, a politics devoid of the rational, willing, autonomous, and self-determining subject of modernity is not so difficult to conceive. Why, then, is putting the subject in question—decentering its constitution, deconstructing its unity, denaturing its origins and components—such a lightning rod for feminist hostility to postfoundational thought?

Seyla Benhabib answers this way: "Carried to its logical consequences, poststructuralism leads to a theory without addressees, to a self without a center. . . . Is not a feminist theory that allies itself with poststructuralism in danger of losing its very reason for being?"[20] Although this worry is rhetorically compelling, it also appears to be slightly disingenuous. After all, the most ardent feminist poststructuralists do not claim that women's pervasive economic subordination, lack of reproductive freedoms, or vulnerability to endemic sexual violence simply evaporates because we cannot fix or circumscribe who or what "woman" is or what it is that "she" wants. Certainly gender can be conceived as a marker of power, a maker of subjects, an axis of subordination, without thereby converting it to a "center" of "selves" understood as foundational.

In fact, postmodern decentering, disunifying, and denaturalizing of the subject is far more threatening to the status of feminism's well of truth than to feminism's *raison d'être*. While often cast as concern with retaining an object of political struggle, feminist attachment to the subject is more critically bound to retaining women's experiences, feelings, and voices as sources and certifications of postfoundational political truth. When the notion of a unified and coherent subject is abandoned, we not only cease to be able to speak of woman or of women in an unproblematic way, we forsake the willing, deliberate, and consenting "I" that liberalism's rational-actor model of the human being proffers, and we surrender the autonomous, rights-bearing fictional unity that liberalism promises to secure. Yet each of these terms and practices—woman, willing, deliberate, consenting, an "I," rational actors, autonomy, and rights—has been challenged by various *modernist* feminisms as masculinist, racist, ethnocentric, heterosexist, culturally imperialist, or all of the above. Moreover, dispensing with the unified subject does not mean ceasing to be able to speak about our experiences as women, only that our words cannot be legitimately deployed or construed as larger or longer than the moments of the lives they speak from; they cannot be anointed as "au-

---

[20] "On Contemporary Feminist Theory," *Dissent* 36 (1989), p. 369.

thentic" or "true" since the experience they announce is linguistically contained, socially constructed, discursively mediated, and never just individually "had."

But this is precisely the point at which many contemporary North Atlantic feminists hesitate and equivocate: while insisting on the constructed character of gender, most also seek to preserve some variant of consciousness-raising as a mode of discerning and delivering the "truth" about women. Consider Catharine MacKinnon's insistence that women are entirely the products of men's construction and her ontologically contradictory project of developing a jurisprudence based on "an account of the world from women's point of view."[21] Consider the similar problematic in other theories of "the feminist standpoint," the sharp but frequently elided tensions between adhering to social construction theory on one hand, and epistemologically privileging women's accounts of social life on the other. "The world from women's point of view" and "the feminist standpoint" attempt resolution of the postfoundational epistemology problem by deriving from within women's experience the grounding for women's accounts. But this resolution requires suspending recognition that women's "experience" is thoroughly constructed, historically and culturally varied, and interpreted without end. Within feminist standpoint theory as well as much other modernist feminist theory, consciousness-raising thus operates as feminism's epistemologically positivist moment. The material excavated there, like the material uncovered in psychoanalysis or delivered in confession, is valued as the hidden truth of women's existence—true because it is hidden, and hidden because women's subordination functions in part through silencing, marginalization, and privatization.[22]

Indeed, those familiar with Foucault's genealogy of confession will have discerned in this argument an implied homology between the epistemological-political operations of consciousness-raising and those he assigns to confessional discourse. In his account of modern sexuality as structured by such discourse, Foucault argues that confession—inaugurated by the Catholic Church as a technique of power that works

---

[21] *Feminism Unmodified: Discourses on Life and Law* (Cambridge: Harvard University Press, 1987), pp. 48–50.

[22] Although I have thus far allowed MacKinnon and Hartsock to be the implicit representatives of "feminist standpoint" theory, Patricia Hill Collins's effort to develop an "Afrocentric feminist epistemology" or a "Black women's standpoint" may be considered here as well. While Collins is far more careful than MacKinnon or Hartsock to avoid claiming that black women have a monopoly on either oppression or truth, she does insist that black women's standpoint derives from her marginalized status as "outsider within" or "neither/nor" within the categories "women and blacks" (where woman is implicitly coded white and black is implicitly coded male). See her *Black Feminist Thought* (New York: Routledge, 1991), chap. 10.

by exposure and individuation—produces "truth" as a secret contained within.[23] Confessional revelations are thus construed as liberation from repression or secrecy, and truth-telling about our desires or experiences is construed as deliverance from the power that silences and represses them (rather than as itself a site and effect of regulatory power). What Foucault terms the "internal ruse of confession" is reducible to this reversal of power and freedom: "Confession frees, but power reduces one to silence; truth does not belong to the order of power, but shares an original affinity with freedom."[24] In believing truth-telling about our experiences to be our liberation, Foucault suggests, we forget that this truth has been established as the secret to our souls not by us but by those who would discipline us through that truth.

Since women's subordination is partly achieved through the construction and positioning of us as private—sexual, familial, emotional—and is produced and inscribed in the domain of both domestic and psychic interiors, then within modernity the voicing of women's experience acquires an inherently confessional cast. Indeed, "breaking silence" is a standard feminist metaphor for what occurs in consciousness-raising sessions, speak-outs against sexual violence, and other forums for feminist truth telling. Consciousness-raising, as/like confession, delivers the "hidden truth" of women and women's experience, which accounts for those symptomatically modernist paradoxes represented in Catharine MacKinnon's work: while women are socially constructed to the core, women's words about their experience, because they issue from an interior space and against an injunction to silence, are anointed as Truth, and constitute the foundations of feminist knowledge. Within the confessional frame, even when social construction is adopted as method for explaining the making of gender, "feelings" and "experiences" acquire a status that is politically if not ontologically essentialist—beyond hermeneutics. This strand of feminist foundationalism transports the domain of Truth from reason to subjectivity, from *Geist* to inner voice, even while femininity itself is submitted to a methodology elaborating its fully fabricated nature.

As a source of truth, the subjectivity of the subject constitutes feminism's alternative to aperspectival and presumably masculinist reason and science. Through articulations of "standpoint" or women's "point of view," this alternative seeks legitimacy as a form of knowledge about the world that, while admitting to being "situated," cannot admit to partiality or contestability, and above all cannot be subjected to hermeneu-

---

[23] *The History of Sexuality,* vol.1, *An Introduction,* trans. R. Hurley (New York: Vintage, 1980), pp. 58–63.

[24] Ibid., p. 60.

tics without giving up its truth value. If feminist anxieties about deconstructing the subject are in this way linked to feminist anxieties about a postfoundational knowledge universe, we may proceed to this problem directly: What is it about feminist politics that cannot survive, or worries that it cannot survive, a radically disenchanted postmodern world? What is it about feminism that fears the replacement of truth with politics, method with contesting interpretations, privileged and systematic knowledge with a cacophony of unequal voices clamoring for position?

. . .

Feminism's complex relationship to Truth—its rejection of Truth's masculine Western modes and its need for grounded knowledges of its own that are equal in potency to those it rejects—has been productively explored by feminist philosophers and historians as an ensemble of epistemological and political conundrums.[25] But in order to fathom our anxiety about a politics unarmed with Truth, I want to explore the problem in Nietzschean terms—the terms of cultural dreads, displacements, ailments, and diagnoses. In this endeavor, it is necessary to retell a portion of a story Nietzsche tells, for Nietzschean "conclusions" have little nonnihilistic force in the absence of Nietzschean genealogies.

In *On the Genealogy of Morals,* Nietzsche inaugurates his deconstruction of morality with an intentionally disturbing query: What if moral goodness were not the telos of the human capacity for splendor and accomplishment but rather, its nemesis? "What if a symptom of regression were inherent in the 'good,' likewise a danger, a seduction, a poison, a narcotic, through which the present was possibly living *at the expense of the future?*"[26] In short, what if morality is not a spur to great human achievements but a strangulation of them? Nietzsche traces these possibilities by hypothesizing morality "as consequence, as symptom, as mask, as tartufferie, as illness, as misunderstanding, but also morality as cause, as remedy, as stimulant, as restraint, as poison."[27] Through a

---

[25] In Donna Haraway's words: "my problem, and 'our' problem, is how to have *simultaneously* an account of radical historical contingency for all knowledge claims and knowing subjects, a critical practice for recognizing our own 'semiotic technologies' for making meanings, *and* a no-nonsense commitment to faithful accounts of a 'real' world" ("Situated Knowledges: The Science Question in Feminism and the Privilege of Partial Perspectives," *Feminist Studies* 14 [1988], p. 579). See also discussions of this problem by Sandra Harding, Evelyn Fox Keller, Catharine MacKinnon, and Nancy Hartsock.

[26] *On the Genealogy of Morals,* trans. W. Kaufmann and R. J. Hollingdale (New York: Vintage, 1969), p. 20.

[27] Ibid., p. 20.

weave of etymological, demographic, literary, and historical fragments, Nietzsche conjures a genealogy of morality that begins with the historical inversion of an aristocratic equation of power with truth, goodness, beauty, happiness, and piety.[28] This ancient equation Nietzsche endorses for its homage to "the noble instincts of man." In his telling, the equation is inverted through "the slave revolt in morality," a 2,000-year-old and -long revolt accompanying the birth of Western civilization, "which we no longer see because it—has been victorious. . . . The slave revolt in morality begins when *ressentiment* itself becomes creative and gives birth to values: the *ressentiment* of natures that are denied the true reaction, that of deeds, and compensate themselves with an imaginary revenge."[29]

In his insistence that morality springs from and compensates powerlessness, Nietzsche challenges the Marxist thesis that all ideology, including ethical and moral codes, issues from class divisions to legitimate the power of the privileged. In Nietzsche's account, morality emerges from the powerless to avenge their incapacity for action; it enacts their resentment of strengths that they cannot match or overthrow. Rather than a codification of domination, moral ideas are a critique of a certain kind of power, a complaint against strength, an effort to shame and discredit domination by securing the ground of the true *and* the good from which to (negatively) judge it. In this way, of course, morality itself becomes a power, a weapon (which is how it eventually triumphs), although this expression of the "will to power" is far from the sort Nietzsche savors or respects: power born of weakness and resentment fashions a culture whose values and ambitions mirror the pettiness of its motivating force. Moreover, *ressentiment*'s acquisition of power is facilitated by what Nietzsche terms the overdeveloped quality of its cleverness; it ascends to power through its cultivation of reason—an "imaginary revenge" taken in lieu of "the true reaction, that of deeds." Because *ressentiment* reacts, needs a hostile external world in order to exist at all,[30] and is preoccupied with discerning and discrediting the nature of what it seeks to undercut, "a race of such men of *ressentiment* is bound to become eventually *cleverer* than any noble race; it will also honor cleverness to a far greater degree: namely, as a condition of existence of the first importance."[31]

[28] Ibid., pp. 32–34.
[29] Ibid., pp. 34, 36.
[30] Ibid., p. 37.
[31] Ibid., p. 38. Nietzsche elaborates: "While the noble man lives in trust and openness with himself . . . , the man of *ressentiment* is neither upright nor naive nor honest and straightforward with himself. His soul *squints;* his spirit loves hiding places, secret paths and back doors, everything covert entices him as *his* world, *his* security, *his* refreshment; he understands how to keep silent, how not to forget, how to wait, how to be provisionally self-deprecating and humble" (p. 38).

Nietzsche means to be telling a generic story about the West and especially about modernity, a story in which "slave morality" has triumphed so completely that "we have lost our love for man," "we are weary of man"—this, and not Nietzsche's analysis, betokens "the true nihilism of our age."[32] I want to suggest that much North Atlantic feminism partakes deeply of both the epistemological spirit and political structure of *ressentiment* and that this constitutes a good deal of our nervousness about moving toward an analysis as thoroughly Nietzschean in its wariness about truth as postfoundational political theory must be. Surrendering epistemological foundations means giving up the ground of specifically *moral* claims against domination—especially the avenging of strength through moral critique of it—and moving instead into the domain of the sheerly political: "wars of position" and amoral contests about the just and the good in which truth is always grasped as coterminous with power, as always already power, as the voice of power.[33] In William Connolly's words, overcoming the demand for epistemological foundations does not foreclose ethics but opens up alternative ethical possibilities.[34] Apparently lacking confidence in our capacity to work and prevail in such domains of the political and the ethical, feminism appears extremely hesitant about this move.

This hesitation is evident first in the feminist worry that postmodern theories of discourse "reduc[e] all discourse to rhetoric, . . . allow[ing] no distinction between reason and power."[35] Presumably, the objection here lies not in the discernment of power, even violence, in discourse itself—most feminists work assiduously at just such discernments—but to the reduction of *all* discourse to rhetoric, to the insistence on the will to power in *all* of reason's purveyors, ourselves included. Consider Nancy Hartsock's "need to be assured that some systematic [undistorted or power-free?] knowledge about our world and ourselves is possible."[36] Now for the morally superior position issuing from *ressentiment* to "work," reason must drape itself in powerlessness or dispossession: it attacks by differentiating itself from the political-ontological *nature* of what it criticizes, by adopting the stance of reason against power, or, in Marx's case, by adopting scientific objectivity against power's inherent

---

[32] Ibid., p. 44.

[33] Foucault, "Truth and Power," in *Power/Knowledge*, p. 133.

[34] Personal communication, April 1994.

[35] Nicholson, introduction to *Feminism/Postmodernism*, p. 11. This is Nicholson's characterization of an objection, not necessarily her own position.

[36] "The Feminist Standpoint: Developing Grounds for a Specifically Feminist Historically Materialism," in *Discovering Reality: Feminist Perspectives on Epistemology, Metaphysics, Methodology, and Philosophy of Science*, ed. Sandra Harding and Merrill Hintikka (Dordrecht: Reidel, 1983), p. 171.

cloaking in ideology. Thus, this desire for accounts of knowledge that position us outside of power would appear to be rooted in the need to make power *answer* to reason/morality and to prohibit demands for accountability in the opposite direction. In Nietzsche's telling, the supreme strategy of morality based in *ressentiment*—the source of its triumph over two thousand years—is denial that it has an involvement with power, that it contains a will to power or seeks to (pre)dominate.

There is no more vivid historical illustration of morality's dependence upon a discursive boundary between truth and power than Plato's attempt to distinguish Socrates from his rivals, the Sophists, by contrasting Socrates' ostensible devotion to truth for its own sake with the Sophists' practice of openly consorting with political interests. In this picture, the impoverished, purely philosophical, and formally powerless Socrates is presented as uncontaminated by power interests or power desires; his life and utterances are cast by Plato as "moral" and "true" because they are not directly hinged to political power, indeed, because philosophy is "out of power." Not surprisingly, Socrates becomes Nietzsche's prime example of (plebeian) *ressentiment*—"One chooses dialectic only when one has no other means. . . . Is dialectic only a form of *revenge* in Socrates?"[37]

A contemporary feminist instance of the Platonic strategy for legitimizing "our truth" through its relation to worldly powerlessness, and discrediting "theirs" through its connection to power, is again provided by Hartsock. Arguing that there can or must be an "epistemological base" such that knowledge of "how the world really works" is possible, she declares:

> Those (simply) critical of modernity can call into question whether we ever really knew the world (and a good case can be made that "they" at least did not). They are in fact right that they have not known the world as it is rather than as they wished and needed it to be; they created their world not only in their own image but in the image of their fantasies.[38]

In this account, powerlessness is implicitly invested in the Truth while power inherently distorts. Truth is always on the side of the damned or the excluded; hence Truth is always clean of power, but therefore also always positioned to reproach power. On the other hand, according to Hartsock, "the vision available to the rulers will be both partial and will reverse the *real* order of things."[39] What would be required for us to live and work politically without such myths, without claiming that our

---

[37] *Twilight of the Idols,* in *The Portable Nietzsche,* trans. W. Kaufmann (New York: Viking, 1954), p. 476.

[38] "Foucault on Power: A Theory for Women?" p. 171.

[39] Ibid., p. 172 (emphasis added).

knowledge is uncorrupted by a will to power, without insisting that our truths are less partial and more moral than "theirs"? Could we learn to contest domination with the strength of an alternative vision of collective life, rather than through moral reproach? In a word, could we develop a feminist politics without *ressentiment?*

. . .

Thus far, I have situated feminist anxieties about postmodernity in its disruption and deauthorization of our moral ground—our subject that harbors truth, and our truth that opposes power. But preference for moral reasoning over open political contest is not the only legacy of the modernist feminist story: modernity also bequeaths to us a preference for deriving *norms* epistemologically over deciding on them politically. Indeed, from Plato to Marx, from natural law theory to Christian idealism, Hobbesian inductivism, and historical materialism, much of Western political theory has derived (and legitimized) the Good from the True, and feminist theory is no exception, notwithstanding the sharply competing conceptions of "truth" harbored under its auspices. Feminist standpoint theory takes this effort furthest in its imitation of the Marxist effort to vest the class that is "in but not of civil society" with the capacity for a situated knowledge capable of achieving universal vision and containing the seeds of universal norms.[40] Not only the truth of oppression but the truth of human existence and human needs is apprehended by, because produced by, the daily experience of society's most exploited and devalued. With their unique capacity for seeing truth and their standing as the new universal class (the class that represents universal interests because its interests lie with the complete abolition of class), this population also has a singular purchase on "the good."[41]

The postmodern exposure of the imposed and created rather than discovered character of all knowledges—of the power-suffused, struggle-

---

[40] This point first emerges, in rough form, in Marx's *Critique of Hegel's Philosophy of Right.* It gains its finest polish from Gyorgy Lukacs's "Reification and the Consciousness of the Proletariat" in *History and Class Consciousness: Studies in Marxist Dialectics,* trans. R. Livingstone (Cambridge: MIT Press, 1971).

[41] Hartsock, "The Feminist Standpoint," pp. 290–300. The "Black women's standpoint" developed by Patricia Hill Collins does not claim the same tight connection between privileged perspective and privileged access to the good. Black women's "outsider within" perspective as developed by Collins is affirmed as an alternative (and undervalued) epistemology rooted in black women's lived experience, not as The Standpoint for knowing The Truth. Nevertheless, one senses that practices she examines such as dialogue and emotional expressiveness in knowledge production are being implicitly valorized as both true and superior ways of knowing, not merely forwarded as black women's way of knowing. See Collins, *Black Feminist Thought,* chap. 10.

produced quality of all truths, including reigning political and scientific ones—simultaneously exposes the groundlessness of discovered norms or visions. It also reveals the exclusionary and regulatory function of these norms: white women who cannot locate themselves in Nancy Hartsock's account of women's experience or women's desires, African American women who do not identify with Patricia Hill Collins's account of black women's ways of knowing, are once again excluded from the Party of Humanism—this time in its feminist variant.

Our alternative to reliance upon such normative claims would seem to be engagement in political struggles in which there are no trump cards such as "morality" or "truth." Our alternative, in other words, is to struggle within an amoral political habitat for temporally bound and fully contestable visions of who we are and how we ought to live. Put still another way, postmodernity unnerves feminist theory not merely because it deprives us of uncomplicated subject standing, as Christine Di Stefano suggests, or of settled ground for knowledge and norms, as Nancy Hartsock argues, or of "centered selves" and "emancipatory knowledge," as Seyla Benhabib avers. Postmodernity unsettles feminism because it erodes the *moral* ground that the subject, truth, and normativity coproduce in modernity. When contemporary feminist political theorists or analysts complain about the antipolitical or unpolitical nature of postmodern thought—thought that apprehends and responds to this erosion—they are protesting, *inter alia,* a Nietzschean analysis of truth and morality as fully implicated in and by power, and thereby delegitimated qua Truth and Morality. Politics, including politics with passionate purpose and vision, can thrive without a strong theory of the subject, without Truth, and without scientifically derived norms—one only need reread Machiavelli, Gramsci, or Emma Goldman to see such a politics flourish without these things. The question is whether *feminist* politics can prosper without a moral apparatus, whether feminist theorists and activists will give up substituting Truth and Morality for politics. Are we willing to engage in struggle rather than recrimination, to develop our faculties rather than avenge our subordination with moral and epistemological gestures, to fight for a world rather than conduct process on the existing one? Nietzsche insisted that extraordinary strengths of character and mind would be necessary to operate in the domain of epistemological and religious nakedness he heralded. But in this he excessively individualized a challenge that more importantly requires the deliberate development of postmoral and antirelativist political spaces, practices of deliberation, and modes of adjudication.

. . .
            The only way through a crisis of space is to invent a new
        space.   —Fredric Jameson, "Postmodernism"

Precisely because of its incessant revelation of settled practices and identities as contingent, its acceleration of the tendency to melt all that is solid
into air, what is called postmodernity poses the opportunity to radically
sever the problem of the good from the problem of the true, to decide
"what we want" rather than derive it from assumptions or arguments
about "who we are." Our capacity to exploit this opportunity positively
will be hinged to our success in developing new modes and criteria for
political judgment. It will also depend upon our willingness to break
certain modernist radical attachments, particularly to Marxism's promise
(however failed) of meticulously articulated connections between a comprehensive critique of the present and norms for a transformed future—a
science of revolution rather than a politics of one.

Resistance, the practice most widely associated with postmodern political discourse, responds to without fully meeting the normativity challenge of postmodernity. A vital *tactic* in much political work as well as for
mere survival, resistance by itself does not contain a critique, a vision, or
grounds for organized collective efforts to enact either. Contemporary
affection for the politics of resistance issues from postmodern criticism's
perennial authority problem: our heightened consciousness of the will to
power in all political "positions" and our wariness about totalizing analyses and visions. Insofar as it eschews rather than revises these problematic practices, resistance-as-politics does not raise the dilemmas of
responsibility and justification entailed in "affirming" political projects
and norms. In this respect, like identity politics, and indeed sharing with
identity politics an excessively local viewpoint and tendency toward positioning without mapping, the contemporary vogue of resistance is
more a symptom of postmodernity's crisis of political space than a coherent response to it. Resistance goes nowhere in particular, has no inherent
attachments, and hails no particular vision; as Foucault makes clear, resistance is an effect of and reaction to power, not an arrogation of it.

What postmodernity disperses and postmodern feminist politics requires are cultivated political *spaces* for posing and questioning feminist
political norms, for discussing the nature of "the good" for women.
Democratic political space is quite undertheorized in contemporary feminist thinking, as it is everywhere in late-twentieth-century political theory, primarily because it is so little in evidence. Dissipated by the
increasing technologizing of would-be political conversations and processes, by the erosion of boundaries around specifically political domains

and activities, and by the decline of movement politics, political spaces
are scarcer and thinner today than even in most immediately prior epochs
of Western history. In this regard, their condition mirrors the splayed and
centrifuged characteristics of postmodern political power. Yet precisely
because of postmodernity's disarming tendencies toward political disorientation, fragmentation, and technologizing, the creation of spaces
where political analyses and norms can be proffered and contested is su-
premely important.

Political space is an old theme in Western political theory, incarnated
by the *polis* practices of Socrates, harshly opposed by Plato in the *Republic*, redeemed and elaborated as metaphysics by Aristotle, resuscitated as
salvation for modernity by Hannah Arendt, and given contemporary
spin in Jurgen Habermas's theories of ideal speech situations and communicative rationality. The project of developing feminist postmodern
political spaces, while enriched by pieces of this tradition, necessarily also
departs from it. In contrast with Aristotle's formulation, feminist political spaces cannot define themselves against the private sphere, bodies,
reproduction and production, mortality, and all the populations and issues implicated in these categories. Unlike Arendt's, these spaces cannot
be pristine, rarified, and policed at their boundaries but are necessarily
cluttered, attuned to earthly concerns and visions, incessantly disrupted,
invaded, and reconfigured. Unlike Habermas, we can harbor no dreams
of nondistorted communication unsullied by power, or even of a "common language," but we recognize as a permanent political condition partiality of understanding and expression, cultural chasms whose nature
may be vigilantly identified but rarely "resolved," and the powers of
words and images that evoke, suggest, and connote rather than transmit
meanings.[42] Our spaces, while requiring some definition and protection,
cannot be clean, sharply bounded, disembodied, or permanent: to engage postmodern modes of power *and* honor specifically feminist knowledges, they must be heterogenous, roving, relatively noninstitution-
alized, and democratic to the point of exhaustion.

Such spaces are crucial for developing the skills and practices of postmodern *judgment*, addressing the problem of "how to produce a discourse
on justice . . . when one no longer relies on ontology or epistemology."[43] Postmodernity's dismantling of metaphysical foundations for
justice renders us quite vulnerable to domination by technical reason un-

---

[42] In "Situated Knowledges," Donna Haraway writes, "feminism loves another science:
the sciences and politics of interpretation, translation, stuttering and the partly understood"
(p. 589).

[43] Emelia Steurman, "Habermas vs. Lyotard: Modernity vs. Postmodernity?" *New
Foundations* 7 (1989), p. 61.

less we seize the opportunity this erosion also creates to develop democratic processes for formulating collective postepistemological and postontological judgments. Such judgments require learning how to have public conversations with each other, arguing from a vision about the common ("what I want for us") rather than from identity ("who I am"), and from explicitly postulated norms and potential common values rather than from false essentialism or unreconstructed private interest.[44] Paradoxically, such public and comparatively impersonal arguments carry potential for greater accountability than arguments from identity or interest. While the former may be interrogated to the ground by others, the latter are insulated from such inquiry with the mantle of "truth" worn by identity-based speech. Moreover, postidentity political positions and conversations potentially replace a politics of difference with a politics of diversity—differences grasped from a perspective larger than simply one point in an ensemble. Postidentity public positioning requires an outlook that discerns structures of dominance within diffused and disorienting orders of power, thereby stretching toward a more politically potent analysis than that which our individuated and fragmented existences can generate. In contrast to Di Stefano's claim that "shared identity" may constitute a more psychologically and politically reliable basis for "attachment and motivation on the part of potential activists,"[45] I am suggesting that political conversation oriented toward diversity and the common, toward world rather than self, and involving conversion of one's knowledge of the world from a situated (subject) position into a public idiom, offers us the greatest possibility of countering postmodern social fragmentations and political disintegrations.

Feminists have learned well to identify and articulate our "subject positions"—we have become experts at politicizing the "I" that is produced through multiple sites of power and subordination. But the very practice so crucial to making these elements of power visible and subjectivity political may be partly at odds with the requisites for developing political conversation among a complex and diverse "we." We may need to learn public speaking and the pleasures of public argument, not to overcome our situatedness, but in order to assume responsibility for our situations and to mobilize a collective discourse that will expand them. For the political making of a feminist future that does not reproach the history on which it is borne, we may need to loosen our attachments to subjectivity, identity, and morality and to redress our underdeveloped taste for political argument.

[44] Haraway makes a similar argument in "Situated Knowledges," pp. 586–87.
[45] "Dilemmas of Difference," p. 76.

CHAPTER THREE

Wounded Attachments

> If something is to stay in the memory, it must be burned in:
> only that which never ceases to *hurt* stays in the memory.
> —Friedrich Nietzsche, *On the Genealogy of Morals*

> . . . this craving for freedom, release, forgetfulness . . .
> —Thomas Mann, *Death in Venice*

TAKING ENORMOUS pleasure in the paradox, Jamaican-born social theorist Stuart Hall tells this story of the postwar, postcolonial "breakup" of English identity:

> . . . in the very moment when finally Britain convinced itself it had to decolonize, it had to get rid of them, we all came back home. As they hauled down the flag [in the colonies], we got on the banana boat and sailed right into London. . . . [T]hey had ruled the world for 300 years and, at last, when they had made up their minds to climb out of the role, at least the others ought to have stayed out there in the rim, behaved themselves, gone somewhere else, or found some other client state. But no, they had always said that this [London] was really home, the streets were paved with gold, and bloody hell, we just came to check out whether that was so or not.[1]

In Hall's mischievous account, the restructuring of collective "First World" identity and democratic practices required by postcoloniality did not remain in the hinterlands but literally, restively, came home to roost. The historical "others" of colonial identity cast free in their own waters sailed in to implode the center of the postcolonial metropoles, came to trouble the last vestiges of centered European identity with its economic and political predicates. They came to make havoc in the master's house after the master relinquished his military-political but not his cultural and metaphysical holdings as *the* metonymy of man.

Hall's narrative of the palace invasion by the newly released subjects might also be pressed into service as metaphor for another historical paradox of late-twentieth-century collective and individual identity formation: in the very moment when modern liberal states fully realize their

---

[1] "The Local and the Global," in *Culture, Globalization, and the World System: Contemporary Conditions for the Representation of Identity,* ed. Anthony King (Albany: SUNY Press, 1989), p. 24.

secularism (as Marx put it in "On the Jewish Question"), just as the mantle of abstract personhood is formally tendered to a whole panoply of those historically excluded from it by humanism's privileging of a single race, gender, and organization of sexuality, the marginalized reject the rubric of humanist inclusion and turn, at least in part, against its very premises. Refusing to be neutralized, to render the differences inconsequential, to be depoliticized as "lifestyles," "diversity," or "persons like any other," we have lately reformulated our historical exclusion as a matter of historically produced and politically rich *alterity*. Insisting that we are not merely positioned but fabricated by this history, we have at the same time insisted that our very production as marginal, deviant, or subhuman is itself constitutive of the centrality and legitimacy of the center, is itself what paves the center's streets with semiotic, political, and psychic gold. Just when polite liberal (not to mention correct leftist) discourse ceased speaking of us as dykes, faggots, colored girls, or natives, we began speaking of ourselves this way. Refusing the invitation to absorption, we insisted instead upon politicizing and working into cultural critique the very constructions that a liberal humanism increasingly exposed in its tacit operations of racial, sexual, and gender privilege was seeking to bring to a formal close.

These paradoxes of late modern liberalism and colonialism, of course, are not a matter of simple historical accident—indeed, they are both incomplete and mutually constitutive to a degree that belies the orderly chronological scheme Hall and I have imposed on them in order to render them pleasurable ironies. Moreover, the ironies do not come to an end with the Jamaican postcolonials sailing into London nor with the historically marginalized constructing an oppositional political culture and critique out of their historical exclusion. Even as the margins assert themselves as margins, the denaturalizing assault they perform on coherent collective identity in the center turns back on them to trouble their own identities. Even as it is being articulated, circulated, and lately institutionalized in a host of legal, political, and cultural practices, identity is unraveling—metaphysically, culturally, geopolitically, and historically— as rapidly as it is being produced. The same vacillation can be seen in the naturalistic legitimating narratives of collective identity known as nationalism. Imploded within by the insurrectionary knowledges and political claims of historically subordinated cultures, and assaulted from without by the spectacular hybridities and supranational articulations of late-twentieth-century global capitalism as well as crises of global ecology, nation formation—loosened from what retrospectively appears as a historically fleeting attachment to states—is today fervently being asserted in cultural-political claims ranging from Islamic to deaf, indigenous to Gypsy, Serbian to queer.

Despite certain convergences, articulations, and parallels between such culturally disparate political formations in the late twentieth century, this chapter does not consider the problematic of politicized identity on a global scale. To the contrary, it is, among other things, an argument for substantial historical, geopolitical, and cultural specificity in exploring the problematic of political identity. Thus, the focus in what follows is on selected contradictory operations of politicized identity *within* late modern democracy; I consider politicized identity as both a production *and* contestation of the political terms of liberalism, disciplinary-bureaucratic regimes, certain forces of global capitalism, and the demographic flows of postcoloniality that together might be taken as constitutive of the contemporary North American political condition. In recent years, enough stalemated argument has transpired about the virtues and vices of something named identity politics to suggest the limited usefulness of a discussion of identity either in terms of the timeless metaphysical or linguistic elements of its constitution or in terms of the ethical–political rubric of good and evil. Beginning instead with the premise that the proliferation and politicization of identities in the United States is not a moral or even political choice but a complex historical production, this chapter seeks to elucidate something of the nature of this production, in order to locate within it both the openings and the perils for a radically democratic political project.

Many have asked how, given what appear as the inherently totalizing and "othering" characteristics of identity in/as language, identity can avoid reiterating such investments in its ostensibly emancipatory mode.[2]

---

[2] "An identity is established in relation to a series of differences that have become socially recognized. These differences are essential to its being. If they did not coexist as differences, it would not exist in its distinctness and solidity. . . . Identity requires difference in order to be, and it converts difference into otherness in order to secure its own self-certainty" (William Connolly, *Identity/Difference: Democratic Negotiations of Political Paradox* [Ithaca: Cornell University Press, 1991], p. 64).

I cite from Connolly rather than the more obvious Derrida because Connolly is exemplary of the effort *within* political theory to think about the political problem of identity working heuristically with its linguistic operation. As well, I cite from Connolly because the present essay is in some ways an extension of a conversation begun in 1991 at an American Political Science Association annual meeting roundtable discussion of his book. In that discussion, noting that Connolly identified late modernity as producing certain problems for identity but did not historicize politicized identity itself, I called for such a historicization. To the degree that the present essay is my own partial response to that call, it—as the footnotes make clear—is indebted to Connolly's book and that public occasion of its discussion.

A short list of others who have struggled to take politicized identity through and past the problem of political exclusion and political closure might include Stuart Hall, Trinh T. Minh-ha, Homi Bhabha, Paul Gilroy, Aiwah Ong, Judith Butler, Gayatri Spivak, and Anne Norton.

I want to make a similar inquiry but in a historically specific cultural-political register, not because the linguistic frame is unimportant but because it is insufficient for discerning the character of contemporary politicized identity's problematic investments. Thus, the concerns framing the work of this chapter are these: First, given the subjectivizing conditions of identity production in a late modern capitalist, liberal, and bureaucratic disciplinary social order, how can reiteration of these production conditions be averted in identity's purportedly emancipatory project? In the specific context of contemporary liberal and bureaucratic disciplinary discourse, what kind of political recognition can identity-based claims seek—and what kind can they be counted on to want—that will not resubordinate a subject itself historically subjugated through identity, through categories such as race or gender that emerged and circulated as terms of power to enact subordination? The question here is not *whether* denaturalizing political strategies subvert the subjugating force of naturalized identity formation, but *what kind* of politicization, produced out of and inserted into *what kind* of political context, might perform such subversion. Second, given the widely averred interest of politicized identity in achieving emancipatory political recognition in a posthumanist discourse, what are the logics of pain in the subject formation processes of late modern polities that might contain or subvert this aim? What are the particular constituents—specific to our time yet roughly generic for a diverse spectrum of identities—of identity's desire for recognition that seem often to breed a politics of recrimination and rancor, of culturally dispersed paralysis and suffering, a tendency to reproach power rather than aspire to it, to disdain freedom rather than practice it? In short, where do the historically and culturally specific elements of politicized identity's investments in itself, and especially in its own history of suffering, come into conflict with the need to give up these investments, to engage in something of a Nietzschean "forgetting" of this history, in the pursuit of an emancipatory democratic project?

Such questions should make clear that this is not an essay about the general worth or accomplishments of identity politics, nor is it a critique of that oppositional political formation. It is, rather, an exploration of the ways in which certain aspects of the specific genealogy of politicized identity are carried in the structure of its political articulation and demands, with consequences that include self-subversion. I approach this exploration by first offering a highly selective account of the discursive historical context of the emergence of identity politics in the United States, and then elaborating, through a reconsideration of Nietzsche's genealogy of the logics of *ressentiment,* the wounded character of politicized identity's desire within this context.

. . .

The tension between particularistic "I's" and a universal "we" in liberalism is sustainable as long as the constituent terms of the "I" remain unpoliticized: indeed, as long as the "I" itself remains unpoliticized on one hand, and the state (as the expression of the ideal of political universality) remains unpoliticized on the other. Thus, the latent conflict in liberalism between universal representation and individualism remains latent, remains unpoliticized, as long as differential powers in civil society remain naturalized, as long as the "I" remains politically unarticulated, as long as it is willing to have its freedom represented abstractly—in effect, subordinating its "I-ness" to the abstract "we" represented by the universal community of the state. This subordination is achieved by the "I" either abstracting from itself in its political representation, thus trivializing its "difference" so as to remain part of the "we" (as in homosexuals who are "just like everyone else except for who we sleep with"), or accepting its construction as a supplement, complement, or partial outsider to the "we" (as in homosexuals who are just "different," or Jews whose communal affiliations lie partly or wholly outside their national identity). The history of liberalism's management of its inherited and constructed others could be read as a history of variations on and vacillations between these two strategies.

The abstract character of liberal political membership and the ideologically naturalized character of liberal individualism together work against politicized identity formation.[3] A formulation of the political state and of citizenship that, as Marx put it in the "Jewish Question," abstracts from the substantive conditions of our lives, works to prevent recognition or articulation of differences *as* political—as effects of power—in their very construction and organization; they are at most the stuff of divergent political or economic *interests*.[4] Equally important, to the extent that political membership in the liberal state involves abstracting from one's social being, it involves abstracting not only from the contingent productions of one's life circumstances but from the *identificatory* processes constitutive of one's social construction and position. Whether read from the frontispiece of Hobbes's *Leviathan,* in which the many are made one through the unity of the sovereign, or from the formulations of tolerance codified by John Locke, John Stuart Mill, and, more currently,

[3] Locke's (1689) *Letter Concerning Toleration* signals this development in intellectual history. The 300-year process of eliminating first the property qualification and then race and gender qualifications in European and North American constitutional states heralds its formal political achievement.

[4] "On the Jewish Question," in *The Marx-Engels Reader,* 2d ed., ed. R. C. Tucker (New York: Norton, 1978), p. 34.

George Kateb, in which the minimalist liberal state is cast as precisely what enables our politically unfettered individuality, we are invited to seek equal deference—equal blindness from—but not equalizing recognition from the state, which is itself liberalism's universal moment.[5] As Marx discerned in his critique of Hegel, the universality of the state is ideologically achieved by turning away from and thus depoliticizing, yet at the same time *presupposing*, our collective particulars—not by embracing them, let alone emancipating us from them.[6] In short, "the political" in liberalism is precisely not a domain for social identification: expected to recognize our political selves in the state, we are not led to expect deep recognition there. Put slightly differently, in a smooth and legitimate liberal order, if the particularistic "I's" must remain unpoliticized, so also must the universalistic "we" remain without specific content or aim, without a common good *other than* abstract universal representation or pluralism. The abstractness of the "we" is precisely what insists upon, reiterates, and even enforces the depoliticized nature of the "I." In Ernesto Laclau's formulation, "if democracy is possible, it is because the universal does not have any necessary body, any necessary content."[7]

While this détente between universal and particular within liberalism is riddled with volatile conceits, it is rather thoroughly unraveled by two features of late modernity, spurred by developments in what Marx and Foucault respectively reveal as liberalism's companion powers: capitalism and disciplinarity. On the one side, the state loses even its guise of universality as it becomes ever more transparently invested in particular economic interests, political ends, and social formations—as it transmogri-

---

[5] John Locke, *Letter Concerning Toleration;* John Stuart Mill, *On Liberty;* George Kateb, "Democratic Individuality and the Claims of Politics," *Political Theory* 12 (1984), pp. 331–60.

[6] In the "Jewish Question," Marx argues, "far from abolishing these *effective* differences [in civil society, the state] only exists so far as they are presupposed; it is conscious of being a *political state* and it manifests its *universality* only in *opposition* to these elements" (p. 33). See also Marx's *Critique of Hegel's Philosophy of Right,* ed. J. O'Malley (Cambridge: Cambridge University Press, 1970), pp. 91, 116.

[7] "Universalism, Particularism, and the Question of Identity," *October* 61 (Summer 1992), p. 90. Laclau is here concerned not with the state but with the possibility of retaining a "universal" in social movement politics where a critique of bourgeois humanist universalism has become quite central. Interestingly, Laclau's effort to preserve a universalist political ideal from this challenge entails making the ideal even more abstract, pulling it further away from any specific configuration or purpose than the distance ordinarily managed by liberal discourse. Laclau's aim in voiding the universal completely of body and content is only partly to permit it to be more completely embracing of all the particulars; it is also intended to recognize the *strategic* value of the discourse of universality, the extent to which "different groups compete to give their particular aims a temporary function of universal representation" (p. 90). But how, if universal discourse may always be revealed to have this strategic function, can it also be taken seriously as a substantive value of democracy?

fies from a relatively minimalist, "night watchman" state to a heavily bureaucratized, managerial, fiscally enormous, and highly intervention- ist welfare-warfare state, a transformation occasioned by the combined imperatives of capital and the auto-proliferating characteristics of bureau- cracy.[8] On the other side, the liberal subject is increasingly disinterred from substantive nation-state identification, not only by the individuat- ing effects of liberal discourse itself but through the social effects of late- twentieth-century economic and political life: deterritorializing demo- graphic flows; the disintegration from within and invasion from without of family and community as (relatively) autonomous sites of social pro- duction and identification; consumer capitalism's marketing discourse in which individual (and subindividual) desires are produced, com- modified, and mobilized as identities; and disciplinary productions of a fantastic array of behavior-based identities ranging from recovering alco- holic professionals to unrepentant "crack mothers."[9] These disciplinary productions work to conjure and regulate subjects through classificatory schemes, naming and normalizing social behaviors as social positions. Operating through what Foucault calls "an anatomy of detail," "disci- plinary power" produces social identities (available for politicization be- cause they are deployed for purposes of political regulation), which cross-cut juridical identities based on abstract right. Thus, for example, the welfare state's production of welfare subjects—themselves subdi- vided through the socially regulated categories of motherhood, disabil- ity, race, age, and so forth—potentially produces political identity through these categories, produces identities *as* these categories.

In this story, the always imminent but increasingly politically manifest failure of liberal universalism to be universal—the transparent fiction of state universality—combines with the increasing individuation of social subjects through capitalist disinterments and disciplinary productions. Together, they breed the emergence of politicized identity rooted in dis- ciplinary productions but oriented by liberal discourse toward protest against exclusion from a discursive formation of universal justice. This

---

[8] Jurgen Habermas's *Legitimation Crisis,* trans. T. McCarthy (Boston: Beacon, 1975), and James O'Connor's *Fiscal Crisis of the State* (New York: St. Martin's, 1973), remain two of the most compelling narratives of this development. Also informing this claim are Max Weber's discussion of bureaucracy and rationalization in *Economy and Society,* ed. G. Roth and C. Wittich (Berkeley: University of California Press, 1978); Sheldon Wolin's discussion of the "mega-state" in *The Presence of the Past: Essays on the State and the Constitution* (Bal- timore: Johns Hopkins University Press, 1989); as well as the researches of Claus Offe, Bob Jessop, and Fred Block.

[9] I draw the latter example from a fascinating dissertation-in-progress by Deborah Con- nolly (Anthropology Board, University of California, Santa Cruz), which examines the contemporary production of "crack mothers" as a totalizing identity through a combina- tion of legal, medical, and social service discourses.

production, however, is not linear or even, but highly contradictory. While the terms of liberalism are part of the ground of production of a politicized identity that reiterates yet exceeds these terms, liberal discourse itself also continuously recolonizes political identity *as* political interest—a conversion that recasts politicized identity's substantive (and often deconstructive) cultural claims and critiques as generic claims of particularism endemic to universalist political culture. Similarly, disciplinary power manages liberalism's production of politicized subjectivity by neutralizing (re-de-politicizing) identity through normalizing practices. As liberal discourse converts political identity into essentialized private interest, disciplinary power converts interest into normativized social identity manageable by regulatory regimes. Thus, disciplinary power politically neutralizes entitlement claims generated by liberal individuation, while liberalism politically neutralizes rights claims generated by disciplinary identities.

In addition to the formations of identity that may be the complex effects of disciplinary and liberal modalities of power, I want to suggest one other historical strand relevant to the production of politicized identity, this one twined more specifically to developments in recent political culture. Although sanguine to varying degrees about the phenomenon they are describing, many on the European and North American Left have argued that identity politics emerges from the demise of class politics attendant upon post-Fordism or pursuant to May '68. Without adjudicating the precise relationship between the breakup of class politics and the proliferation of other sites of political identification, I want to refigure this claim by suggesting that what we have come to call identity politics is partly dependent upon the demise of a critique of capitalism and of bourgeois cultural and economic values.[10] In a reading that links the new identity claims to a certain relegitimation of capitalism, identity politics concerned with race, sexuality, and gender will appear not as a supplement to class politics, not as an expansion of left categories of oppression and emancipation, not as an enriching augmentation of progressive formulations of power and persons—all of which they also are—but as tethered to a formulation of justice that reinscribes a bourgeois (masculinist) ideal as its measure.

If it is this ideal that signifies educational and vocational opportunity,

[10] To be fully persuasive, this claim would have to reckon with the ways in which the articulation of African American, feminist, queer, or Native American "values" and cultural styles have figured centrally in many contemporary political projects. It would have to encounter the ways that the critique of cultural assimilation to which I alluded on pages 52–53 of this chapter has been a critical dimension of identity politics. Space prohibits such a reckoning but I think its terms would be those of capitalism and style, economics and culture, counterhegemonic projects and the politics of resistance.

upward mobility, relative protection against arbitrary violence, and re-
ward in proportion to effort, and if it is this ideal against which many of
the exclusions and privations of people of color, gays and lesbians, and
women are articulated, then the political purchase of contemporary
American identity politics would seem to be achieved in part *through* a
certain renaturalization of capitalism that can be said to have marked progressive discourse since the 1970s. What this also suggests is that identity
politics may be partly configured by a peculiarly shaped and peculiarly
disguised form of class resentment, a resentment that is displaced onto
discourses of injustice other than class, but a resentment, like all resentments, that retains the real or imagined holdings of its reviled subject as
objects of desire. In other words, the enunciation of politicized identities
through race, gender, and sexuality may require—rather than incidentally produce—a limited identification through class, specifically abjur-
ing a critique of class power and class norms precisely insofar as these
identities are established vis-à-vis a bourgeois norm of social acceptance,
legal protection, and relative material comfort. Yet, when not only economic stratification but other injuries to the human body and psyche
enacted by capitalism—alienation, commodification, exploitation, displacement, disintegration of sustaining albeit contradictory social forms
such as families and neighborhoods—when these are discursively normalized and thus depoliticized, other markers of social difference may
come to bear an inordinate weight; indeed, they may bear all the weight
of the sufferings produced by capitalism in addition to that attributable to
the explicitly politicized marking.[11]

If there is one class that articulates and even politicizes itself in late
modern North American life, it is that which gives itself the name of the
"middle class." But the foregoing suggests that this is not a reactive identity in the sense, for example, of "white" or "straight" in contemporary
political discourse. Rather it is an articulation by the figure of the class
that represents, indeed depends upon, the naturalization rather than the
politicization of capitalism, the denial of capitalism's power effects in
ordering social life, the representation of the ideal of capitalism to provide the good life for all. Poised between the rich and poor, feeling itself
to be protected from the encroachments of neither, the phantasmic mid-

---

[11] It is, of course, also the abstraction of politicized identity from political economy that
produces the failure of politicized identities to encompass and unify their "members." Striated not only in a formal sense by class but divided as well by the extent to which the
suffering entailed, for example, in gender and racial subordination can be substantially
offset by economic privilege, insistent definitions of Black, or Queer, or Woman sustain
the same kind of exclusions and policing previously enacted by the tacitly white male heterosexual figure of the "working class."

dle class signifies the natural and the good between the decadent or the corrupt on one side, the aberrant or the decaying on the other. It is a conservative identity in the sense that it semiotically recurs to a phantasmic past, an imagined idyllic, unfettered, and uncorrupted historical moment (implicitly located around 1955) when life was good—housing was affordable, men supported families on single incomes, drugs were confined to urban ghettos. But it is not a reactionary identity in the sense of reacting to an insurgent politicized identity from below. Rather, it precisely embodies the ideal to which nonclass identities refer for proof of their exclusion or injury: homosexuals, who lack the protections of marriage, guarantees of child custody or job security, and freedom from harassment; single women, who are strained and impoverished by trying to raise children and hold paid jobs simultaneously; and people of color, who are not only disproportionately affected by unemployment, punishing urban housing costs, and inadequate health care programs, but disproportionately subjected to unwarranted harassment, figured as criminals, ignored by cab drivers.

The point is not that these privations are trivial but that without recourse to the white masculine middle-class ideal, politicized identities would forfeit a good deal of their claims to injury and exclusion, their claims to the political significance of their difference. If they thus require this ideal for the potency and poignancy of their political claims, we might ask to what extent a critique of capitalism is foreclosed by the current configuration of oppositional politics, and not simply by the "loss of the socialist alternative" or the ostensible "triumph of liberalism" in the global order. In contrast with the Marxist critique of a social whole and Marxist vision of total transformation, to what extent do identity politics require a standard internal to existing society against which to pitch their claims, a standard that not only preserves capitalism from critique, but sustains the invisibility and inarticulateness of class—not accidentally, but endemically? Could we have stumbled upon one reason why class is invariably named but rarely theorized or developed in the multiculturalist mantra, "race, class, gender, sexuality"?

. . .

The story of the emergence of contemporary identity politics could be told in many other ways—as the development of "new social antagonisms" rooted in consumer capitalism's commodification of all spheres of social life, as the relentless denaturalization of all social relations occasioned by the fabrications and border violations of postmodern technologies and cultural productions, as a form of political consciousness precipitated by the black Civil Rights movement in the United States.[12] I have told the story this way in order to emphasize the *discursive political context* of its emergence, its disciplinary, capitalist, and liberal parentage, and this in order to comprehend politicized identity's genealogical structure as comprising and not only opposing these very modalities of political power. Indeed, if the ostensibly oppositional character of identity politics also render them something of the "illegitimate offspring" of liberal, capitalist, disciplinary discourses, their absent fathers are not, as Donna Haraway suggests, "inessential" but are installed in the very structure of *desire* fueling identity-based political claims: the psyche of the bastard child is hardly independent of its family of origin.[13] And if we are interested in developing the politically subversive or transformative elements of identity-based claims, we need to know the implications of the particular genealogy and production conditions of identity's desire for recognition. We need to be able to ask: Given what produced it, given what shapes and suffuses it, what does politicized identity want?

We might profitably begin these investigations with a reflection on their curious elision by the philosopher who also frames them, Michel Foucault. For Foucault, the constraints of emancipatory politics in late modern democracy pertain to the ubiquity and pervasiveness of power—the impossibility of eschewing power in human affairs—as well as to the ways in which subjects and practices are always at risk of being resubordinated through the discourses naming and politicizing them. Best known for his formulation of this dual problem in the domain of sexual liberation, Foucault offers a more generic theoretical account in his discussion of the disinterment of the "insurrectionary knowledges" of marginalized populations and practices:

> Is the relation of forces today still such as to allow these disinterred knowledges some kind of autonomous life? Can they be isolated by these means from every subjugating relationship? What force do they have taken in themselves? . . . Is it not perhaps the case that these fragments of genealogies are no sooner

---

[12] See Ernesto Laclau and Chantal Mouffe, *Hegemony and Socialist Strategy* (London: Verso, 1985), p. 161; Scott Lash and John Urry, *The End of Organized Capitalism* (Madison: University of Wisconsin Press, 1987), chap. 9; David Harvey, *The Condition of Postmodernity* (Oxford: Blackwell, 1989), chap. 26; and Bernice Johnson Reagon, "Coalition Politics: Turning the Century," in *Home Girls: A Black Feminist Anthology,* ed. Barbara Smith (New York: Kitchen Table: Woman of Color, 1983), p. 362.

[13] In "A Manifesto for Cyborgs: Science, Technology, and Socialist Feminism and the Privilege of Partial Perspective" (in *Feminism/Postmodernism,* ed. Linda Nicholson [New York: Routledge, 1990]), Donna Haraway writes: "cyborgs . . . are the illegitimate offspring of militarism and patriarchal capitalism, not to mention state socialism. But illegitimate offspring are often exceedingly unfaithful to their origins. Their fathers, after all, are inessential" (p. 193).

brought to light, that the particular elements of the knowledge that one seeks to disinter are no sooner accredited and put into circulation, than they run the risk of re-codification, re-colonisation? In fact, those unitary discourses which first disqualified and then ignored them when they made their appearance are, it seems, quite ready now to annex them, to take them back within the fold of their own discourse and to invest them with everything this implies in terms of their effects of knowledge and power. And if we want to protect these only lately liberated fragments, are we not in danger of ourselves constructing, with our own hands, that unitary discourse?[14]

Foucault's caution about the annexing, colonizing effects of invariably unifying discourses is an important one. But the question of the emancipatory orientation of historically subordinated discourse is not limited to the risk of cooptation or resubordination by extant or newly formed unitary discourses—whether those of humanism on one side, or of cultural studies, multiculturalism, subaltern studies, and minority discourse on the other. Nor is it reducible to that unexamined Frankfurt School strain in Foucault, the extent to which the Foucaultian subject originally desirous of freedom comes to will its own domination, or (in Foucault's rubric) becomes a good disciplinary subject. Rather, I think that for Foucault, insofar as power always produces resistance, even the disciplinary subject is perversely capable of resistance, and in practicing it, practices freedom. Discernible here is the basis of a curious optimism, even volunteerism in Foucault, namely his oddly physicalist and insistently nonpsychic account of power, practices, and subject formation. His removal of the "will to power" from Nietzsche's complex psychology of need, frustration, impotence, and compensatory deeds is what permits Foucault to feature resistance as always possible and as equivalent to practicing freedom.

In an interview with Paul Rabinow, Foucault muses:

> I do not think that it is possible to say that one thing is of the order of "liberation" and another is of the order of "oppression." . . . No matter how terrifying a given system may be, there always remain the possibilities of resistance, disobedience, and oppositional groupings. On the other hand, I do not think that there is anything that is functionally . . . absolutely liberating. Liberty is a *practice*. . . . The liberty of men is never assured by the institutions and laws that are intended to guarantee them. . . . Not because they are ambiguous, but simply because "liberty" is what must be exercised. . . . The guarantee of freedom is freedom.[15]

[14] "Two Lectures," in *Power/Knowledge: Selected Interviews and Other Writings, 1972–1977*, ed. C. Gordon (New York: Pantheon, 1980), p. 86.
[15] "Space, Knowledge, and Power," interview by Paul Rabinow in *The Foucault Reader*, ed. Rabinow (New York: Pantheon, 1984), p. 245.

My quarrel here is not with Foucault's valuable insistence upon freedom as a practice but with his distinct lack of attention to what might constitute, negate, or redirect the desire for freedom.[16] Notwithstanding his critique of the repressive hypothesis and his postulation of the subject as an effect of power, Foucault seems to tacitly assume the givenness and resilience of the desire for freedom, a givenness that arises consequent to his implicit conflation of the will to power in the practice of resistance with a will to freedom. Thus, Foucault's confidence about the possibilities of "practicing" or "exercising" liberty resides in a quasi-empirical concern with the relative *capacity* or space for action in the context of certain regimes of domination. But whether or not resistance is possible is a different question from what its aim is, what it is for, and especially whether or not it resubjugates the resisting subject. Foucault's rejection of psychoanalysis and his arrested reading of Nietzsche (his utter neglect of Nietzsche's diagnosis of the culture of modernity as the triumph of "slave morality") combine to define the problem of freedom for Foucault as one of domain and discourse, rather than the problem of "will" that it is for Nietzsche. Indeed, what requires for its answer a profoundly more psychological Nietzsche than the one Foucault embraces is not a question about when or where the practice of freedom is possible but a question about *the direction of the will to power*, a will that potentially, but only potentially, animates a desire for freedom. Especially for the Nietzsche of *On the Genealogy of Morals*, the modern subject does not simply cease to desire freedom as is the case with Foucault's disciplinary subject but, much more problematically, loathes freedom.[17] Let us now consider why.

.   .   .

Contemporary politicized identity in the United States contests the terms of liberal discourse insofar as it challenges liberalism's universal "we" as a strategic fiction of historically hegemonic groups and asserts liberalism's "I" as social—both relational and constructed by power—rather than contingent, private, or autarkic. Yet it reiterates the terms of liberal discourse insofar as it posits a sovereign and unified "I" that is disen-

[16] John Rajchman insists that Foucault's philosophy *is* "the endless question of freedom" (*Michel Foucault: The Freedom of Philosophy* [New York: Columbia University Press, 1985], p. 124), but Rajchman, too, eschews the question of desire in his account of Foucault's freedom as the "motor and principle of his skepticism: the endless questioning of constituted experience" (p. 7).

[17] "This *instinct for freedom* forcibly made latent— . . . this instinct for freedom pushed back and repressed, incarcerated within and finally able to discharge and vent itself only on itself . . . " (*On the Genealogy of Morals*, trans. W. Kaufmann and R. J. Hollindale [New York: Vintage, 1969], p. 87).

franchised by an exclusive "we." Indeed, I have suggested that politicized identity emerges and obtains its unifying coherence through the politicization of *exclusion* from an ostensible universal, as a protest against exclusion: a protest premised on the fiction of an inclusive/universal community, a protest that thus reinstalls the humanist ideal—and a specific white, middle-class, masculinist expression of this ideal—insofar as it premises itself upon exclusion from it. Put the other way around, politicized identities generated out of liberal, disciplinary societies, insofar as they are premised on exclusion from a universal ideal, require that ideal, as well as their exclusion from it, for their own continuing existence as identities.[18]

Contemporary politicized identity is also potentially reiterative of regulatory, disciplinary society in its configuration of a disciplinary subject. It is both produced by and potentially accelerates the production of that aspect of disciplinary society which "ceaselessly characterizes, classifies, and specializes," which works through "surveillance, continuous registration, perpetual assessment, and classification," through a social machinery "that is both immense and minute."[19] An example from the world of local politics makes clear politicized identity's imbrication in disciplinary power, as well as the way in which, as Foucault reminds us, disciplinary power "infiltrates" rather than replaces liberal juridical modalities.[20]

Recently, the city council of my town reviewed an ordinance, devised and promulgated by a broad coalition of identity-based political groups, which aimed to ban discrimination in employment, housing, and public accommodations on the basis of "sexual orientation, transsexuality, age, height, weight, personal appearance, physical characteristics, race, color, creed, religion, national origin, ancestry, disability, marital status, sex, or gender."[21] Here is a perfect instance of the universal juridical ideal of liberalism and the normalizing principle of disciplinary regimes conjoined and taken up within the discourse of politicized identity. This ordinance—variously called the "purple hair ordinance" or the "ugly or-

[18] As Connolly argues, politicized identity also reiterates the structure of liberalism in its configuration of a sovereign, unified, accountable individual. Connolly urges a different configuration of identity—one that understood itself as contingent, relational, contestatory, and social—although it is not clear what would motivate identity's transformed orientation. See *Identity/Difference,* especially pp. 171–84.

[19] Michel Foucault, *Discipline and Punish: The Birth of the Prison,* trans. A. Sheridan (New York: Vintage, 1979), pp. 209, 212.

[20] Ibid., p. 206.

[21] From an early draft of "An Ordinance of the City of Santa Cruz Adding Chapter 9.83 to the Santa Cruz Municipal Code Pertaining to the Prohibition of Discrimination." A somewhat amended form of the ordinance was eventually adopted by the city council in 1994.

dinance" by state and national news media—aims to count every difference as no difference, as part of the seamless whole, but also to count every potentially subversive rejection of culturally enforced norms as themselves normal, as normalizable, and as normativizable through law. Indeed, through the definitional, procedural, and remedies sections of this ordinance (e.g., "sexual orientation shall mean known or assumed homosexuality, heterosexuality, or bisexuality") persons are reduced to observable social attributes and practices defined empirically, positivistically, as if their existence were intrinsic and factual, rather than effects of discursive and institutional power; and these positivist definitions of persons as their attributes and practices are written into law, ensuring that persons describable according to them will now become regulated through them. Bentham couldn't have done it better. Indeed, here is a perfect instance of how the language of recognition becomes the language of unfreedom, how articulation in language, in the context of liberal and disciplinary discourse, becomes a vehicle of subordination through individualization, normalization, and regulation, even as it strives to produce visibility and acceptance. Here, also, is a perfect instance of the way in which "differences" that are the effects of social power are neutralized through their articulation as attributes and their circulation through liberal administrative discourse: what do we make of a document that renders as juridical equivalents the denial of employment to an African American, an obese woman, and a white middle-class youth festooned with tattoos, a pierced tongue, and fuchsia hair?

What I want to consider, though, is why this strikingly unemancipatory political project emerges from a potentially more radical critique of liberal juridical and disciplinary modalities of power. For this ordinance, I want to suggest, is not simply misguided in its complicity with the rationalizing and disciplinary elements of late modern culture; it is not simply naive with regard to the regulatory apparatus within which it operates. Rather, it is symptomatic of a feature of politicized identity's *desire* within liberal-bureaucratic regimes, its foreclosure of its own freedom, its impulse to inscribe in the law and in other political registers its historical and present pain rather than conjure an imagined future of power to make itself. To see what this symptom is a symptom of, we need to return once more to a schematic consideration of liberalism, this time in order to read it through Nietzsche's account of the complex logics of *ressentiment*.

. . .

Liberalism contains from its inception a generalized incitement to what Nietzsche terms *ressentiment,* the moralizing revenge of the powerless, "the triumph of the weak as weak."[22] This incitement to *ressentiment* inheres in two related constitutive paradoxes of liberalism: that between individual liberty and social egalitarianism, a paradox which produces failure turned to recrimination by the subordinated, and guilt turned to resentment by the "successful"; and that between the individualism that legitimates liberalism and the cultural homogeneity required by its commitment to political universality, a paradox which stimulates the articulation of politically significant differences on the one hand, and the suppression of them on the other, and which offers a form of articulation that presses against the limits of universalist discourse even while that which is being articulated seeks to be harbored within—included in—the terms of that universalism.

Premising itself on the natural equality of human beings, liberalism makes a political promise of universal individual freedom in order to arrive at social equality, or achieve a civilized retrieval of the equality postulated in the state of nature. It is the tension between the promises of individualistic liberty and the requisites of equality that yields *ressentiment* in one of two directions, depending on the way in which the paradox is brokered. A strong commitment to freedom vitiates the fulfillment of the equality promise and breeds *ressentiment* as welfare state liberalism— attenuations of the unmitigated license of the rich and powerful on behalf of the "disadvantaged." Conversely, a strong commitment to equality, requiring heavy state interventionism and economic redistribution, attenuates the commitment to freedom and breeds *ressentiment* expressed as neoconservative anti-statism, racism, charges of reverse racism, and so forth.

However, it is not only the tension between freedom and equality but the prior presumption of the self-reliant and self-made capacities of liberal subjects, conjoined with their unavowed dependence on and construction by a variety of social relations and forces, that makes *all* liberal subjects, and not only markedly disenfranchised ones, vulnerable to *ressentiment:* it is their situatedness within power, their production by power, and liberal discourse's denial of this situatedness and production that cast the liberal subject into failure, the failure to make itself in the context of a discourse in which its self-making is assumed, indeed, is its assumed nature. This failure, which Nietzsche calls suffering, must either find a reason within itself (which redoubles the failure) or a site of external blame upon which to avenge its hurt and redistribute its pain. Here is Nietzsche's account of this moment in the production of *ressentiment:*

---

[22] A number of political theorists have advanced this argument. For a cogent account, see Connolly, *Identity/Difference*, pp. 21–27.

> For every sufferer instinctively seeks a cause for his suffering, more exactly, an agent; still more specifically, a *guilty* agent who is susceptible to suffering—in short, some living thing upon which he can, on some pretext or other, vent his affects, actually or in effigy. . . . This . . . constitutes the actual physiological cause of *ressentiment*, vengefulness, and the like: a desire to *deaden pain by means of affects*, . . . to *deaden*, by means of a more violent emotion of any kind, a tormenting, secret pain that is becoming unendurable, and to drive it out of consciousness at least for the moment: for that one requires an affect, as savage an affect as possible, and, in order to excite that, any pretext at all.[23]

Ressentiment in this context is a triple achievement: it produces an affect (rage, righteousness) that overwhelms the hurt; it produces a culprit responsible for the hurt; and it produces a site of revenge to displace the hurt (a place to inflict hurt as the sufferer has been hurt). Together these operations both ameliorate (in Nietzsche's term, "anaesthetize") and externalize what is otherwise "unendurable."

In a culture already streaked with the pathos of *ressentiment* for the reasons just discussed, there are several distinctive characteristics of late modern postindustrial societies that accelerate and expand the conditions of its production. My listing will necessarily be highly schematic: First, the phenomenon William Connolly names "increased global contingency" combines with the expanding pervasiveness and complexity of domination by capital and bureaucratic state and social networks to create an unparalleled individual powerlessness over the fate and direction of one's own life, intensifying the experiences of impotence, dependence, and gratitude inherent in liberal capitalist orders and constitutive of *ressentiment*.[24] Second, the steady desacralization of all regions of life—what Weber called disenchantment, what Nietzsche called the death of god—would seem to add yet another reversal to Nietzsche's genealogy of *ressentiment* as perpetually available to "alternation of direction." In Nietzsche's account, the ascetic priest deployed notions of "guilt, sin, sinfulness, depravity, damnation" to "direct the *ressentiment* of the less severely afflicted sternly back upon themselves . . . and in this way *exploit[ed]* the bad instincts of all sufferers for the purpose of self-discipline, self-surveillance, and self-overcoming."[25] However, the desacralizing tendencies of late modernity undermine the efficacy of this deployment and turn suffering's need for exculpation back toward a site of external agency.[26] Third, the increased fragmentation, if not disintegration, of all

[23] *Genealogy of Morals*, p. 127.

[24] *Identity/Difference*, pp. 24–26.

[25] *Genealogy of Morals*, p. 128.

[26] A striking example of this is the way that contemporary natural disasters, such as the 1989 earthquake in California or the 1992 hurricanes in Florida and Hawaii, produced popu-

forms of association not organized until recently by the commodities market—communities, churches, families—and the ubiquitousness of the classificatory, individuating schemes of disciplinary society, combine to produce an utterly *unrelieved* individual, one without insulation from the inevitable failure entailed in liberalism's individualistic construction.[27] In short, the characteristics of late modern secular society, in which individuals are buffeted and controlled by global configurations of disciplinary and capitalist power of extraordinary proportions, and are at the same time nakedly individuated, stripped of reprieve from relentless exposure and accountability for themselves, together add up to an incitement to *ressentiment* that might have stunned even the finest philosopher of its occasions and logics. Starkly accountable yet dramatically impotent, the late modern liberal subject quite literally seethes with *ressentiment*.

Enter politicized identity, now conceivable in part as both product of and reaction to this condition, where "reaction" acquires the meaning Nietzsche ascribed to it: namely, an effect of domination that reiterates impotence, a substitute for action, for power, for self-affirmation that reinscribes incapacity, powerlessness, and rejection. For Nietzsche, *ressentiment* itself is rooted in reaction—the substitution of reasons, norms, and ethics for deeds—and he suggests that not only moral systems but identities themselves take their bearings in this reaction. As Tracy Strong reads this element of Nietzsche's thought:

> Identity . . . does not consist of an active component, but is reaction to something outside; action in itself, with its inevitable self-assertive qualities, must then become something evil, since it is identified with that against which one is reacting. The will to power of slave morality must constantly reassert that which gives definition to the slave: the pain he suffers by being in the world.

---

lar and media discourse about relevant state and federal agencies (e.g., the Federal Emergency Management Agency [FEMA]), that came close to displacing onto the agencies themselves responsibility for the suffering of the victims.

[27] In a personal communication (Spring 1994), Kathy Ferguson suggested that given "all the people I know, from a variety of classes, colors, and sexualities, who struggle mightily, and often happily, to create and maintain families and communities—might the death of families be greatly exaggerated?" I want to affirm the existence of these efforts and at the same time note that the struggle she cites is taking place precisely because the family is a disintegrating social form (a process that is several centuries old and not, as the Christian Right would have it, a recent tear in the social fabric). Moreover, the numbers grow annually for those who have lost or abandoned such struggles, those who live without any significant geographically based familial or community ties, "Internet communities" notwithstanding. And it is this nonemancipatory individuation that renders late modern subjects more intensely vulnerable to social powers that in turn undermine their capacity for self-making. Indeed, it is the increased vulnerability attendant upon this kind of individuation that most powerfully exposes the fallacy of the sovereign subject of liberalism.

Hence any attempt to escape that pain will merely result in the reaffirmation of painful structures.[28]

If the "cause" of *ressentiment* is suffering, its "creative deed" is the reworking of this pain into a negative form of action, the "imaginary revenge" of what Nietzsche terms "natures denied the true reaction, that of deeds."[29] This revenge is achieved through the imposition of suffering "on whatever does not feel wrath and displeasure as he does"[30] (accomplished especially through the production of guilt), through the establishment of suffering as the measure of social virtue, and through casting strength and good fortune ("privilege," as we say today) as selfrecriminating, as its own indictment in a culture of suffering: "it is disgraceful to be fortunate, there is too much misery."[31]

But in its attempt to displace its suffering, identity structured by *ressentiment* at the same time becomes invested in its own subjection. This investment lies not only in its discovery of a site of blame for its hurt will, not only in its acquisition of recognition through its history of subjection (a recognition predicated on injury, now righteously revalued), but also in the satisfactions of revenge, which ceaselessly reenact even as they redistribute the injuries of marginalization and subordination in a liberal discursive order that alternately denies the very possibility of these things and blames those who experience them for their own condition. Identity politics structured by *ressentiment* reverse without subverting this blaming structure: they do not subject to critique the sovereign subject of accountability that liberal individualism presupposes, nor the economy of inclusion and exclusion that liberal universalism establishes. Thus, politicized identity that presents itself as a self-affirmation now appears as the opposite, as predicated on and requiring its sustained rejection by a "hostile external world."[32]

Insofar as what Nietzsche calls slave morality produces identity in reaction to power, insofar as identity rooted in this reaction achieves its moral superiority by reproaching power and action themselves as evil, identity structured by this ethos becomes deeply invested in its own impotence, even while it seeks to assuage the pain of its powerlessness through its vengeful moralizing, through its wide distribution of suffering, through its reproach of power as such. Politicized identity, premised

---

[28] Tracy Strong, *Friedrich Nietzsche and the Politics of Transfiguration*, expanded ed. (Berkeley: University of California Press, 1988), p. 242.

[29] *Genealogy of Morals*, p. 36.

[30] *Thus Spoke Zarathustra*, in *The Portable Nietzsche*, ed. W. Kaufmann (New York: Viking, 1954), p. 252.

[31] *Genealogy of Morals*, pp. 123, 124.

[32] Ibid. p. 34.

on exclusion and fueled by the humiliation and suffering imposed by its historically structured impotence in the context of a discourse of sovereign individuals, is as likely to seek generalized political paralysis, to feast on generalized political impotence, as it is to seek its own or collective liberation through empowerment. Indeed, it is more likely to punish and reproach—"punishment is what revenge calls itself; with a hypocritical lie it creates a good conscience for itself"[33]—than to find venues of self-affirming action.

But contemporary politicized identity's desire is not only shaped by the extent to which the sovereign will of the liberal subject, articulated ever more nakedly by disciplinary individuation and capitalist disinternments, is dominated by late-twentieth-century configurations of political and economic powers. It is shaped as well by the contemporary problematic of history itself, by the late modern rupture of history as a narrative, history as ended because it has lost its end—a rupture that paradoxically gives history an immeasurable weight. As the grim experience of reading *Discipline and Punish* makes clear, there is a sense in which the gravitational force of history is multiplied at precisely the moment that history's narrative coherence and objectivist foundation is refuted. As the problematic of power in history is resituated from subject positioning to subject construction; as power is seen to operate spatially, infiltrationally, "microphysically" rather than only temporally, permeating every heretofore designated "interior" *space* in social lives and individuals; as eroding historical metanarratives take with them both laws of history and the futurity such laws purported to assure; as the presumed continuity of history is replaced with a sense of its violent, contingent, and ubiquitous *force*—history becomes that which has weight but no trajectory, mass but no coherence, force but no direction: it is war without ends or end. Thus, the extent to which "the tradition of all the dead generations weighs like a nightmare on the brain of the living"[34] is today unparalleled, even as history itself disintegrates as a coherent category or practice. We know ourselves to be saturated by history, we feel the extraordinary force of its determinations; we are also steeped in a discourse of its insignificance, and, above all, we know that history will no longer (always already did not) act as our redeemer.

I raise the question of history because in thinking about late modern politicized identity's structuring by *ressentiment,* I have thus far focused on its foundation in the sufferings of a subordinated sovereign subject. But Nietzsche's account of the logic of *ressentiment* is also linked to that

---

[33] *Zarathustra*, p. 252.
[34] Marx, "The Eighteenth Brumaire of Louis Bonaparte," in *Marx-Engels Reader*, p. 595.

feature of the will that is stricken by history, that rails against time itself, that cannot "will backwards," that cannot exert its power over the past—either as a specific set of events or as time itself.

> Willing liberates; but what is it that puts even the liberator himself in fetters? "It was"—that is the name of the will's gnashing of teeth and most secret melancholy. Powerless against what has been done, he is an angry spectator of all that is past. . . . He cannot break time and time's covetousness, that is the will's loneliest melancholy.[35]

Although Nietzsche appears here to be speaking of the will as such, Zarathustra's own relationship to the will as a "redeemer of history" makes clear that this "angry spectatorship" can with great difficulty be reworked as a perverse kind of mastery, a mastery that triumphs over the past by reducing its power, by remaking the present against the terms of the past—in short, by a project of self-transformation that arrays itself against its own genealogical consciousness. In contrast with the human ruin he sees everywhere around him—"fragments and limbs and dreadful accidents"—it is Zarathustra's own capacity to discern and to make a future that spares him from a rancorous sensibility, from crushing disappointment in the liberatory promise of his will:

> The now and the past on earth—alas, my friends, that is what *I* find most unendurable; and I should not know how to live if I were not also a seer of that which must come. A seer, a willer, a creator, a future himself and a bridge to the future—and alas, also, as it were, a cripple at this bridge: all this is Zarathustra.[36]

Nietzsche here discerns both the necessity and the near impossibility—the extraordinary and fragile achievement—of formulating oneself as a creator of the future and a bridge to the future in order to appease the otherwise inevitable rancor of the will against time, in order to redeem the past by lifting the weight of it, by reducing the scope of its determinations. "And how could I bear to be a man if man were not also a creator and guesser of riddles and redeemer of accidents?"[37]

Of course, Zarathustra's exceptionality in what he is willing to confront and bear, in his capacities to overcome in order to create, is Nietzsche's device for revealing us to ourselves. The ordinary will, steeped in the economy of slave morality, devises means "to get rid of his melancholy and to mock his dungeon," means that reiterate the cause of the melancholy, that continually reinfect the narcissistic wound to its capa-

[35] *Zarathustra*, p. 251.
[36] Ibid., pp. 250–51.
[37] Ibid., p. 251.

ciousness inflicted by the past. "Alas," says Nietzsche, "every prisoner becomes a fool; and the imprisoned will redeems himself foolishly."[38] From this foolish redemption—foolish because it does not resolve the will's rancor but only makes a world in its image—is born the wrath of revenge:

> "that which was" is the name of the stone [the will] cannot move. And so he moves stones out of wrath and displeasure, and he wreaks revenge on whatever does not feel wrath and displeasure as he does. Thus the will, the liberator, took to hurting; and on all who can suffer he wreaks revenge for his inability to go backwards. This . . . is what *revenge* is: the will's ill will against time and its "it was."[39]

Revenge as a "reaction," a substitute for the capacity to act, produces identity as both bound to the history that produced it and as a reproach to the present which embodies that history. The will that "took to hurting" in its own impotence against its past becomes (in the form of an identity whose very existence is due to heightened consciousness of the immovability of its "it was," its history of subordination) a will that makes not only a psychological but a political practice of revenge, a practice that reiterates the existence of an identity whose present past is one of insistently unredeemable injury. This past cannot be redeemed *unless* the identity ceases to be invested in it, and it cannot cease to be invested in it without giving up its identity as such, thus giving up its economy of avenging and at the same time perpetuating its hurt—"when he then stills the pain of the wound *he at the same time infects the wound*."[40]

In its emergence as a protest against marginalization or subordination, politicized identity thus becomes attached to its own exclusion both because it is premised on this exclusion for its very existence as identity and because the formation of identity at the site of exclusion, as exclusion,

---

[38] Ibid., p. 251.

[39] Ibid., pp. 251–52.

[40] *Genealogy of Morals*, p. 126. In what could easily characterize the rancorous quality of many contemporary institutions and gatherings—academic, political, cultural—in which politicized identity is strongly and permissibly at play, Nietzsche offers an elaborate account of this replacement of pain with a "more violent emotion" that is the stock in trade of "the suffering":

> The suffering are one and all dreadfully eager and inventive in discovering occasions for painful affects; they enjoy being mistrustful and dwelling on nasty deeds and imaginary slights; they scour the entrails of their past and present for obscure and questionable occurrences that offer them the opportunity to revel in tormenting suspicions and to intoxicate themselves with the poison of their own malice: they tear open their oldest wounds, they bleed from long-healed scars, they make evildoers out of their friends, wives, children, and whoever else stands closest to them. "I suffer: someone must be to blame for it"—thus thinks every sickly sheep. (pp. 127–28)

augments or "alters the direction of the suffering" entailed in subordination or marginalization by finding a site of blame for it. But in so doing, it installs its pain over its unredeemed history in the very foundation of its political claim, in its demand for recognition as identity. In locating a site of blame for its powerlessness over its past—a past of injury, a past as a hurt will—and locating a "reason" for the "unendurable pain" of social powerlessness in the present, it converts this reasoning into an ethicizing politics, a politics of recrimination that seeks to avenge the hurt even while it reaffirms it, discursively codifies it. Politicized identity thus enunciates itself, makes claims for itself, only by entrenching, restating, dramatizing, and inscribing its pain in politics; it can hold out no future—for itself or others—that triumphs over this pain. The loss of historical direction, and with it the loss of futurity characteristic of the late modern age, is thus homologically refigured in the structure of desire of the dominant political expression of the age: identity politics. In the same way, the generalized political impotence produced by the ubiquitous yet discontinuous networks of late modern political and economic power is reiterated in the investments of late modern democracy's primary oppositional political formations.

What might be entailed in transforming these investments in an effort to fashion a more radically democratic and emancipatory political culture? One avenue of exploration may lie in Nietzsche's counsel on the virtues of "forgetting," for if identity structured in part by *ressentiment* resubjugates itself through its investment in its own pain, through its refusal to make itself in the present, memory is the house of this activity and this refusal. Yet erased histories and historical invisibility are themselves such integral elements of the pain inscribed in most subjugated identities that the counsel of forgetting, at least in its unreconstructed Nietzschean form, seems inappropriate if not cruel.[41] Indeed, it is also possible that we have reached a pass where we ought to part with Nietzsche, whose skills as diagnostician often reach the limits of their political efficacy in his privileging of individual character and capacity over the transformative possibilities of collective political invention, in his remove from the refigurative possibilities of political conversation or transformative cultural practices. For if I am right about the problematic of pain installed at the heart of many contemporary contradictory demands for political recognition, all that such pain may long for—more than revenge—is the chance to be heard into a certain release, recognized into self-overcoming, incited into possibilities for triumphing over, and hence

---

[41] This point has been made by many, but for a recent, quite powerful phenomenological exploration of the relationship between historical erasure and lived identity, see Patricia Williams, *The Alchemy of Race and Rights* (Cambridge: Harvard University Press, 1991).

losing, itself. Our challenge, then, would be to configure a radically democratic political culture that can sustain such a project in its midst without being overtaken by it, a challenge that includes guarding against abetting the steady slide of political into therapeutic discourse, even as we acknowledge the elements of suffering and healing we might be negotiating.

What if it were possible to incite a slight shift in the character of political expression and political claims common to much politicized identity? What if we sought to supplant the language of "I am"—with its defensive closure on identity, its insistence on the fixity of position, its equation of social with moral positioning—with the language of "I want this for us"? (This is an "I want" that distinguishes itself from a liberal expression of self-interest by virtue of its figuring of a political or collective good as its desire.) What if we were to rehabilitate the memory of desire within identificatory processes, the moment in desire—either "to have" or "to be"—prior to its wounding?[42] What if "wanting to be" or "wanting to have" were taken up as modes of political speech that could destabilize the formulation of identity as fixed position, as entrenchment by history, and as having necessary moral entailments, even as they affirm "position" and "history" as that which makes the speaking subject intelligible and locatable, as that which contributes to a hermeneutics for adjudicating desires? If every "I am" is something of a resolution of the movement of desire into fixed and sovereign identity, then this project might involve not only learning to speak but to *read* "I am" this way: as potentially in motion, as temporal, as not-I, as deconstructable according to a genealogy of want rather than as fixed interests or experiences.[43] The subject understood as an effect of an (ongoing) genealogy of desire, including the social processes constitutive of, fulfilling, or frustrating desire, is in this way revealed as neither sovereign nor conclusive even as it is affirmed as an "I." In short, if framed in a political language, this deconstruction could be that which reopens a desire for futurity where Nietzsche saw it foreclosed by the logics of rancor and *ressentiment*.

Such a slight shift in the character of the political discourse of identity eschews the kinds of ahistorical or utopian turns against identity politics

---

[42] Jesse Jackson's 1988 "keep hope alive" presidential campaign strikes me as having sought to configure the relationship between injury, identity, and desire in something like this way and to have succeeded in forging a "rainbow coalition" *because* of the idiom of futurity it employed—want, hope, desires, dreams—among those whose postures and demands had previously had a rancorous quality.

[43] In Trinh T. Minh-ha's formulation, "to seek is to lose, for seeking presupposes a separation between the seeker and the sought, the continuing me and the changes it undergoes" ("Not You/Like You: Post-Colonial Women and the Interlocking Questions of Identity and Difference," *Inscriptions* 3–4 [1988], p. 72).

made by a nostalgic and broken humanist Left as well as the reactionary and disingenuous assaults on politicized identity tendered by the Right. Rather than opposing or seeking to transcend identity investments, the replacement—even the admixture—of the language of "being" with "wanting" would seek to exploit politically a recovery of the more expansive moments in the genealogy of identity formation, a recovery of the moment prior to its own foreclosure against its want, prior to the point at which its sovereign subjectivity is established through such foreclosure and through eternal repetition of its pain. How might democratic discourse itself be invigorated by such a shift from ontological claims to these kinds of more expressly political ones, claims that, rather than dispensing blame for an unlivable present, inhabited a necessarily agonistic theater of discursively forging an alternative future?

CHAPTER FOUR

The Mirror of Pornography

> Too much freedom seems to change into nothing but too
> much slavery, both for private man and the city. Well then,
> tyranny is probably established out of no other regime than
> democracy, I suppose—the greatest and most savage slavery
> out of the extreme of freedom.
> —"Socrates," in *Plato's Republic*

> To lead a life soaked in the passionate consciousness of one's
> gender at every single moment, to will to be a sex with a
> vengeance—these are impossibilities, and far from the aims of
> feminism.   —Denise Riley, *"Am I That Name?"*

THIS EFFORT to apprehend the *rhetorical* power of Catharine MacKinnon's social theory of gender is compelled by an aim that exceeds critique of her depiction of women as always and only sexually violable, her pornography politics, or her arguments about the First Amendment. Insofar as MacKinnon's work has extraordinary political purchase, this essay seeks to discern something of the composition and constituency of this power in her theoretical project. How and why does MacKinnon's complicatedly radical political analysis and voice acquire such hold? And what are the possibilities that other feminisms could rival such power with analyses more multivalent in their representation of gender subordination and gender construction, more attentive to the race and class of gender, more compatible with the rich diversity of female sexual experience, more complex in their representations of sexuality and sexual power, more extravagant and democratic in their political vision? In other words, while MacKinnon might be "wrong" about Marxism, gender, sexuality, power, the state, or the relation between freedom and equality, those issues are of less concern here than the potent order of "truth" she produces. How did MacKinnon so successfully deploy a militant feminism during the 1980s, a decade markedly unsympathetic to all militancies to the left of center?

Whether developing antipornography ordinances in midwestern cities and, more recently, Canada, or articulating an analysis of sexual harassment on the MacNeil/Lehrer News Hour, Catharine MacKinnon has been taken up and taken seriously by those in mainstream judicial and media institutions as well as in august corners of academe, an unusual phenomenon in any event and certainly rare for a feminist who is no liberal. Featured in fall 1991 as the cover story of the *New York Times* magazine, she was anointed in the same season by philosopher Richard Rorty as the new prophet of our age. Named NBC "person of the week" during the Hill-Thomas hearings, shortly after which she delivered the prestigious Gauss Lectures at Princeton University, she has also appeared frequently in other commercial media venues to discuss issues ranging from pornography and sexual harassment to hate speech.

While MacKinnon has made an unusual splash in the mainstream, her following among radical feminists is equally significant. The unquestioned theoretical lodestar of the feminist antipornography movement, she is an important figure in the rapidly developing field of feminist jurisprudence, and her rhetorical persuasiveness also shows its measure on ordinary undergraduates: young women and men across political and sexual orientations, racial and class formations, find themselves compelled, disturbed, and convinced by her work.

Anyone who has seen or heard MacKinnon knows that she is extremely smart, articulate, charismatic, and a master of an oratorical style in which righteous rage is alloyed with icy rationality, hammering empiricism, and a beseeching feminine anguish—all of which must be mentioned in an analysis that purports to account for her power and purchase in American politics, the law school classroom, and the feminist activist community. However, without diminishing the importance of these elements, nor the sheer brilliance and deftness of some of her arguments, I want to ask a different set of questions about MacKinnon's political hold, questions concerned with the logical and narrative structures of her prose, with rhetorical strategies and contemporary political resonances in her writing.

To some degree, discerning MacKinnon's analytic potency entails debunking the putative radicalism of MacKinnon's work. It involves exploring the ways in which MacKinnon's formulation of gender, notwithstanding its flirtations with social construction and its concern to supplant arguments from difference with arguments from inequality, closely echoes the universalizing, transcultural, and transhistorical arguments about the sexual order of things proffered by orthodox political conservatives. But elaborating the purchase of her arguments is not only a matter of locating the conservative body beneath the radical attire. Indeed, MacKinnon's complex residual attachments to Marxism and to monological, structural analyses of oppression also produce a set of questions about the rhetorical powers of certain kinds of logical and narrative structures. Here, the problem for which a study of MacKinnon's work provides only an occasion could be put this way: Can a radical postfoundationalist feminist political discourse about women, sexuality, and the law—with its necessarily partial logics and provisional truths, situated knowledges, fluid subjects, and decentered sovereignty—work to claim power, or to contest hegemonic power, to the degree that MacKinnon's discourse does? Or do the commitments of postfoundationalist feminist analysis condemn it to a certain political marginalization, to permanent gadfly status, to a philosopher's self-consolation that she is on the side of "truth" rather than power? In the domain of late modern political life, and especially the domain of the law, can political-theoretical strategies of subversion, displacement, proliferation, and resignification compare or compete with the kinds of systematic and ontological claims MacKinnon makes about the condition of women and the good for women? And is any answer we might venture to this question specific to the resonant range of the contemporary discursive field into which these claims are inserted, a field that remains formally dominated by a modernist political idiom? Or might we venture some more quasi-transcendental postulates about the powers of systematic analytical structures and syllogistic logical forms, about the ways in which (scientistic) modes of analysis that totalize, reduce, systematize, and close achieve their superior power effects precisely through such discursive violence and can effectively ignore or dominate "postmodern" incursions because of this greater violence? While these are not questions to be fully answered here, they frame and animate this investigation of the rhetorical structure of MacKinnon's work.

.   .   .

> Sexuality is to feminism what work is to Marxism.
> —Catharine MacKinnon, *Toward a
> Feminist Theory of the State*

MacKinnon's social theory of gender is an adaptation of Marxism, which, somewhat paradoxically, it intends both to parallel and displace.[1] Paralleling the systemic and totalizing explanatory logic of the realm of production and the materiality of labor in explaining and criticizing class

---

[1] Early in *Toward a Feminist Theory of the State* (Cambridge: Harvard University Press, 1989), MacKinnon refers to Marxism and feminism as two social theories of power, defining and tracking two "basic social processes" (p. 4). However, when she is engaged in a critical analysis of Marxist method for feminism, she refers to feminism as "stand[ing] in relation to marxism as marxism does to classical political economy: its final conclusion and ultimate critique" (p. 125).

society, MacKinnon develops an analogical account of sexuality and gender. Yet by simultaneously displacing the Marxist emphasis on the primacy of class, and of economics, as the constructing and positioning feature of women and men, MacKinnon identifies Marxism as a partial rather than inclusive social theory and positions feminism as that which can "turn marxism inside out and on its head."[2] Her desire to match and displace Marxism's systematicity is captured in the following statement:

> Feminism has not been perceived as having a method, or even a central argument. It has been perceived [by whom?] not as a systematic analysis but as a loose collection of complaints and issues that, taken together, describe rather than explain the misfortunes of the female sex. The challenge is to demonstrate that feminism systematically converges upon a central explanation of sex inequality through an approach distinctive to its subject yet applicable to the whole of social life, including class.[3]

MacKinnon's social theory of gender rests upon a crucial conceptual identification and a crucial conceptual equivalence: it depends upon an identity—not merely a relation—between sexuality and gender, and an equivalence—not merely an analogy—between the capital-labor relation in Marxism and the male-female relation in feminism. For Marx, the organization of production expressed by the capital-labor relation *is* the material of class in capitalism; for MacKinnon, the organization of sexuality expressed in the male-female relation *is* the material of gender in male dominance. Sexuality is the stuff of gender *because* labor is the stuff of class, and class is like gender—both are relations of dominance and subordination rooted in fundamental social processes, sexual activity and production respectively. Thus the organization of desire is to gender as the organization of labor is to class—fully constitutive but masked in the ideologically naturalized form that legitimates the regime. If sexuality signifies the organization of human desire and labor signifies the organization of human productive power, the former makes gender and the latter makes class: together they make history, the social world, ideology, the state, and the individual. "As the organized appropriation of the work of some for the benefit of others defines a class, workers, the organized expropriation of the sexuality of some for the use of others defines the sex, woman."[4]

---

[2] Ibid., p. 125.
[3] Ibid., p. 108.
[4] Ibid., p. 3. One can begin to discern here a number of problems with the parallel MacKinnon is attempting to establish between work and sex, class and gender. Sexuality, which MacKinnon defines at times as the organization of desire—leaving open an ensemble of questions about the ontological status of desire—and at other times as "whatever a given society eroticizes"—leaving open questions about the ontological status of society and the

In MacKinnon's account, the sexiness of the social process she calls desire closes a loop in gender formation that is not closed in Marx's account of class formation. If gender is a relation of domination and subordination in male dominant societies, and gender is constituted by sexuality, then, argues MacKinnon, sexuality in such societies *is* the eroticization of dominance and submission.[5] Thus, female sexuality is not only expropriated by men (as labor is expropriated by capital), heterosexual desire itself constitutes, insofar as it eroticizes, gender subordination by eroticizing dominance and submission as gendered positions. Sexuality in male dominant societies *is* the eroticization of male dominance, an eroticization that *produces* gender as this dominance, a gendering that *reproduces* the erotics of this dominance. Thus, "feminism is a theory of how the eroticization of dominance and submission creates gender, creates woman and man in the social form in which we know them."[6] For MacKinnon, if sex is to gender what work is to class—only more so, because the sexiness of sex eroticizes gender inequality and does not simply coercively or ideologically enforce it—then every feminist issue, every injustice and injury suffered by women, devolves upon sexuality: the construction of femininity is the making of female vulnerability and violation as womanhood; the construction of female economic dependence is sexual availability to men; incest, sexual harassment, rape, and prostitution are all modes of sexual subordination; women's lack of authoritative speech is women's always already sexually violated condition.[7]

However, it is pornography that MacKinnon isolates as the most potent and tangible vehicle of women's subordination in contemporary culture. Neither a "harmless fantasy nor a corrupt and confused misrepresentation of an otherwise natural and healthy sexual situation,"

---

erotic—is the "linchpin of gender inequality" because sexuality is a form of power, indeed, the form of power that creates gender. Marx, of course, rooted his argument about labor as power in labor's generativity—its capacity to produce a surplus that could be commodified as labor power, appropriated as surplus value, and congealed as capital. While MacKinnon posits the "organized expropriation of the sexuality of some for the use of others" as defining the sex, woman, and posits "gender and family as its congealed forms" (*Toward a Feminist Theory of the State*, pp. 3–4), she never quite specifies how—through what generativity—the political economy of sexuality is orchestrated. Thus, where Marx's argument is logical (dialectical) and developmental (progressive), MacKinnon's is tautological (circular) and static (rooted in equivalents and syllogisms). As will become clear in the last portion of this chapter, this has political implications that exceed the mere irritant of its analytic incoherence.

[5] Ibid., p. 113.

[6] *Feminism Unmodified: Discourses on Life and Law* (Cambridge: Harvard University Press, 1987), p. 50.

[7] *Toward a Feminist Theory of the State*, pp. 109–12.

pornography "institutionalizes the sexuality of male supremacy, fusing the erotization of dominance and submission with the social construction of male and female."[8] For MacKinnon, pornography is the distillate of gender relations in male dominant regimes, not merely an expression but the legitimating institution of male dominance:

> Pornography, in the feminist view, is a form of forced sex, a practice of sexual politics, an institution of gender inequality. In this perspective, pornography is not harmless fantasy or a corrupt and confused misrepresentation of an otherwise natural and healthy sexuality. Along with the rape and prostitution in which it participates, pornography institutionalizes the sexuality of male supremacy, which fuses the eroticization of dominance and submission with the social construction of male and female. Gender is sexual. Pornography constitutes the meaning of that sexuality. Men treat women as who they see women as being. Pornography constructs who that is. Men's power over women means that the way men see women defines who women can be. Pornography is that way.[9]

Although MacKinnon never says so explicitly, pornography presumably is to male dominance as, for Marx, liberalism is to capitalism— something institutionally securing, discursively naturalizing, ideologically obscuring, and historically perpetrating the power of the dominant.

.   .   .

There are any number of questions to be raised about MacKinnon's effort to install gender and sexuality into categories and dynamics used to explain the making of class through labor. We might begin by wondering at her failure to develop a specific theory of sexuality and gender—as opposed to adapting a theory of work and class for this project. If sex is to gender what work is to class, then presumably a theory of sexuality, rather than a theory of work applied to sex, is required for a feminist critique and theory of emancipation. Moreover, given the importance to Marx's theory of class of the capacity to generate a surplus—and hence to produce surplus value and to support the revolutionary aim dependent on the possibility of collectivizing work and collectively sharing in the benefits of such surplus generativity—and given the absence of this element in the power(s) constitutive of gender or organizing desire, we might also wonder about the fit of a Marxist theory of class to a theory of gender based on sexuality. Even if it were granted that a single social relation, called sexuality, produced gender, would it therefore be eligible

---

[8] *Feminism Unmodified,* p. 172.
[9] Ibid, p. 148.

for a theoretical apparatus designed to apprehend class? And what if sexuality is not reducible to a single social relation but is itself a complex nonschema of discourses and economies, which are constitutive not only of the semiotics of gender but of race and class formations? What if gender generally and women's subordination in particular do not devolve on a single social relation but have manifold sites and sources of production and reproduction—for example, in discourses organizing motherhood, race, philosophical truth, citizenship, class, heterosexuality, war, science, and so forth? Does sexuality's inability to be systematized and the lack of a single mechanism on which gender turns make gender subordination less real than class distinctions, or sexual violation less injurious than exploited labor? Or does it instead make gender less conducive to a monological theoretical form and unified political practice? In this regard, might MacKinnon's anxiety about supplying feminism with a systematicity, with a single logic, mechanism, and explanatory principle, betoken a distinctly late modernist (as well as phallogocentric) anxiety about what constitutes the real and the potent?

Insofar as MacKinnon's Marxism is intended to be less doctrinal than methodological, it gives the illusion of being surgically reconfigured to fit its subject and thus to elide one of MacKinnon's chief anxieties—namely, that the intercourse of Marxism and feminism will inevitably subordinate the latter.[10] However, MacKinnon's adoption of Marxism as method and worldview may ultimately constitute problems more insidious for feminism than did more patently limited efforts to assimilate feminist concerns to an unreconstructed Marxist lexicon, efforts that revealed the character of women's work (caretaking and service), domain of injury (bodily, private, subjective), consciousness (always exceeding a relation to the mode of production), and social location (isolated, private) to make it a poor candidate for intelligent apprehension within terms such as "production of surplus value" or "history of class struggle." In MacKinnon's own words, the abiding significance and value of Marxist theory pertains to its critical analysis of "society's dynamic laws of motion in their totality, materiality, and historicity, combining determinacy with agency, thought with situation, complexly based on interest."[11] In other words, MacKinnon intends to appropriate from Marxist theory not its categories, its theory of history, nor even its historical approach to social life, but an extract from its *science* of domination. Indeed, hers is a strikingly nonhistorical and nondialectical account of antagonistic social

---

[10] "Underlying marxist attempts to accommodate or respond to feminism, including most socialist-feminist theories, is one of three approaches: equate and collapse, derive and subordinate, and substitute contradictions" (*Toward a Feminist Theory of the State*, p. 60).

[11] Ibid., p. 39.

dynamics constitutive of an apprehensible social totality. In this MacKinnon not only takes over but exaggerates Marxism's totalizing constructions of social life—including and especially its reduction of subjects and subjectivity to subject *positions*—and its ontological generalization of historically specific subject production (about which more shortly).

MacKinnon's conceptual equivalent between the absolute domination of capital and the absolute domination of men—"as many work and few gain . . . some fuck and others get fucked"[12]—de-essentializes gender, by making it fully a production of power. At the same time, this conceptual equivalent unifies and universalizes gender by dehistoricizing it; by divesting it of any greater specifiability through class, age, sexuality, race, or culture; by exhaustively identifying it with respectively dominant and subordinate social positions; and by making gender fully a function of such positions, giving it no plasticity, complex and diverse interiors, variability, or domain of invention. In this replacement of mystified political subjects with reified ones, in this subversion of denaturalizing analytic strategies with dehistoricizing and totalizing ones, MacKinnon is operating both within and outside a Marxist framework. She is repeating a certain Marxist limitation but repeating it with a difference that, as we shall see, intensifies the force of the limitation.

First, what is she repeating? By Baudrillard as well as Arendt, we are reminded that Marx's powerful analytic critique of nineteenth-century political economy may have been less Archimedean with respect to its specific historical context than Marx had imagined or than his followers ordinarily acknowledge. In Baudrillard's analysis, Marx was so steeped in the milieu of capitalist political economy that he rendered its cultural productions and effects in a vein more ontological than historical and thus reified the *activity* of the nineteenth-century proletarian as an eternal verity of man and the *culture* of nineteenth-century European industrialization as the soul of history. In Baudrillard's reading, the mid-nineteenth-century resolution of industrializing European societies into two great oppositional classes led Marx to regard history as fully constituted by class struggle and labor as fully constitutive of man. This is Baudrillard:

> If on the one hand Marx is interested in the later fate of the labor power objectified in the production process as abstract social labor[,] . . . Marxist theory, on the other hand, never challenges human capacity of production[,] . . . this productive potential of every man in every society "of transforming his environment into ends useful for the individual or society." . . . Criticism and history are strangely arrested before this anthropological postulate: a curious fate for a Marxist concept. . . . Radical in its *logical* analysis of capital, Marxist

[12] Ibid., p. 4.

theory nonetheless maintains an *anthropological* consensus with the options of Western rationalism in its definitive form acquired in eighteenth-century bourgeois thought.[13]

"Overwhelmed," as Hannah Arendt puts the matter, "by the unprecedented actual productivity of Western mankind [in the modern age]," Marx deduces "man" from this epoch and thus dehistoricizes the relative valences of political economy and its components—labor, labor power, and relations of production—even while treating the development of specific modes of production as a problem of dialectics and history.[14] "But," as Baudrillard reminds us, "differentiating modes of production renders unchallengeable the evidence of production as the determinant instance. It generalizes the economic mode of rationality over the entire expanse of human history, as the generic mode of human becoming." Thus, failing to grasp his critical ontology of man the producer as itself historically produced, Marx posits a *homo faber* who mirrors rather than criticizes the age of political economy—"the abstract and generalized development of productivity (the developed form of political economy) is what makes *the concept of production* itself appear as man's movement and generic."[15] Production as the determinant instance, Baudrillard argues,

> circumscribes the entire history of man in a gigantic simulation model. It tries somehow to turn against the order of capital by using as an analytic instrument the most subtle ideological phantasm that capital has itself elaborated. Is this a "dialectical" reversal? Isn't the system pursuing its dialectic of universal reproduction here? If one hypothesizes that *there has never been and will never be anything but the single mode of production ruled by capitalist political economy*—a concept that makes sense only in relation to the economic formation that produced it (indeed, to the theory that analyzes this economic formation)—then even the "dialectical" generalization of this concept is merely the *ideological* universalization [the mirror] of this system's postulates.[16]

Just as Baudrillard suggests that Marx "generalizes the economic mode of rationality over the entire expanse of human history, as the generic mode of human becoming," so MacKinnon's thesis that sexuality is fully constitutive of gender, and that heterosexuality is gender's male dominant form, also "generalizes the [pornographic heterosexual sexual] mode of rationality over the entire expanse of human history, as the generic mode of [gender] becoming." As Marx's "discovery" that eco-

---

[13] "The Mirror of Production," in *Selected Writings,* ed. Mark Poster (Stanford: Stanford University Press, 1988), pp. 104–5.

[14] *The Human Condition* (Chicago: University of Chicago Press, 1958), p. 87.

[15] "Mirror of Production," pp. 105, 104.

[16] Ibid., p. 105.

nomic production is the ontological ground of humanity mirrors the age in which it occurred, MacKinnon's thesis mirrors a hyperbolic expression of gender as sexuality in the late-twentieth-century United States and reveals the extent to which construction and regulation of gender by a panoply of discourses, activities, and distinctions other than sexuality have been sharply eroded and destabilized. These would include the privatization and pervasive feminization of reproductive work; a gendered division of labor predicated on the exchange between household labor and socialized production; gendered religious, political, and civic codes; and other sharply gendered spheres of activity and social norms—in short, all elements of the construction of gender that are institutionalized, hence enforced, elsewhere than through the organization of desire. The destabilization of these other domains of the production and regulation of gender lead not only MacKinnon but feminist theorists putatively quite different from her—those theorizing gender as performativity vis-à-vis heterosexual norms, for example—to read gender as almost wholly constituted by the (heterosexual) organization of *desire*.[17]

While a clearly delineated and complexly arrayed sexual division of labor may have constituted regimes of gender—gendered social locations, productions of subjectivity, and mechanisms of subordination—more profoundly in other times and places, the culturally normative heterosexual organization of desire, including its pornographic commercial expression, emerges most fiercely inscribed in our own.[18] Moreover, as in Baudrillard's reading "the system of political economy does not produce only the individual as labor power that is sold and exchanged . . . [but] the very conception of labor power as the fundamental human potential," the pornographic sexual order, of which MacKinnon's theory is

[17] Baudrillard himself mentions psychoanalytic categories as taking flight from the history that produces them—"What we have said about the Marxist concepts holds for the unconscious, repression, Oedipus complex, etc. as well" ("Mirror of Production," p. 113)—but it is not a point that he develops. Moreover, Baudrillard implies that the problem with the psychoanalytic concepts is their complicity with the Marxist economic one. My point, which could not be Baudrillard's, given his inattention to the construction of gender, is that their dehistoricized character is linked to the naturalized constituents of gender.

[18] This is, crucially, a different argument from Hegel's argument about the relation of philosophy to history in which the "owl of Minerva flies at dusk." For I am suggesting that the reduction of gender construction and regulation to heterosexual sexual orders is a historical process of our time, not that MacKinnon is only retrospectively grasping what held together an order now unraveling. Yet I also want to make the second argument: Evidence of the unraveling of the heterosexual gender regime is everywhere in popular culture, from Madonna and Michael Jackson to Ronald Reagan's possibly queer son and PeeWee Herman. In short, MacKinnon is theorizing a very peculiar historical moment, as Marx did when he described "society as a whole as more and more splitting up into two great hostile camps, into two great classes directly facing each other" (*Manifesto of the Communist Party*, in *The Marx-Engels Reader*, 2d ed., ed. R. C. Tucker [New York: Norton, 1978], p. 474).

a mirror, does not produce only women as sexuality but the very conception of sexuality as the fundamental feature of gender. In Baudrillard's
elaboration:

> More deeply than in the fiction of individuals freely selling their labor power in
> the market, the system is rooted in the identification of individuals with their
> labor power and with their acts of "transforming nature according to human
> ends." In a word, man is not only quantitatively exploited as a productive
> force by the *system* of capitalist political economy, but is also metaphysically
> overdetermined as a producer by the *code* of political economy. In the last
> instance, the system rationalizes its power here. *And in this Marxism assists the*
> *cunning of capital.*[19]

I am suggesting that MacKinnon's theory of gender as fully constituted by sexuality and of pornography as the ultimate expression of male
dominance is itself historically produced by, on the one hand, the erosion
of other sites of gender production and gender effects, and on the other,
the profusion, proliferation, and radical deprivatization and diffusion of
sexuality in the late twentieth century. The phenomenon Marcuse called
repressive desublimation, which Foucault reconceived as the production
of a specific regime of sexuality, is what we might call the pornographic
age that MacKinnon's theory "mirrors" rather than historically or analytically decodes. So, too, does her social theory of gender mirror rather
than deconstruct the *subjects* of heterosexual male pornography—both
the male consumer and the female model—subjects that, we may specu-
late, function largely (and futilely) to shore up or stabilize a sexual/
gender dominance itself destabilized by the erosions of other elements of
gender subordination in the late twentieth century.

In other words, if not only gendered divisions of labor and activity,
but a regime of sexual binarism—heterosexuality—itself is decentered
by the political-economic-cultural forces of late modernity, then Mac-
Kinnon's theory of gender unwittingly consolidates gender out of symp-
toms of a crisis moment in male dominance. In this way, MacKinnon
formulates as the deep, universal, and transhistorical structure of gender
what is really a hyperpornographic expression: indeed, it marks the crisis
attendant upon the transmutation from overdetermined gender dualism
and gender subordination (here underspecified) to a present and future
characterized by the erosion of compulsory heterosexuality itself as constitutive of everyday gender constructions.[20]

MacKinnon's move to read gender off of pornography, her construc-

---

[19] "Mirror of Production," p. 104.

[20] MacKinnon herself glimpses this: "[I]f you understand that pornography literally
means what it says, you might conclude that sexuality has become the fascism of contemporary America and we are moving into the last days of Weimar" (*Feminism Unmodified*,
p. 15).

tion of a social theory of gender that mirrors heterosexual male pornography, not only convenes a pervasively, totally, and singly determined gendered subject, it encodes the pornographic age as the truth rather than the hyperbole of gender production: it fails to read the $10 billion a year porn industry as a "state of emergency" (as Nietzsche spoke of the hyperrationality of classical Greek philosophy) of a male dominant heterosexual regime.[21] Moreover, her move to read pornography as the literal and essential representation of gendered heterosexuality precisely identifies the pornographic male consumer and pornographic female subject as ontologically male and female. In arguing that "pornography literally means what it says,"[22] MacKinnon not only begs questions about the workings of representation and fantasy, of hermeneutics and interpellation, she ontologizes pornography *as* gender. In short, MacKinnon's theory of gender mirrors the straight male pornography it means to criticize, a mirroring that manifests in a number of ways.

First, in MacKinnon's theory of gender as in the heterosexual male porn she analyzes, the subject positions of male and female are depicted as relentlessly dualistic and absolute, figured literally, not metaphorically or qualifiedly, as subject and object, person and thing, dominant and subordinate: or, as Drucilla Cornell puts it in *Beyond Accommodation,* "fuckor and fuckee."[23]

Second, in MacKinnon's theory of gender as in the heterosexual male porn she analyzes, the subject positions of male and female are formed only and totally by sexuality. Not only does gender lack other constituents, but the making of gender is not seen to vary substantively across other formations and vectors of power—for example, race—except insofar as these differences are expressed sexually. Sexuality may be racialized, racial subordination may be sexualized; but differences among women dissolve when sexuality is grasped as the universal axis of subordination. In this metaphysical overdetermination of gender as sexual, MacKinnon assists in the cunning of pornography. (Recall Baudrillard's argument that Marxism assists in the cunning of capital in its complicity with the metaphysical overdetermination of man as a producer by the code of political economy.)

Third, in MacKinnon's theory as in the heterosexual male porn she analyzes, the sexual subject positions of male and female are also made

[21] Nietzsche, *Twilight of the Idols,* in *The Portable Nietzsche,* ed. W. Kaufmann (New York: Viking, 1954). Nietzsche argues that the hyperrationality of the Greeks should be read as a symptom: "The fanaticism with which all Greek reflection throws itself upon rationality betrays a desperate situation; there was danger, there was but one choice: either to perish or—to be *absurdly rational*" (p. 478).

[22] *Feminism Unmodified,* p. 15.

[23] *Beyond Accommodation: Ethical Feminism, Deconstruction, and the Law* (New York: Routledge, 1991), p. 119.

one with the *subjectivity* of male and female, with the consequence that male and female subjectivities are totalized, dichotomized, and pervasively sexualized. This is MacKinnon:

> [A] woman is a being who identifies and is identified as one whose sexuality exists for someone else, who is socially male. What is termed women's sexuality is the capacity to arouse desire in that someone. Considering women's sexuality in this way forces confrontation with whether there is, in the possessive sense of "women's," any such thing. Is women's sexuality its absence?[24]

If gender is sexuality as it appears in heterosexual male pornography, then not only female sexuality but the totality of female consciousness consist solely of what men (now also unified as a consumer subject) require. Thus, MacKinnon concludes, "if women are socially defined such that female sexuality cannot be lived or spoken or felt or even somatically sensed apart from its enforced definition, then there is no such thing as a woman as such; there are only walking embodiments of men's projected needs."[25] Of course, this evacuation of female subjectivity of any element not transparent on the pornographic page renders any emancipatory project nearly impossible. MacKinnon is no more able to answer her own question about consciousness—"how can woman, 'thingified in the head,' complicit in the body, see her condition as such?"[26]—than she is able to imagine the making of a feminist female sexual future.

Fourth, in MacKinnon's theory as in the pornography she analyzes, heterosexuality is the past, present, and eternal future of gender. If gender is sexuality, sexuality is always gendered and women are sex for men, then, for example, lesbian sexuality either doesn't exist, is sex for men, or imitates heterosexuality—all of which are indeed tropes of lesbian representation in straight male porn as well as MacKinnon's account of lesbianism: "If being for another is women's sexual construction, it can be no more escaped by . . . men's temporary concrete absence, than it can be eliminated . . . by sexual permissiveness, which, in this context, looks like women emulating male roles."[27] And, "lesbian sex, simply as sex between women, given a social definition of gender and sexuality, does not by definition transcend the erotization of dominance and submission and their social equation with masculinity and femininity."[28]

Finally, and here the ground is more speculative, MacKinnon's social

---

[24] *Toward a Feminist Theory of the State*, p. 118.
[25] Ibid., p. 119.
[26] Ibid., p. 124.
[27] Ibid., p. 118.
[28] Ibid., p. 119. In "Does Sexuality Have a History?" (*Discourses of Sexuality: From Aristotle to AIDS*, ed. Domna Stanton [Ann Arbor: University of Michigan Press, 1992]), MacKinnon comments further on lesbian sexuality, but not in ways that are either analytically compelling or politically consistent. Here is a sample:

theory of gender mirrors pornography in its prose structure and rhetorical effect, in a fashion similar to what Baudrillard identified as Marxism's
mirroring of the *code* of political economy. The pornographic rhetorical
structure of MacKinnon's writing and speech would appear to inhere in
the insistent and pounding quality of her prose: in the rhythmic pulses of
her simple subject-verb-object sentences in which a single point is incessantly reiterated, reworked, driven, and thrust at its audience; in an over-
burdened syllogistic structure, which makes the syllogistic logic more
proliferative, intoxicating, overstimulating, agitated, and less contestable; in the literalism and force of her abstract claims—"pornography is
that way"—which simultaneously structure the scene and permit any
(man) his own imaginative entry into the scene; in the use of simple,
active verbs, hyperbolic adverbs, and strategically deployed sentence
fragments; in the slippage between representation and action; in the direct and personalized form of address; in the repeated insistence on gender, sexuality, and representation as "the real"; and in the personification
and activation of things or concepts. Consider:

> In pornography, women desire dispossession and cruelty. Men, permitted to
> put words (and other things) in women's mouths, create scenes in which
> women desperately want to be bound, battered, tortured, humiliated, and
> killed. Or merely taken and used. This is erotic to the male point of view.
> Subjection itself is the content of women's sexual desire and desirability.
> Women are there to be violated and possessed, men to violate and possess
> them, either on screen or by camera or pen, on behalf of the viewer.[29]

Listen again:

> What looks like love and romance in the liberal view looks a lot like hatred and
> torture in the feminist view. Pleasure and eroticism become violation. Desire
> appears as lust for dominance and submission. The vulnerability of women's
> projected sexual availability—that acting we are allowed; asking to be acted
> upon [a brief lingering, a tease, before returning to . . .] is victimization. Play
> conforms to scripted roles, fantasy expresses ideology[,] . . . and admiration
> of natural physical beauty becomes objectification.[30]

Women and men are still women and men in the world, even when they are gay or lesbian.
That makes lesbian women distinctively subordinated within a subordinate group, women,
and gay men distinctively subordinated within a dominant group, men.

Heterosexuality is constructed around gender, as the dominant paradigm of sex; homosexuality is constructed around gender, as the subordinated paradigm of sex. Both are
deeply invested in gender, if in different ways. (p. 135)

[29] *Feminism Unmodified*, p. 148.
[30] Ibid., p. 149.

I am suggesting that MacKinnon repeats one of Marxism's most problematic but also most rhetorically compelling features: the stylistic mirroring of its subject of critique. MacKinnon's analysis acquires much of its potency from the cultural resonance it strikes, the libidinal excitation it incites, the pornographic guilt it taps and reworks—all under the sign of radical critique. This is a slightly different claim from Drucilla Cornell's bold suggestion that MacKinnon "fucks her audiences," yet it also converges with that view: MacKinnon's theory of gender transpires within a pornographic genre, suspending us in a complex pornographic experience in which MacKinnon is both purveyor and object of desire and her analysis is proffered as substitute for the sex she abuses us for wanting. This substitution itself participates in a pornographic chain; pornography *as* substitute for sex and the endless substitutability of all the parties to pornography are mirrored in MacKinnon's insistence on sexual equality as substitute for sexual pleasure and the endless substitutability of all parties to the figure of male and female in the regime of masculine dominance. MacKinnon's analysis takes part as well in the pornographic chain of prohibition and transgression: as pornography is premised upon desire constructed out of prohibition and must therefore continually reestablish the prohibitions it purports to undo through transgression, MacKinnon's analysis participates in this project by proliferating prohibitions, speaking transgressively, working our desire into a political opposition to itself. If she assists in this way in the "cunning of pornography," perhaps literally abetting its production, her rhetoric also mirrors pornographic strategy insofar as she marks repeatedly the prohibitions against her work, its transgressiveness, and its unspeakability, even as she persists in it. And as with pornography, this economy of transgression and prohibition is a closed one: as the sexiness of porn lies in its temporal repetitiveness and spatial sequestering, the power of MacKinnon's analysis is bound to its oft-noted theoretical closures and political foreclosures. "There's no way out" is among students' most frequent responses to her work.

In short, in its rehearsal of a powerful underground (pornographic) code of gender and sexuality, reinscribing and exploiting the power of this code even while denouncing its contents, MacKinnon's theory permits easy cultural identification and recognition, giving her "radicalism" a seductively familiar rather than threatening resonance and cultural location. In this way, her putative radicalism simultaneously sustains the pleasure of the familiar, the pleasure of the illicit, the pleasure of moralizing against the illicit, and the comforts of conservatism—gender is eternal and sexual pleasure is opprobrious—in an era of despair about substantive political transformation.

. . .

While the potency of MacKinnon's analysis is drawn in part from the Marxist method she seeks to appropriate for feminism, she also intensifies one of its more problematic tendencies by shearing it of history, dialectics, and a dynamic of change. For Marx, the resolution of society into "two great classes directly facing each other" is a historical achievement—"complete" only in the mid-nineteenth century.[31] (This "completion" turned out to be, as I am arguing hyperheterosexual gendering is, a fairly brief moment in the history of capitalism, a dualistic social formation that was probably unraveling even as Marx wrote, to be reconfigured by the rise of the middle class, corporate capital, the decline of the bourgeoisie, and so forth.) Moreover, as a historical process structured by the inherent contradiction of class domination and exploitation, capitalism produces in the proletariat not merely a class that serves the needs of capital but also "its own gravediggers."[32]

By contrast, MacKinnon's utterly static account of sexual antagonism, conjoined with a Marxist view of the socially pervasive quality of this antagonism—its function as a structure of domination rather than mere or random "interest"—theoretically forecloses both the mechanism and trajectory of political transformation proffered by Marxist theory, namely, the movement of history according to struggle conditioned by systemic contradictions. So also does she foreclose one of the transformative possibilities held out by Marxism, by refusing to vest the class of women with the kind of power Marx vested in the proletariat: anxious not to sentimentalize femininity or female sexual power, she eliminates the very dynamic of social change on which Marx counted for emancipatory praxis, namely, that the class that is "in but not of society" harbors all of the productive force but none of the social or political power of society.[33] In Marx's account, "for the oppressed class to be able to emancipate itself, it is necessary that the productive powers already acquired and the existing social relations should no longer be capable of existing side by side."[34] But unlike the contradictions of capital, sexism for

[31] *Communist Manifesto*, p. 474.

[32] Ibid., p. 483.

[33] See Drucilla Cornell's critique of MacKinnon, in which she argues that "the feminine" is not reducible to what women are made to be for men: "Put very simply, MacKinnon's central error is to reduce feminine 'reality' to the sexualized object we are for *them* by *identifying* the feminine totally with the 'real world' as it is seen and constructed through the male gaze" (*Beyond Accommodation*, p. 130). Cornell seeks to avoid MacKinnon's totalization on the one side and an essentialized femininity, on the other, by mobilizing a "feminine imaginary" that is productive even as it is without specific content (see *Beyond Accommodation*, p. 17).

[34] "The Poverty of Philosophy," in *Marx-Engels Reader*, p. 218.

MacKinnon is "metaphysically nearly perfect" and utterly static—without a history or a dynamic of transformation to open a different future.[35] Moreover, while labor is exploited for profit and is exploitable because of its capacity to generate a surplus, sexuality lacks such a dimension; thus the *raison d'être* of sexism would seem to recur, darkly, to the intrinsic pleasures of male sexual dominance.

This evisceration of history, generativity, and dialectics from Marxism transforms it from radical political theory into an implicitly positivist, conservative project. The very meaning of a radical critique is transformed when there is no historical prospect of redressing the critique, when there is no social dynamic, and when the power deployed by the dominant class is not retrievable by the subordinate class because it never belonged to the latter and, indeed, is foreign to it. Prospects for radical social change evaporate when the oppressed class is only derivative of the dominant class, when it has no cultural meaning or existence other than this derivation, and when the oppressed have no inner resources for the development of consciousness or agency, precisely because they have been produced subjectively, and not only positioned, by dominant power. Whereas Marx distinguished between the conditions in which the proletarian found himself and his potential consciousness of his situation as being in contradiction with the dominant ideology—indeed, Marx counted on the contradictions between material conditions, proletarian consciousness, and dominant ideology for revolutionary possibility—MacKinnon's formulation of the organization of sexuality as the organization of gender erases this distinction. Male dominance does not simply organize a class to serve it but, in producing a class whose identity is "to be for men," makes a class whose subjectivity is its social position and vice versa.

In this regard, MacKinnon is not, as she suggests, merely methodologically post-Marxist but historically post-Marxist; in fact, she is posthistorical. She is a Marxist for whom history either never existed or never mattered, for whom the past has been erased and the future is an abyss, but for whom what Marx called the weight of the nightmare of dead generations on the brains of the living is incalculably heavy. As a total analysis of a social totality, a Marxism voided of historical struggle, contingency, and variation, as well as of prospects of change from within, is precisely totalitarianism. Indeed, a "Communist Manifesto" written without history or historical reason, without dialectics, without a dynamic of change, would not only transform in tone from exhilarating to depressing, but would become an argument for the condition it describes as being in the nature of things; capitalist domination would ap-

---

[35] *Toward a Feminist Theory of the State*, p. 115.

pear rooted in a will to dominate combined with the intrinsic power to dominate, and its "victims" would thus appear to be in need of protection rather than emancipation. Not surprisingly, sexual emancipation is what MacKinnon is always insisting women do not need more of.

In other words, theory in a Marxist modality without history and without dialectics is conservative insofar as it becomes hermeneutically and ontologically positivist—the condition it describes loses its historically contingent and socially dynamic character. A different past never existed and the future contains no openings, no promises. I want to suggest that this core of MacKinnon's theory speaks directly to the anxieties of an age in the throes of a theoretical and political crisis about the end of history, an era defined by lost faith in progressivist or teleological movement in history. Indeed, in gutting Marxist social theory of historical laws of development and dynamics of change, MacKinnon's analysis converges with certain poststructural critiques of Marxist historiography, dialectics, and logics of systemic contradictions, critiques that figure all of these as part of Marx's uncritical and problematic assumption of Enlightenment premises.

This "end of history" phenomenon—articulated in one domain by contemporary theoretical challenges to progressivist historiography, in another by both the global collapse of socialist aspirations and the retrenchment of liberal-democratic promises of social improvement— breeds for many an ensemble of anxious questions about political identity, strategy, possibility, and future. For what the combination of theoretical critiques and apparent political refutations of progressivist historiography appears to configure is an unrelieved past, present, and future of domination: precisely what is articulated in MacKinnon's totalizing, circular theory of masculinist power and female subordination. Thus, not only MacKinnon's depiction of women as relentlessly victimized by their gendered construction but also the character of her political interventions—her insistence on the need to insulate us from the worst abuses of such domination not through emancipatory strategies but by curtailing and regulating sexuality, speech, and so forth—betoken radical despair in the face of this moment in history. With the lost promise of forward movement, when substantive political freedom no longer seems possible or even intelligible, the best we might hope for is some minor relief from domination's excess. Not freedom but censorship; not First Amendment guarantees but more rights to sue for damages; not risky experiments with resignification and emancipation but more police, more regulation, better dead-bolt locks on the doors.

But to note how MacKinnon's account has elements of convergence with late modern theoretical critiques and global political developments is not to say they all amount to the same thing. Indeed, MacKinnon's postulations of a social totality, of a single socially pervasive dualism structuring that totality, and of that dualism relentlessly and universally governing the production of all subjects—these are at odds with post-structuralist insights about the character of multiply constructed social orders and social subjects who bear some capacity for subversive resignification. Where much contemporary theory and many contemporary political developments cast into question—that is, deconstruct and destabilize—the categories of subject, identity, and society so central to modern and more specifically liberal societies, MacKinnon resurrects, restores, and reworks these categories. In her account, there are men and women, dominators and dominated, exploiters and exploited, social systems and social wholes. Thus, MacKinnon gives us the comfort of recognizing ourselves in modernist terms, even as she exploits a growing popular and academic sentiment that we have no modernist future.

From this perspective, it would appear that the very structure and categories of her theory—its tautological and totalizing dimensions, its dualisms and absolutes, its strange syllogisms and forced equivalences—articulate a profound late modern anxiety, channeling it into a certain militance while doing nothing to resolve its constituents. Thus the rhetorical force of MacKinnon's theory of gender may inhere as much in its homological refiguring of a late modern political despair as in its pornographic cadences, and perhaps especially in the potentially fascistic interplay of manipulated despair and libidinal arousal.

CHAPTER FIVE

Rights and Losses

> For the historically disempowered, the conferring of rights is symbolic of all the denied aspects of their humanity: rights imply a respect that places one in the referential range of self and others, that elevates one's status from human body to social being.
> —Patricia Williams, *The Alchemy of Race and Rights*

> [I]t is not through recourse to sovereignty against discipline that the effects of disciplinary power can be limited, because sovereignty and disciplinary mechanisms are two absolutely integral constituents of the general mechanism of power in our society. If one wants to . . . struggle against disciplines and disciplinary power, it is not towards the ancient right of sovereignty that one should turn, but towards the possibility of a new form of right, one which must indeed be anti-disciplinarian, but at the same time liberated from the principle of sovereignty.
> —Michel Foucault, "Two Lectures"

> Minority people committed themselves to these struggles [for rights], not to attain some hegemonically functioning reification leading to false consciousness, but a seat in the front of the bus, repatriation of treaty-guaranteed sacred lands, or a union card to carry into the grape vineyards.
> —Robert A. Williams, Jr., "Taking Rights Aggressively"

WHAT IS the emancipatory force of rights claims on behalf of politicized identities in late-twentieth-century North American political life? If, historically, rights have been claimed to secure formal emancipation for individuals stigmatized, traumatized, and subordinated by particular social identities, to secure a place for such individuals in a humanist discourse of universal personhood, what does it mean to deploy rights on behalf of identities that aim to confound the humanist conceit? What are the consequences of installing politicized identity in the universal discourse of liberal jurisprudence? And what does it mean to use a discourse of generic personhood—the discourse of rights—against the privileges that such discourse has traditionally secured?

In pursuing these kinds of questions about the contemporary deployment of rights, I am not asking whether rights as such are emancipatory. Nor am I concerned with the theoretical question of whether the sovereign subject of rights can be squared with contemporary deconstruction of such subjects.[1] Rather, I want to begin by recognizing rights as protean and irresolute signifiers, varying not only across time and culture, but across the other vectors of power whose crossing indeed they are sometimes deployed to effect—class, race, ethnicity, gender, sexuality, age, wealth, education.[2] I want to acknowledge the diverse, inconstant, even contradictory ways that rights operate across various histories, cultures, and social strata.[3]

But an inquiry into the relationship between identity formation and rights claims in late-twentieth-century politics requires more than registering the indeterminacy and contingency of rights. Those concerned with emancipatory political practices in our time confront as well a set of paradoxes about rights, perhaps the central one of which is this: The question of the liberatory or egalitarian force of rights is always historically and culturally circumscribed; rights have no inherent political semiotic, no innate capacity either to advance or impede radical democratic ideals. Yet rights necessarily operate in and as an ahistorical, acultural, acontextual idiom: they claim distance from specific political contexts and historical vicissitudes, and they necessarily participate in a discourse of enduring universality rather than provisionality or partiality. Thus, while the measure of their political efficacy requires a high degree of historical and social specificity, rights operate as a political discourse of the general, the generic, and universal.[4]

This paradox between the universal idiom and the local effect of rights

[1] Drucilla Cornell offers one of the most interesting speculations on this topic in "Dismembered Selves and Wandering Wombs," chap. 2 of *The Imaginary Domain* (forthcoming from Routledge).

[2] See, on a related but somewhat different point, Ernesto Laclau and Chantal Mouffe, who argue that "the meaning of liberal discourse on individual rights is not definitively fixed" (*Hegemony and Socialist Strategy* [London: Verso, 1985], p. 176).

[3] Consider: rights as boundary, and as access; rights as markers of power, and as masking lack; rights as claims, and as protection; rights as organization of social space, and as defense against incursion; rights as articulation, and as mystification; rights as disciplinary, and as antidisciplinary; rights as a mark of one's humanity, and as a reduction of one's humanity; rights as expression of desire, and as foreclosure of desire.

[4] To put this matter in an old-fashioned way, rights work within the dissimulating ideology of modernism, and in this regard there will always be something of a chasm between the discourses of rights and their concrete operations.

itself transpires on both a temporal and spatial level. On the temporal level: While rights may operate as an indisputable force of emancipation at one moment in history—the American Civil Rights movement, or the struggle for rights by subjects of colonial domination such as black South Africans or Palestinians—they may become at another time a regulatory discourse, a means of obstructing or coopting more radical political demands, or simply the most hollow of empty promises.[5] This paradox is captured in part by Nietzsche's insistence that liberal institutions cease to be liberal as soon as they are attained.[6] It is expressed as well in the irony that rights sought by a politically defined *group* are conferred upon depoliticized *individuals;* at the moment a particular "we" succeeds in obtaining rights, it loses its "we-ness" and dissolves into individuals. On the spatial or social level: Rights that empower those in one social location or strata may disempower those in another. The classic example is property rights, which not only buttress the power of landlords and capital but help to constitute the subjects called tenant and worker. Less obvious examples would be the right to free speech, which some feminists argue fortifies the "speech" of pornographers that in turn "silences" women; or the right to privacy, a highly ambiguous right that differentially serves those differentially situated in the murky sphere demarcated as "the private." The point is that rights converge with powers of social stratification and lines of social demarcation in ways that extend as often as attenuate these powers and lines. And when the temporal and spatial dimensions of the paradox of the universalistic idiom and particularistic force of rights are combined, we can see quite clearly the impossibility of saying anything generic about the political value of rights: it makes little sense to argue for them or against them separately from an analysis of the historical conditions, social powers, and political discourses with which they converge or which they interdict.

The universal-local paradox of rights is itself paradoxical insofar as this "discovery"—that the value of rights is tethered to history, and that the political efficacy of rights shifts according to which social group is wielding them and what social powers situate them—occurs as "history" unravels and social "identity" destabilizes. Thus, we historicize rights in late modernity even as we discredit history as such, and we try to take the measure of the political effectiveness of rights according to an analysis of

---

[5] I take this to be the force of Derrick Bell's argument in *Faces at the Bottom of the Well* (New York: Basic Books, 1992): namely, that whatever extraordinary historical and political event the Civil Rights movement was at the time, the emancipatory power of civil rights practices *and* ideology does not necessarily endure over time. See also Kristin Bumiller's *The Civil Rights Society* (Baltimore: Johns Hopkins University Press, 1992).

[6] *Twilight of the Idols,* in *The Portable Nietzsche,* ed. W. Kaufmann (New York: Viking, 1954), p. 541.

social stratification even as we place in question the structures and fixity of the identities that such measurement presumes. And within this paradox lies still another: The late modern effort to critically rework the individualist and universalist legacy of rights for a formulation that offers a potentially more fecund form of political recognition—namely, "group rights," rights of "difference," or rights of "cultural minorities"—is an effort also beset by the contemporary historical, geopolitical, and analytical destabilization of identity upon which such formulations depend. Here we circle back to the first paradox: If contemporary rights claims are deployed to protect historically and contextually contingent identities, might the relationship of the universal idiom of rights to the contingency of the protected identities be such that the former operates inadvertently to resubordinate by renaturalizing that which it was intended to emancipate by articulating? In the context of this paradox, our question acquires an analytic as well as historical form: If, as Robert Meister paraphrases Hegel, "for itself, representation is a means for the people to transform the state [while] in itself, it is a means for the state to control the people,"[7] when do rights sought by identity "for itself" become "in themselves" a means of administration? When does identity articulated through rights become production and regulation of identity through law and bureaucracy? When does legal recognition become an instrument of regulation, and political recognition become an instrument of subordination?

Here is yet another way of casting this paradox: Historically, rights emerged in modernity both as a vehicle of emancipation from political disenfranchisement or institutionalized servitude and as a means of privileging an emerging bourgeois class within a discourse of formal egalitarianism and universal citizenship. Thus, they emerged both as a means of protection against arbitrary use and abuse by sovereign and social power and as a mode of securing and naturalizing dominant social powers— class, gender, and so forth. Not only did bourgeois rights discourse mask by depoliticizing the social power of institutions such as private property or the family, it organized mass populations for exploitation and regulation, thus functioning as a modality of what Foucault termed "biopower."[8] But, like the others, this paradox is not merely of anachronistic

---

[7] *Political Identity: Thinking Through Marx*(Oxford: Blackwell, 1990), p. 172.

[8] In this regard, I am distancing myself slightly from Foucault's suggestion that disciplinary discourses historically displace or converge with discourses of rights, suggesting instead that rights are from the beginning a potentially disciplinary practice.

Rosalind Petchesky and Eli Zaretsky have both argued that the juridical recognition of women in the late nineteenth century corresponded with expanded state and medical control over women's reproductive and sexual conduct. See Petchesky, *Abortion and Women's Choice: The State, Sexuality, and Reproductive Freedom* (New York: Longman, 1984), and

interest. How, we might ask, does this historical function of rights as operating both to emancipate and dominate, both to protect and regulate, resurface in contemporary articulations of rights, especially those sought for subjects recently, and patently, produced through regulatory discourses—subjects such as welfare mothers, surrogate mothers, or lesbian mothers?[9]

I begin with this nest of paradoxes not to resolve them—paradox designates a condition in which resolution is the most uninteresting aim—but to avoid misconstrual of my critical engagement with contemporary rights discourse. I do not want to participate in an argument for or against rights as such—for example, the disagreement between Critical Legal Studies thinkers and Critical Race Theorists—precisely because such an argument eschews the significance of historical timing, social power, and political cultural context in adjudicating the emancipatory value of rights discourse. Rather, I want to reflect upon the place of rights in the politics of politicized identities—rights of "inclusion" as well as rights of "difference" currently sought for people of color, homosexuals, and women in the late-twentieth-century United States.

. . .

In the service of such reflection, let us reconsider the critique of "political emancipation" embedded in Marx's essay "On the Jewish Question." Arguably one of Marx's most philosophically and politically complex as well as least programmatic pieces of writing, the "Jewish Question" was

---

Zaretsky, "The Place of the Family in the Origins of the Welfare State," in *Rethinking the Family: Some Feminist Questions,* ed. Barrie Thorne (New York: Longman, 1982). Through Michael Grossberg's study of nineteenth-century family law, Martha Minow makes a similar point about the effect of children's rights in enlarging state power over both children and adults. Minow cites Grossberg's *Governing the Hearth: Law and the Family in Nineteenth-Century America* (Chapel Hill: University of North Carolina Press, 1985), pp. 287–307, in "Interpreting Rights: An Essay for Robert Cover," *The Yale Law Review* 96 (1987), p. 1882, n. 82.

9 While the traditional left critique of rights focuses on the law's decontextualization of persons from social power, the critique of contemporary legal efforts to *achieve* such contextualization, to recognize subjects as "effects" of social power, might be precisely that it reifies these effects, marking with a reactionary permanence the production of social subjects through, for example, "race," "gender," or "sexuality." A critique of contemporary efforts to install difference in the law would worry as well about the analytical slide from social construction and constructions of subjectivity to social position and constructions of identity. It would worry about the conversion of articulations of modes of power complexly and temporally constitutive of subjectivity into static analyses of social position that are then installed in the ahistorical discourse of the law.

and remains an occasion to inquire into the formulations of identity, state, and law configured by modernity, by liberal constitutional polities, and by capitalist economies. The quest for Jewish citizenship in a Prussian, Christian, or even ostensibly secular state raised for Marx and for his left-Hegelian protagonist Bruno Bauer an ensemble of questions about the nature of religious identity, the state, citizenship, political consciousness, and political freedom. Do Jews want political recognition and rights as Jews or as persons? How does the demand for recognition construct Jewishness, personhood, and citizenship? How does this demand figure the state and political life—what is the state being asked to see or recognize, to disregard in its seeing, and to disavow in itself? Do Jews seeking emancipation want to be free from Judaism, free of Judaism, or free to be Jewish? What does it mean to turn to the state for such emancipation? What is the relationship between political representation, political identity, social identity, and religious identity? How does the nature of the political state transform one's social identity when one turns to the state for political resolution of one's subordination, exclusion, or suffering? What kind of subject is being held out to the state for what kind of redress or redemption?

While there are substantial riches to be mined from an essay concerned with such questions, there are also stumbling blocks in using the "Jewish Question" to reconsider the formulations of identity, rights, and the state it poses. These include the anti-Semitism evinced in the essay, an anti-Semitism that has led some to dismiss it (and Marx) altogether. Others have ignored the extent to which the essay is concerned with Jews and Judaism, treating it either as an immanent critique of Hegelian philosophy or as a critique of liberal constitutional precepts—in either case, for them the Jewish question is only an heuristic device.[10] I will try to steer a

---

[10] Two provisional notes about the putative anti-Semitism of the "Jewish Question." Since there is good evidence that Marx was as racist as he was anti-Semitic, and it is a certainty that he took Jewish men more seriously than he took any woman, we need to ask *ourselves:* What precisely vexes us here? Is his anti-Semitism at issue because he was writing *about* the "Jewish Question"? Or is it the possible specter of self-hatred and dissimulation within the quest for assimilation that produces anxiety? Why isn't J. S. Mill's sexism as bothersome to us? Is the problem anti-Semitism, Marx as a Jew, or Marx as a Jewish anti-Semite writing on the Jewish question? Insofar as Marx criticized religion as such and criticized Christianity with vehemence, what specifically constitutes his critique of Judaism as anti-Semitism? These questions are not intended to defend Marx but rather to suggest that in objecting to his anti-Semitism, we may not know the real nature of our objections, what unique place the charge of anti-Semitism occupies in our psyches, what psychic place is held by the self-hating Jew, and why it is this and not Marx's terrible remarks about Africans or silences about women that is at issue.

The second point responds to the impossibility of the answering the first in anything short of a separate study of the problem. If there is something of potential value in Marx's essay, but it is not easily extricable from the deprecations of Judaism and Jews, then we need

third course, dismissing neither the essay nor its engagement with Judaism. Particularly in light of twentieth century formations of European anti-Semitism, including those of the present, Marx's rough distillation of Judaism into "practical need, egoism,"[11] is certainly disturbing, as is his consequent resolution of the "Jewish Question" into the "general question of the age"—the domination of civil society by capital. But this is not the whole story of his treatment of Judaism in the essay, nor can his critique of Judaism be isolated from his more general critique of religion; his caricature of Christianity is at least as savage.

Rather than inquiring into the anti-Semitic elements of the Jewish assimilationist formulations of which Marx's essay is a particular expression, I want to consider the essay's characterizations of Judaism along different lines. The variations on the "Jewish question" across European states spurred Marx to attempt to diagnose politically, and resolve theoretically, the historically specific making and meaning of the Jewish quest for political membership in a variety of states, some of which were tacitly rather than explicitly invested in Christianity.[12] And it is this formulation of the problem that may be of use in thinking about contemporary campaigns by feminists, gay activists, indigenous peoples, and people of color for emancipation through and for rather than in spite of their "difference," for recognition from a state whose masculinism, heterosexism, and whiteness is also frequently tacit rather than explicit. In other words, precisely because Jews sought political rights as secular Jews in Christian as well as "secular" states, precisely because the Jewish question does not issue from a wholly liberal claim to generic personhood on the part of the historically disenfranchised, Marx's essay has potentially rich contemporary resonances. Insofar as the analysis concerns the complex political claims and aspirations of a marked identity not constituted *solely* through subjugation and exclusion, not reducible to a socioeconomic category, and not figurable as a "difference" entirely attributable to a form of social power as class is attributable to property relations, the quest for Jewish

---

to proceed with the double consciousness such a paradox demands. In this kind of consciousness, one attends both to the exoteric argument or narrative of a novel or philosophical work and, simultaneously, to the effect of the anti-Semitism on the shape and turns of this argument. This reading strategy offers not simply a mode of "correcting" Marx's prejudice but, even more importantly, of learning, rather than preconceiving, how this prejudice operates both as philosophy and politics.

[11] "On the Jewish Question," *The Marx-Engels Reader*, 2d ed., ed. R. C. Tucker (New York: Norton, 1978), p. 50.

[12] See Carlebach's *Karl Marx and the Radical Critique of Judaism* (London: Routledge, 1978), for a discussion of the ways in which assimilation in general, and conversion and baptism in particular, figured in both the background and foreground of the "Jewish question" in Marx's time.

civil and political rights in European nation states in the nineteenth century bears some (incomplete) parallels to antiassimilationist juridical claims generated by contemporary identity politics.[13]

. . .

Marx begins with a notoriously ungenerous engagement with Bruno Bauer's own attempt to "resolve" the Jewish question. But Marx is ultimately less interested in the left Hegelianism Bauer espouses than in the historical condition of which Marx takes Bauer (as well as Hegelianism, right and left) to be a political and philosophical symptom. For Bauer, the Jewish question arises as a consequence of the unemancipated *consciousness* of Jews on the one hand and the state on the other: as long as the Jew privileges his Judaism (his partial nature) above his universal personhood, and as long as the state privileges its Christianity above its universal (secular) nature, this partiality (in both senses of the word) prevents the recognition and realization of "the universal humanity of man."[14]

Marx's objection to Bauer's formulation is that within its terms, both the state and the Jew could give up their religious "prejudice" and in so doing be "politically emancipated" without being emancipated from religion. What, Marx asks, is the nature of the emancipation Bauer advocates such that it addresses only the way the state and the Jew respectively *represent* themselves, the way each thinks of itself in a political way, such that the formal secularism demanded from each in no way affects the "actual religiosity" of either? What does it mean to render "prejudice" a matter of attitude and freedom, a matter of words and representation, a matter of pose? And why does Bauer's (idealist) formulation of freedom so closely resemble that represented by the state itself? Is it significant that the left-Hegelian formulation of freedom as a problem of consciousness, representation, and state proclamations is precisely the formulation of freedom animating and legitimating the liberal constitutional state?

In contending that the "actual religiosity" of the state and its citizens is undiminished by the declared irrelevance of religion to politics, Marx is concerned not simply with the religious *belief* harbored by Jews or the state, but, more importantly, with the conditions that give rise to reli-

---

[13] This, notwithstanding Marx's own effort to reduce Judaism to an "empirical essence of . . . huckstering and its conditions," and thus to render Judaism as a "historically produced need" and "the Jewish question" as a *symptom* of an age materially dominated by relations of capital and spiritually dominated by Christianity. At the extreme, Marx casts Judaism as the avatar of "material egoism" and civil society, dialectically opposed to Christianity as the avatar of "spiritual egoism," imaginary transcendence, and the state ("Jewish Question," p. 52).

[14] Ibid., p. 28.

gious consciousness, the conditions that produce and require religion. While Marx and Bauer share a view of religious consciousness as "a defect," Marx regards this consciousness, and the state's participation in it (expressed in the very declaration that it is *free* of religion when it ceases to determine political membership on the basis of religion), as historically necessary rather than contingent. To the extent that religious consciousness is historically produced rather than freely adopted, it cannot, as Bauer would have it, be "cast off like snake skins." Rather, for Marx,

> The question is: what is the relation between *complete* political emancipation and religion? If we find in the country which has attained full political emancipation [the United States], that religion not only continues to *exist* but is *fresh* and *vigorous*, this is proof that the existence of religion is not at all opposed to the perfection of the state. But since the existence of religion is the existence of a defect, the source of this defect must be sought in the *nature* of the state itself. Religion no longer appears as the basis, but as the *manifestation* of secular narrowness. That is why we explain the religious constraints upon the free citizens by the secular constraints upon them. We do not claim that they must transcend their religious narrowness in order to get rid of their secular limitations. We claim that they will transcend their religious narrowness once they have overcome their secular limitations. We do not turn secular questions into theological questions; we turn theological questions into secular ones.[15]

Critical here is Marx's effort to reveal the metalepsis in Hegelian thinking about the relation between religious and secular life, consciousness and institutions. This effort is most apparent in his insistence that religious consciousness is a *manifestation* of rather than the *basis* of what he calls "secular narrowness"—the social and political constraints upon substantive freedom, equality, and community. This, in a vernacular foreign to the one we now speak, is Marx's method of de-essentializing in order to deconstruct political expressions of cultural, ethnic, or religious identity. Reading religious consciousness as a political symptom, even a site of injury and despair about freedom in *this* world, Marx seeks to avoid responding to it as a political demand issuing from fixed political identities or interests.

What Marx calls religious narrowness, what we might term investments in particular identities, is not blamed by him as it is by Bauer upon those who have such investments and fail to understand their place in the

---

[15] Ibid., p. 31. Marx's point about the fresh, vigorous character of religion in the nineteenth-century United States was repeated on September 16, 1992, almost verbatim, by Clinton during his presidential campaign as he argued for the continuation of religious tolerance and separation of church and state. "In no other advanced nation," Clinton remarked, "is religion so widely practiced, do so many people go to church, synagogues, temples, and mosques."

world of universal humanity, nor upon the state's failure to look beyond such investments to the universal humanity of its subjects. Marx's critique of Bauer's Hegelian emphasis upon the independence of consciousness—either in individuals or in the state—turns on his derivation of "religious narrowness" from the specific political conditions that require this "narrowness," conditions that, importantly, are obscured rather than redressed through formal emancipation, through acquiring the right to be free of the political stigma of this narrowness. In fact, Marx argues, the limits of political emancipation "appear at once in the fact that the state can liberate itself from a constraint without man himself really being liberated."[16]

The political "constraint" to which Marx refers is the state's vulnerability to reproach for a religious bearing, for its appearance of failed or incomplete secularism. Yet the state is no more liberated from religion by declaring itself religiously tolerant than it is liberated from private property through the "abolition of the property qualification" for suffrage.[17] Insofar as Marx *deliteralizes* both religion and secularism, he is able to establish the state's religiosity as inhering not in express religious statements but in its transcendent ideology, its representation of universal humanity above the mortal particulars of civil society. The constitutional state he is analyzing is homologically Christian in its reduction of freedom to pronouncements of freedom, in its equation of equality with the declaration that it regards us as equal, in its creation of equality through its ideology of popular sovereignty; in short, in its *idealist* resolution of our relative lack of freedom, equality, and community.

The "constraint" from which political emancipation "frees" the individual is politicized identity—the treatment of a particular social identity as the basis for deprivation of suffrage, rights, or citizenship. But, Marx repeats, emancipation from this constraint does not liberate the individual from the conditions constitutive or reiterative of the identity. To the contrary, it is only in abstraction from such conditions that the individual can be "emancipated" by the universal state:

> man frees himself from a constraint in a *political* way, through the state, when he transcends his limitations, in contradiction with himself, and in an *abstract, narrow and partial* way. Furthermore, by emancipating himself *politically*, man emancipates himself in a *devious* way, through an intermediary, however *necessary* this intermediary might be.[18]

Marx's characterization of political emancipation as "devious" does not constitute a moral objection to the evident hypocrisy of the liberal state.

[16] "Jewish Question," p. 31.
[17] Ibid., p. 33.
[18] Ibid., p. 32.

Such an objection would remain within the rubric of liberalism in which certain attitudes or postures on the part of the state become eligible for moral criticism and, potentially, reform; this is exactly the kind of criticism in which Marx considered left Hegelians like Bauer to be wrongheadedly engaged. Rather, "deviousness" here signals a ruse of power necessitated when the requisites of power's legitimacy generate a promise upon which it cannot deliver; deviousness connotes the political culture of indirection and mediation inherent within, rather than accidental to, this political condition.[19]

In Marx's account, the ruse of power peculiar to liberal constitutionalism centers upon granting freedom, equality, and representation to abstract rather than concrete subjects. The substitution of abstract political subjects for actual ones not only forfeits the project of emancipation but resubjugates us precisely by emancipating substitutes for us—by emancipating our abstracted representatives in the state and naming this process "freedom." The subject is thus *ideally emancipated* through its anointing as an abstract person, a formally free and equal human being, and is *practically resubordinated* through this idealist disavowal of the material constituents of personhood, which constrain and contain our freedom. Thus, because we are in this way subjugated by the very discourse of our freedom, liberal freedom is structurally, not merely definitionally, ambiguous. The notion of "representative" and the process by which, according to Hobbes's *Leviathan,* we "author" the state exemplify this condition, and Rousseau makes a similar point in his critique of representative government in the "Discourse on Inequality" and the *Social Contract.*[20] Marx himself develops this point through an analogy between the state and Christianity:

> Religion is simply the recognition of man in a roundabout fashion; that is, through an intermediary. The state is the intermediary between man and human liberty. Just as Christ is the intermediary to whom man attributes all his own divinity and all his religious *bonds,* so the state is the intermediary to which man confides all his non-divinity and all his *human freedom.*[21]

Here again it becomes clear not only why Marx considers political emancipation partial, narrow, and contradictory, but why he insists that the "secular" state is Christian in character: As Christ represents man's holiness, the state represents man's freedom, and in both cases, this represen-

---

[19] Using the notion of the camera obscura, Marx will offer a more substantial account of this feature of political power in the theory of the relationship between consciousness and power developed in *The German Ideology.*

[20] Hobbes, *Leviathan,* chap. 16, and Rousseau, "Discourse on Inequality" and *The Social Contract.*

[21] "Jewish Question," p. 32.

tation abstracts from the unfree and unholy conditions of man's actual life. Moreover, these unfree and unholy conditions are the basis of both state and Christianity: as the conditions of real as opposed to abstract human beings, they are the conditions that *necessitate* the state and Christianity. As Christianity consecrates a ghostly ideal of man as divine and leaves actual man to suffer on earth, so the state liberates its ideal of man and abandons actual man to the actual powers that construct, buffet, and subject him.

In one of his earliest formulations of the *political* structure of alienation in modern society, Marx then argues that both Christianity and the constitutional state require that "man lea[d], not only in thought . . . but in reality, in life, a double existence—celestial and terrestrial";[22] this "double existence" is one in which heavenly life is inaccessible and earthly life is degraded. Insofar as Christianity and the bourgeois state are the available discourses for self-understanding and political articulation, it is in what Marx calls "real life"—life in civil society and on earth—that man will be most illusory to himself, while the "imaginary domains" of the state and heaven articulate the "real nature" of man:

> [Man] lives in the *political community,* where he regards himself as a *communal being,* and in *civil society* where he acts simply as a *private individual,* treats other men as means, degrades himself to the role of a mere means, and becomes the plaything of alien powers. The political state, in relation to civil society, is just as spiritual as is heaven in relation to earth. It stands in the same opposition to civil society, and overcomes it in the same manner as religion overcomes the narrowness of the profane world; i.e. it has always to acknowledge it again, reestablish it, and allow itself to be dominated by it. . . . In the state, . . . where he is regarded as a species-being, man is the imaginary member of an imaginary sovereignty, divested of his real, individual life, and infused with an unreal universality.[23]

In the political state, "man treats political life, which is remote from his own individual existence, as if it were his own true life"; this formulation constitutes the religious consciousness of the state. However, Marx also insists that "religion is here the spirit of civil society" insofar as it "expresses the separation and withdrawal of man from man," and insofar as every man is "considered a sovereign being, a supreme being," but as alienated man, man "lost to himself."[24] The Christian dimension of the liberal ideological formulation of the state and civil society ordered by capitalism rests here: although anointed as a sovereign, even a supreme

[22] Ibid., p. 34.
[23] Ibid., p. 34.
[24] Ibid., p. 39.

being, man's sovereignty is ghostly, alienated, and finally punishing, insofar as it casts this isolated and impotent creature as fully accountable for himself. Man is proclaimed king but limited by his powerlessness and alienation; his crown ultimately serves to bewilder, isolate, and humiliate him.[25]

Remarking that "the political elevation of man above religion shares the weaknesses and merits of all such political measures," Marx makes clear that he is not against political emancipation, which he deems "a great progress[,] . . . the final form of human emancipation *within* the framework of the prevailing social order";[26] rather, he seeks to articulate the historical conditions of its emergence and its consequent limitations. The deviousness of political emancipation—its removal of a stratifying social power from political standing—calls not for refusal of this form of emancipation but for analysis of the kind of social and political relations engendering and engendered by it. In particular, Marx is interested in how the state's "emancipation" from particular social powers operates as a form of political suppression that tacitly legitimates these powers, and how, at the same time, this process itself *constitutes* the power and legitimacy of the liberal state. Thus, for example, the elimination of the "property qualification" for citizenship constitutes the "ideal abolition" of private property, since the "property qualification is the last *political* form in which private property is recognized." Yet

> the political suppression of private property not only does not abolish private property; it actually presupposes its existence. The state abolishes, after its fashion, the distinctions established by *birth, social rank, education, occupation,* when it decrees that [these] are *non-political* distinctions; when it proclaims, without regard to these distinctions, that every member of society is an *equal* partner in popular sovereignty. . . . But the state, none the less, allows private

[25] If Marx's analysis is difficult to follow at this point, this is because he is doing three things at once: he is criticizing religion and the state, establishing a homology between them, *and* establishing their philosophical, as well as material and historical, presupposition of each other. This is Marx, in other words, in his least economistic and most deconstructive mode, but it is deconstruction in a historically progressive register, governed by the dialectic, by reason in history, and by analytically coherent, if contradictory, social totalities. While it is Marx's genius to sustain the analysis on all three levels at once, it may also be this genius, steeped in Hegelianism, that leads Marx to overstate the theological dimension of the constitutional state. Here is the extended passage from which the citation in the text is drawn:

> The members of the political state are religious because of the dualism between individual life and species-life, between the life of civil society and political life. They are religious in the sense that man treats political life, which is remote from his own individual existence, as if it were his true life; and in the sense that religion is here the spirit of civil society, and expresses the separation and withdrawal of man from man. (Ibid., p. 39)

[26] Ibid., pp. 33, 35.

property, education, occupation, to *act* after *their* own fashion, namely as private property, education, occupation, and to manifest their *particular* nature. Far from abolishing these *effective* differences, it only exists so far as they are presupposed; it is conscious of being a *political* state and it manifests its *universality* only in opposition to these elements. . . . Only in this manner, *above* the *particular* elements, can the state constitute itself as universality.[27]

If civil society is striated by forms of social power that the state declares politically insignificant, and the state's universality or "perfected secularism" is premised upon its transcendence of the particularism of civil society, then the state is premised upon that which it pretends to transcend and requires that which it claims to abolish; it reinforces by politically suppressing (removing from political discourse) that which grounds its *raison d'être*. But in addition to its legitimacy, the state achieves a good deal of its power through its devious claims to resolve the very inequalities that it actually entrenches by depoliticizing. Achieving its "universality" and reinstantiating the "particularity" of civil society through this depoliticization, by this ruse it also acquires its own "right" to govern—to legislate and adjudicate, to mobilize and deploy force.[28]

.   .   .

If, according to Marx, the bourgeois constitutional state is premised upon depoliticized inegalitarian social powers, if it depends upon naturalizing egoistic civil society and abstract representations of equality and community, then *rights* are the modern political form that secure and

[27] *Ibid.* p. 33.

[28] It may be appropriate here to mark the way in which Marx's critique of universalism, and the constitutional state's embodiment of it, differs from many contemporary critiques, particularly those trafficking under the sign of postmodernism, post-Marxism, or poststructuralism. For Marx, the false universalism of the state presupposes *and* entrenches unresolved particulars, stratifying social powers that not only enact subordination and sustain poverty, but estrange human beings from one another and divide us against our respective selves. For post-Marxist critics of liberal universalism, the problem is of a different order: universalism is less an unrealized political ideal than an unrealizable one, a bad political metonymy in which particular kinds of humans and positions masquerade as generic or universal. Marx is not without sympathy for this position—indeed, he clearly appreciates the extent to which universalist discourse is always strategically deployed by the dominant or the would-be dominant: "For each new class which puts itself in the place of one ruling before it, is compelled, merely in order to carry through its aim, to represent its interest as the common interest of all the members of society, that is, expressed in ideal form: it has to give its ideas the form of universality, and represent them as the only rational, universally valid ones" (*The German Ideology*, in *The Marx-Engels Reader*, p. 174). But especially for the early Marx, history is making its way toward true, as opposed to strategic, universalism; for post-Marxist critics, universalism is unredeemable insofar as it is always one with the hegemonic aims of the historically dominant.

legitimate these tendencies. Rights emblematize the ghostly sovereignty of the unemancipated individual in modernity. In order to see the connections as Marx makes them, we must return briefly to his engagement with Bauer on the question of Jews' entitlement to rights.

According to Marx, Bauer argued that the Jew could neither acquire nor concede to others the universal rights of man because his "Jewish nature," and more particularly his avowal of its effect in *separating* him from other men (Gentiles), prohibited his entitlement to rights that *associate* all men with each other.[29] In Bauer's view, "man has to sacrifice the 'privilege of faith' in order to acquire the general rights of man," in order to acquire membership in the community which delivers these rights. But why should this be, Marx asks, when the rights of man are nothing more than the rights of "a member of civil society[,] . . . of egoistic man, of man separated from other men and from the community?"[30] Nothing about these rights, Marx notes, pertains to human association, membership, or participation in political community; consequently there is no basis for withholding them from anyone, regardless of particulars of social station, faith, or consciousness.

It is within this analytical vein, where rights are figured as both manifestations and entrenchments of a specific historical production of egoistic man in civil society, that Marx proffers his (in)famous critique of bourgeois rights. This critique does not condemn but exposes the way rights encode rather than emancipate us from the social powers and social formations that are the conditions of our unfreedom. Thus Marx calls the constitutional right to liberty the right of "separation" from other men, the "right of the *circumscribed* individual, withdrawn into himself." The right to private property, as the practical "application" of the right of liberty, is only "the right of self-interest." And equality, putatively the most profound political achievement of liberalism, Marx identifies as a "term [that] has here no political significance," since it is "only the equal right to liberty [in which] every man is equally regarded as a self-sufficient monad."[31] Liberal equality, insofar as it neither constitutes political community nor achieves substantive equality, guarantees only that all individuals will be treated *as if* they were sovereign and isolated individuals. Liberal equality guarantees that the state will regard us all as equally abstracted from the social powers constituting our existence, equally decontextualized from the unequal conditions of our lives.

Marx concludes this brief assessment of rights with a consideration of the constitutional guarantee of security, "the supreme social concept of society; the concept of the *police*." Underpinning the basic bargain of the

---

[29] "Jewish Question," p. 40.
[30] Ibid., pp. 40, 42.
[31] Ibid., p. 42.

social contract in which we largely surrender to the state the power to protect our lives and our property, the concept of "security," imprecisely termed a right, reveals the essential character of this society and the historically configured obsession of its members: "The concept of security is not enough to raise civil society above its egoism. Security is, rather, the *assurance* of its egoism."[32] The state founded on the promise to secure its members against each other is thus the state that provides an antipolitical "resolution" of the historically produced Hobbesian character of civil society. Like rights themselves, the state's constitutional guarantee of security, embodied in "the concept of the police," reifies a historical condition as an ontological one, naturalizing rather than redressing it.

.   .   .

Certainly Marx's polemical treatment of the civil liberties foundational to the liberal state could be criticized for the undeconstructed binary oppositions it deploys: ideal versus material, theological versus secular, state versus civil society, mediated versus unmediated freedom, egoism versus association, universal versus particular. It could also be impugned for presenting as immanent critique what is actually bound to a panoply of normative referents: radical egalitarianism, "real" popular sovereignty, and "true" political community unmediated by the state. Moreover, insofar as rights are not tethered to the values Marx endorses but serve other ends, he could be faulted for demanding from them what they were not intended to figure or deliver. His criticism of the liberal state for reducing the political to a "mere means" glosses the possibilities that on the one hand, rights need not be the *end* of liberal political states, and that on the other, liberal individuals, even socially subordinated ones, may want nothing more than state-secured rights and protection—they may bear no desire for radical freedom or community.

We shall return shortly to the problems of binarisms and progressive historiography in Marx's critique. For the moment, I want to suggest that while Marx's critique of the "egoism" of rights is fueled by ideals of political and economic life that exceed liberal aims, its force is not wholly dependent on these norms nor on the extent to which liberalism forecloses them. Rather, it depends upon a critical reading of the form of political life produced by the social relations of capital; it depends upon understanding the domination and alienation entailed in capitalist social relations as simultaneously reiterated and obscured by the political life they generate.

In Marx's view, the transition from feudal monarchy to bourgeois de-

[32] Ibid., p. 43.

mocracy entailed a form of economic and political revolution that "abolished the political character of civil society," that is, put an end to the ways in which "elements of civil life such as property, the family, and types of occupation had been raised, in the form of lordship, caste and guilds, to elements of political life." The European political revolutions that abolished monarchy at the same time shattered the expressly political form of social and economic stratifications, the estates and corporations. "The political revolution therefore *abolished* the *political character of civil society*" such that "a specific activity and situation in life no longer had any but an individual significance."[33] Marx is again underscoring how certain modalities of social and economic domination are less eliminated than *depoliticized* by the political revolutions heralding formal equality, although these modalities are transformed in the process, losing their formal representation in the state as estates. At the same time, Marx is seeking to articulate the extent to which the modern *individual* is produced by and through, indeed *as,* this depoliticization and in the image of it. He is proffering a political genealogy of the sovereign individual, whose crucial site of production is the depoliticization of social relations. Put the other way around, Marx exposes the modern formulation of sovereignty as itself a modality of discursive depoliticization. Power as circulating and relational—as located not in the state but in social relations and the movement of history—is ideologically suppressed in the congealed and static persona of sovereignty.

Marx's criticism does not stop with depicting the political emancipation or declared sovereignty of the individual as its effective depoliticization. He also posits the depoliticization of civil society as the "consummation" of the materialism of civil society, and the removal of political community to the realm of the state as the "consummation" of the idealism of the state.[34] Community is figured in a ghostly way in the state, and social atomism is the concrete reality of civil society. But in becoming celestial and otherworldly, abstracted from the real character of its subjects, the state also figures its future overcoming, its future irrelevance. And in becoming thoroughly material and egoistical, civil society forecasts its disintegration: "The bonds which had restrained the egoistic spirit of civil society were removed along with the political yoke. Political emancipation was at the same time an emancipation of civil society from politics and from even the *semblance* of a general content."[35] Establishing the breakup of the feudal state as that which "frees" civil society in a double sense—from feudal bondage but also from the bonds

[33] Ibid., pp. 44, 45.
[34] *Vollendung,* which Tucker translates as "consummation," means completion, termination, ending, perfection.
[35] "Jewish Question," p. 45.

of association that express our ontological sociality, "from even the semblance of a general content"—Marx signals the ambiguity that for him characterizes not only bourgeois rights but the spirit of capitalism. (Recall that this double freedom is also how Marx ironically frames the condition of the proletariat in *Capital*. In contrast with the serf, the proletarian is free to sell his labor power to any buyer. But he is also "free" in the sense of being unburdened and deracinated: he lacks any means of survival other than selling his labor power. The proletarian's "freedom" is thus the source of his radical exploitability *and* of his expanded political capaciousness.) Similarly, when Marx refers to the representation of man in the political state as the "ideal" of man, he is identifying the state representation of community and equality as directly contradicted by the egoism of rights-bearing sovereign individuals in the depoliticized domain of civil society. And he is identifying rights as fundamentally ambiguous: a marker both of our unfreedom and of our expanded political capaciousness.

What should be evident by now is that in contrast with some Critical Legal Studies scholars' anxieties about the individualism of rights, Marx's analysis in the "Jewish Question" is neither a moral critique nor an ontological claim about the "nature of rights." Rather, Marx's characterization of rights as egoistic rests on a reading of the ways in which the historical emergence of the "rights of man" naturalizes and thus entrenches historically specific, unavowed social powers that set us against each other, preoccupy us with property, security, and freedom of movement, and economically and socially stratify us. "The liberty of egoistic man, and the recognition of this liberty . . . is the recognition of the *frenzied* movement of the cultural and material elements which form the content of his life."[36] In other words, the kind of liberty that bourgeois rights discourse casts as natural is actually the *effect* of the historically specific elements constitutive of life in civil society. Through rights discourse, bourgeois social relations are reified as bourgeois man, and the rights required by this "frenzied" (*zugellosen;* actually, "unbridled") social order are misapprehended as required by and confirming the naturalness of the man it produces.

For Marx, then, the political culture of "egoism" and rights produces not mere individualism but anxious, defended, self-absorbed, and alienated Hobbesian subjects who are driven to accumulate, diffident toward others, obligated to none, made impossibly accountable for themselves, and subjected by the very powers their sovereignty is supposed to claim. "Egoism" also connotes the discursive depoliticization of this production: an order of sovereign, self-made, and privatized subjects who sub-

[36] Ibid.

jectively experience their own powerlessness as their own failure vis-à-vis other sovereign subjects. In sum, even as they emancipate certain groups and certain energies from historical suppression, bourgeois rights codify the social needs generated by historically specific, traumatic social powers as natural, unhistorical, and permanent.

Marx's criticisms of bourgeois rights might be distilled thus: (1) Bourgeois rights are rendered necessary by the depoliticized material conditions of unemancipated, inegalitarian civil society, conditions that rights themselves depoliticize rather than articulate or resolve. (2) They entrench by naturalizing the egoism of capitalist society, reifying the "frenzied movement of the material elements" of this society as the nature of man, thereby masking social power and mistaking its effects—atomistic individuals—for its wellspring and agents. (3) They construct an illusory politics of equality, liberty, and community in the domain of the state, a politics that is contradicted by the unequal, unfree, and individualistic domain of civil society. (4) They legitimize by naturalizing various stratifying social powers in civil society, and they disguise the state's collusion with this social power, thereby also legitimating the state as a neutral and universal representative of the people. Thus they disguise the actual power constitutive of both civil society and the state through the ruse of establishing fictional sovereignty in the domain of civil society and illusory liberty, equality, and community in the state.

Marx's enthusiasm for political emancipation, including bourgeois rights, could be distilled thus: (1) Being regarded by the state *as if* we were free and equal is an improvement over being treated as if we were naturally subjected and unequal vis-à-vis stratifying social powers. Insofar as personhood and membership in community is ideally cast as unconstrained by these social powers, political emancipation constitutes *progress*. (Here, a discerning contemporary eye might see an analysis concerned with the way ideological idealism masks social power sliding into one that emphasizes the discursive production of political possibility.) (2) The ideals of freedom, equality, and community in the bourgeois state figure the (historically unrealized) *desire* for these goods and, in a historical process governed by dialectical materialism, they will be realized through the establishment of the material conditions for them. (3) Political emancipation in the form of civil and political rights can be embraced precisely because it represents a "stage" of emancipation. In dialectical analysis, the failure of rights to procure "true human emancipation" is made manifest in our experienced unfreedom and alienation, and it is overcome by the development of forms of association appropriate to a society that has "revolutionized its elements" and transcended its egoism.

. . .

Marx's essay produces two sets of questions for contemporary political struggles waged under the rubric of identity politics. First, if the desire for rights in liberalism is, in part, a desire to depoliticize or unmark one's social existence, to be free of the politicization of subordinating social powers, and if, in this respect, rights entail a turn away from the political, how do they also advance a political struggle to transform the social conditions of one's making? What, if anything, guarantees their instrumental deployment in this direction? Marx's account could be cast in a more Foucaultian register: To the extent that the egoism of rights—their discursive formation of the sovereign individual—obscures the social forces *producing* rather than merely marking particular groups or behaviors as subhuman, rights appear to discursively bury the very powers they are designed to contest. To the extent that the "egoism of society" both provokes rights claims and is entrenched by them, the social relations iterating class, sexuality, race, and gender would appear to be individualized through rights discourse, ascribed to persons as attribute or internal content rather than social effect. If rights thus reify the social power they are designed to protect against, what are the political implications of doing both? What happens when we understand individual rights as a form of protection against certain social powers of which the ostensibly protected individual is actually an effect? If, to paraphrase Marx, rights do not liberate us from relations of class, gender, sexuality, or race, but only from formal recognition of these elements as politically significant, thereby liberating them "to *act* after their own fashion," how does the project of political emancipation square with the project of transforming the conditions against which rights are sought as protection?

The second set of questions pertains to the place of rights in legitimating the humanist dimensions of liberal discourse. To what extent is the power of a humanist fiction of universality affirmed as the mantle of generic personhood sought by the historically disenfranchised? How is the metonymic operation of the generic person obscured by the increasingly wide distribution of its political attributes? How can the invidious dimensions of universalist claims be contested even as the historically disenfranchised seek a place under their auspices?

These questions become more vexed when the progressive historiography presumed by Marx is excised from his critique of rights, when the contradiction between "political emancipation" and "true, human emancipation" is no more likely to erupt as radical consciousness or be transcended through revolution than various contradictions within capitalism are likely to explode into a socialist alternative. Absent this teleology, instead of rights constituting a "historical stage" of the progress toward emancipation, they figure a political culture that daily recapitulates its value in anointing and protecting personhood and daily reiterates the egoism out of which rights emerge. Operating as a discursive regime rather than a stage in the history of emancipation, rights appear as political ends rather than historical or political instruments. And situated within the larger context of Weberian rationalization in modernity, a process whereby instrumental rationality cancerously supplants all other values as all means become ends, the so-called litigious culture disparaged across the contemporary political spectrum becomes more than a contingent item for political criticism.[37] In this recasting, rights discourse appears in opposition to—rather than a stage in the progress toward—alternative modes of redressing social subjugation expressed as politicized identity. When "history" is no longer regarded as driven by structural contradictions and tethered to the telos of freedom, the delusion is no longer possible that "every emancipation is a restoration of the human world and of human relationships to man himself."[38]

Yet it is also the case that when we cease to regard history as composed of coherent social totalities and single threads of progress, viewing it instead in terms of converging and conflicting discourses and genealogies, a different order of political thinking becomes possible. Consider the difference in the relationship between history and freedom conceived by Marx and by Foucault: For Marx, political promise inheres in the dialectical movement of history toward freedom. (Animated generally by a drive to overcome scarcity expressed in the developmental aspect of modes of production, history is specifically powered by the class struggles that occur at the point of contradictions between the means, mode, and relations of production.) Thus, for Marxists, history voided of a teleological project—an emptiness achieved by exposing the reli-

[37] The political range of critics of the "litigious society" is quite wide: from George Bush's 1992 campaign attack on "trial lawyers" to Mary Ann Glendon's *Rights Talk: The Impoverishment of Political Discourse* (New York: Free Press, 1991), to Ben Barber's worry over the contemporary privatizing turn of rights discourse ("Constitutional Rights: Democratic Institution or Democratic Obstacle?" in *The Framers and Fundamental Rights*, ed. Robert A. Licht (Washington, D.C.: AIE, 1992), and Michael Walzer's kindred worry in *What It Means to Be an American*, especially the essay therein entitled "Constitutional Rights and the Shape of Civil Society" (New York: Marsilio, 1992).

[38] "Jewish Question," p. 46. There is a question, at least in my mind, about whether poststructuralist critiques of historical metanarrative should be historicized such that only *in our time* does progressive historiography collapse, or whether the stronger poststructuralist claim that all progressive notions of history were thoroughgoing fictions should be advocated. I remain enough of a Marxist to find it difficult to surrender the notion of "development" in a historiography that accounts for the "transition" from feudalism to capitalism, from competitive capitalism to corporate capitalism, and from industrial to postindustrial capitalism in the global economic core (Europe and North America).

gious Hegelian metanarrative at the core of Marxist historiography—implies the political nightmare of nihilism or of eternal daylight, of time frozen. The forfeiture of historical design implied by the "end of history," by the bankruptcy of the principle of temporal (dialectical) movement forward, signals the political crisis of a total present. It heralds totalitarianism insofar as the pervasive domination in the social totality Marxism depicts is left without a principle of self-overcoming. Marxist critique absent redemption through dialectic, it may be recalled, was precisely the logic structuring the dark conclusions of Marcuse's *One-Dimensional Man*.

For Foucault, on the other hand, the end of history is less a political problem than a political relief. The critique of metanarrative offers reprieve not only from humanist conceits but from temporal or structural models of power: economic models in which power is figured as a wieldable commodity, and repressive models, in which power is figured as suppressing the capacities of a transcendent subject. The critique of teleology in history releases us as well from models of the political subject framed in the (global) narrative of identity, subjugation, and redemption. Reason in history, which requires both the fiction of social totalities and the fiction of epochal periodization, is made to give way to genealogical analyses of selected regimes of truth, analyses that make no claim to spatial or temporal comprehensiveness. We are also urged to conceive the problematic of power in spatial yet nonstructural terms and temporal yet nonlinear terms: space is refigured as the domain in which multiple and contestable discourses operate, time as a domain of imprecise and refigurable repetition. Intervention or resignification is possible in both dimensions insofar as power is reconceived outside discourses of structures, laws of history, and even hegemony. In this regard, Foucault's insistence on the spatialization of power means that "history" finally becomes human.

Yet if Foucault's critique of progressivist historiography offers a reprieve from historical and political perspectives tied to social totalities and temporal stages, thereby varying and widening the field of political intervention, his investigations into the nature of power also complicates the problem posed by depoliticizing discourses such as those of rights. In his concern with disciplinary power, in his articulation of how certain discourses are forged into *regimes* of truth, and in his formulation of power as that which *produces* subjects rather than simply suppressing or positioning them, Foucault conjures a political field with relatively little open space and none of the tricks of self-overcoming, of forward motion, contained in Marxist historiography. This Foucaultian discernment of power where neither Marxism nor liberalism perceives it forces a rethinking of the Marxist formulation of politicized identity and rights claims. Foucault's account not only severs "political emancipation" from a phantasmic progress of emancipation, it also problematizes the Marxist presumption that the quest for such emancipation issues from historically subordinated or excluded subjects seeking a place in a discourse of universal personhood. It suggests instead that these claims may issue from contemporary productions of the subject by regulatory norms, productions that may be entrenched as much as challenged or loosened through political recognition and acquisition of rights. In other words, the collapse of a progressivist historiography becomes more serious given the extent to which contemporary discourses of rights converge with the disciplinary production of identities seeking them, given the extent to which contemporary discourses of political emancipation may be products not simply of stratified and egoistic civil society, but of disciplinary modalities of power producing the very subjects whose rights become a method of administering them. Here, one additional comparison between Marxist and post-Marxist social theory will indicate how certain limitations in Marx's formulation of power interact in a complex way with his problematic historiography.

For Marx, subordination is a function of social position, of where one is positioned within hierarchical relations of power constitutive of a social order. At its most economistic, the Marxist formula for measuring subordination involves ascertaining a subject's relationship to the means of production within a particular mode of production. In its less economistic moments (for example, in the "Jewish Question" or "The Holy Family"), elements of social power other than production may be considered relevant, but the issue remains one of positioning. The problem of political consciousness thus becomes one of accurately apprehending one's social positioning and hence the truth of the social totality, a matter that requires "piercing the ideological veil" in which the order is shrouded and, in particular, reversing the "camera obscura" by which it disguises its power. Political consciousness in inegalitarian societies is thus a matter of perceiving the power by which such societies are objectively stratified, a perception that depends upon a critique of the ideological mystification (and especially naturalization) of stratification in order to recognize its achievement by power. (This process is mapped in the discussion of ideology in the *The German Ideology* and is modeled in the discussion of commodification in volume 1 of *Capital*.) For Marx and in many social theories heavily indebted to Marxism—for example, Catharine MacKinnon's—subject position is social position; determined by social relations that structure stratification, subject position can be apprehended through scientific discernment of these relations, a science elaborated in various incarnations of standpoint epistemology.

While critical theories of gender, race, and sexuality probably cannot dispense entirely with a notion of subject position, the formulations of power and of the subject entailed by this notion are also inadequate to the aspirations of such theories. Consequently, much contemporary critical theory has moved to augment the Marxist account of subordination as a function of social positioning. Post-Marxist feminist theory, for example, figures the political problem of women both as a problem of constructed subjectivities (local, particular, unfixable, always exceeding the denotations of woman or women) *and* as one of social positioning (nameable, tangible yet always abstract, a potent designation evacuated of any particular inhabitant). If "identity" "occurs," is named or produced, at the point where these touch, where the particulars of subject formation intersect with vectors of social stratification such as race or gender, then the richest accounts of racial formation or gendering will prevail when subjectivity and social positioning are figured simultaneously.[39] More than simply recognizing the importance of both analytic registers, this requires interlacing them such that social "positioning" is formulated as part of subject production and the construction of subjectivity is formulated as an element in the making of social hierarchy and political domination.

What are the implications for the emancipatory potential of rights of replacing an account of subjugation as subject position with an understanding of "subject formation" and with an understanding of power as "something which circulates[,] . . . which is never appropriated as a commodity or piece of wealth . . . but is employed and exercised through a net-like organization"? What happens when we come to understand subjects as not only *positioned by* power, as not only created out of the expropriation or exploitation of their powers, but as *effects of* power, as formed or produced by power, *and* as "simultaneously undergoing and exercising . . . power"?[40] What happens when we understand subjects of racial or sexual domination to be the partial *effects* of *regimes*

[39] Yet this project is made difficult by virtue of the articulation of subject positioning and formations of subjectivity in such different registers. While subjectivity is local, particular, psychoanalytic, concerned with the problem of consciousness and unconscious, body and psyche, and desire and culture, social positioning invariably refers to orders or structures of power; it involves reading them historically and deducing how subjects are located within a field of power rather than how subjects are formed by specific operations of power. Many (but not all) contemporary battles about the "discursive" versus the "material" elements of power are drawn over this line, where those most concerned with subjectivity insist that all is discourse while those who see only social positioning insist on the pre- or extradiscursive materiality of that positioning. Resolving this matter will undoubtedly require a more thoroughly developed notion of discursive materiality and the different valences of, for example, political discourses of race and discourses of racial subjectivity.

[40] Michel Foucault, "Two Lectures," in *Power/Knowledge: Selected Interviews and Other Writings, 1972–1977,* ed. C. Gordon (New York: Pantheon, 1980), p. 98.

and *formations* of race and sexuality, rather than positioned within and fully formed by totalizing *systems*? What is implied for rights when we understand politicized identity as a regulatory production of a disciplinary society and not only as political consciousness of one's social positioning in orders stratified by hierarchical social power? Might rights then appear as a means both of contesting state power by asserting individual autonomy and of more deeply articulating identity by forgetting the social norms and regulatory discourses that constitute it? Do rights affixed to identities partly function to imprison us within the subject positions they are secured to affirm or protect?

. . .

Contemporary reflection on Marx's critique of right portrays its value as mixed. On the one hand, a number of Marx's operative assumptions are called into question by post-Marxist theory: the "real universality" embodied in "true human emancipation"; the progress toward this universalism secured by a Hegelian historiography rooted in the resolution of systemic contradictions through dialectic; the ontological, historical, and epistemological distinctions between state and civil society, politics and economy, ideal and material orders; and the distinction between social position and subjectivity presumed by the possibility of scientific critique and rational consciousness. On the other hand, the experience of late modernity poses questions about the emancipatory function of rights never entertained by Marx: these include attention to disciplinary power, subjectivity, and subject production; political culture understood in spatial rather than temporal dimensions; and power and politics formulated in the metaphor of "battle" or permanent contestation rather than the metaphors of contradiction, progress, and transcendence.

Yet for all the limitations and aporias in Marx's formulation of rights and political emancipation, there are strong claims to be made for its contemporary relevance. In fact, rather than vitiating the Marxist critique of rights, the suspension of certain Marxist assumptions and the addition of certain Foucaultian insights may intensify its force. Indeed, post-Marxist theory permits us to understand how rights pervasively configure a political culture (rather than merely occupying a niche within it) and discursively produce the political subject (rather than serving as the instrument of such a subject). It also permits us to grasp the way in which disciplinary productions of identity may become the site of rights struggles that naturalize and thus entrench the powers of which those identities are the effects.[41]

[41] See n. 6 above. The point here is that naming may be *simultaneously* a form of empowering recognition and a site of regulation: this is the ambiguity about identity that Foucault articulated in his concern that we might be excavating only to then inter insurrec-

But to suggest that rights sought by politicized identities may cut two (or more) ways—naturalizing identity even as they reduce elements of its stigma, depoliticizing even as they protect recently produced political subjects, empowering what they also regulate—is not to condemn them. Rather, it is to refuse them any predetermined place in an emancipatory politics and to insist instead upon the importance of incessantly querying that place. I want to proceed with such querying now by reflecting on the formulation of rights by two of their progressive exponents in contemporary law and politics, Patricia Williams and Catharine MacKinnon.

. . .

What happens, in the kind of culture Marx diagnosed as producing the need and desire for rights, to those without them, or to those largely sequestered in domains marked "private" or "natural" where rights do not apply? What happens to the "frenzied" order of egoistic civil society where those subordinated via race, sexuality, gender, or age—locked out or thrust into the ontological basement of the social structure—are routinely exploited or violated by those armed with rights, social power, and social legitimacy? What happens when the lack of a right to property or speech, bodily integrity or sexual conduct, is conjoined with the vulnerability and dependence created by relative social powerlessness and marginalization?

This is the perspective, in her terms "the subject position," from which Patricia Williams's defense of rights issues in *The Alchemy of Race and Rights*. This defense is mindful of critiques from the left wing of the legal establishment as well as of the failure of civil rights, once gained, to substantially augment the socioeconomic condition of the majority of blacks in the United States. It is also a defense that de-emphasizes the ways the emergence of rights interlocked with the triumph of the bourgeoisie in postfeudal Europe, with capital's pressing need for the free circulation of land and labor, and with individual propertied male ownership of the members and elements of his household. It is a defense that eschews the way that, historically, rights discourse legitimated the new class formations as well as a constitutional state designed to secure and naturalize them. Williams's account begins already inside this history, presumes the Hobbesian/Adam Smithian culture it figures, and dwells

---

tionary discourses. Moreover the emancipatory function of rights cannot be adjudicated in abstraction from the bureaucratic juridical apparatus through which they are negotiated. Who, today, defends their rights without an army of lawyers and reams of complex legal documents? In this regard, rights, rather than being the "popular and available" currency depicted by Patricia Williams, may subject us to intense forms of bureaucratic domination and regulatory power even at the moment that we assert them in our own defense.

upon the experience of those explicitly deprived of rights within it: those whom, *Dred Scott* opined, "were so far inferior, that they had no rights which the white man was bound to respect."[42] For Patricia Williams, in whose analysis of the law "subject position is everything,"[43] thinking about rights is unavoidably tethered to the experience of those persons historically denied them in a political culture in which political membership, civic belonging, bodily, emotional, and sexual boundary, social respect, legitimacy as an actor, capacity as a transactor, autonomy, privacy, visibility, and generative independence are all negotiated through the language and practice of rights and rightlessness.

While the importance of this link cannot be overstated, neither can its partiality. For deprivation on this scale is not merely lack but the creation of desire through lack. As homosexuals may crave the legitimacy conferred by the institution of marriage from which we are debarred—and thus reinscribe the very mechanism of our subjection in our yearning for that which is *premised* on our exclusion—Patricia Williams's defense of rights on the basis that it is "a symbol too deeply enmeshed in the psyche of the oppressed to lose without trauma and much resistance" poses a conundrum.[44] What if this deeply enmeshed symbol operates not only in but against that psyche, working as self-reproach, depoliticized suffering, and dissimulation of extralegal forms of power? To see how this might be the case, I want to consider three strands of Williams's argument in *The Alchemy of Race and Rights:* her critique of the phenomenon she calls "privatization," her analysis of black women's cultural positioning, and her effort to proliferate and resignify the meaning and distribution of rights.

For Patricia Williams, the "over-expanded mental state we call 'privacy' " is among the most pernicious and subtle enemies of contemporary democracy, as well as a powerful mode of legitimizing class and race inequalities. "The tyranny of what we call the private," she argues, risks reducing us to "the life-crushing disenfranchisement of an entirely owned world," where "permission must be sought to walk upon the face of the earth." Williams spies the corrosive effects of privatization in contemporary arguments about "reverse discrimination" and for "employer preference," in Supreme Court decisions permitting states to determine levels of indigent support, in police commissioner complaints about being singled out for media attention during police brutality investigations, in John Tower's promise to give up drinking if confirmed as Bush's de-

[42] Quoted in *The Alchemy of Race and Rights* (Cambridge: Harvard University Press, 1991), p. 162.

[43] Ibid., p. 3.

[44] Ibid., p. 165.

fense secretary. Criticizing not only privatization of public functions *by* the economy (workfare or school vouchers), Williams also assails increased privatization *of* the economy, represented by restricted access in commerce. The latter frames an incident in which a young white Benetton salesman refused her entry to a buzzer-controlled shop in New York and characterizes as well a sign she saw in a Greenwich Village boutique—"Sale! $2 overcoats. No bums, no booze"—which commodifies poverty while excluding the poor.[45]

Williams also traces forms of privatization that, like the design of corporate parks and shopping malls, effectively resegregate populations along lines of race and class. Reflecting on Mayor Koch's plea for black compassion toward white Howard Beach residents unhappy about an interracial protest march through "their" streets, she writes: "Koch was, in effect, pleading for acceptance of the privatization of public space. This is the de facto equivalent of segregation; it is exclusion in the guise of deep-moated property 'interests' and 'values.' Lost is the fact that the object of discussion, the street, is public."[46] Williams also examines how the language of privacy and its cousin, "choice," are used to mask state coercion as private desire. When defendants in child abuse or rape cases are "offered a 'choice' between . . . jail and sterilization[,] . . . the defendant is positioned as a purchaser, as 'buying' . . . freedom by paying the price of her womb" or by "choosing" castration.[47] This repackaging of state domination as the market freedom of individuals, she argues, imperils both public morality and the meaning of citizenship. It vandalizes a language of public obligation and at the same time legitimizes the de facto racism, misogyny, and hatred of the poor that, in her analysis, it is the task of the political to mitigate. In short, "privatization" violates public space, depoliticizes socially constructed problems and injustices, exonerates public representatives from public responsibility, and undermines a notion of political life as concerned with the common and obligating us in common.

How is this searing political critique reconcilable with Williams's unalloyed defense of rights? Rights in liberal capitalist orders, Marx reminds us, are bits of discursive power that quintessentially privatize and depoliticize, that mystify and reify social powers (property and wealth, but also race, sexuality, and gender) as the natural possessions of private persons, that analytically abstract individuals from social and political context, that are in fact *effects* of the social power they obfuscate. Indeed, to the extent that rights discursively mask stratifying social powers

---

[45] Ibid., pp. 43, 42.
[46] Ibid., p. 69.
[47] Ibid., pp. 32, 33.

through their constitution of sovereign subjects rendered formally equal before the law, they would appear to be among the most basic strategies of the privatization Williams condemns. As the Reagan-Bush years made clear, rights discourse is precisely what furnishes the claims of reverse discrimination and employer preference, the justifications for school voucher systems, regressive tax reform, union busting, and the prerogatives of store owners and neighborhoods to restrict access. Rights discourse in liberal capitalist culture casts as private potentially political contests about distribution of resources and about relevant parties to decision making. It converts social problems into matters of individualized, dehistoricized injury and entitlement, into matters in which there is no harm if there is no agent and no tangibly violated subject. And if we shift here from Marx to Foucault in querying the incommensurability of Williams's critique of privatization and defense of rights, we can ask: What more thoroughly obscures domination by regulatory norms—the "whiteness" or "maleness" of certain standards of excellence—than the figure of the sovereign subject of rights? And what would more neatly converge with the late modern disciplinary production of identity, and regulation through identity, than the proliferation of rights Williams counsels?[48]

None of this is to suggest that those without rights in a rights-governed universe should abandon the effort to acquire and use them. Williams and others make clear enough that such counsel, especially from white middle-class academics, is at once strategically naive and a disavowal of cultural prerogatives.[49] But to argue for the importance of having rights where rights are currency is not yet an assessment of how they operate politically nor of the political culture they create. Rather, that argument underscores both the foolishness of walking into a pitched battle unarmed and the crippling force of being deemed unworthy of whatever a given culture uses to designate humanity. The question Williams's defense leaves unasked is whether the proliferation of rights she advocates might not abet the phenomenon she calls privatization, the encroachment of "a completely owned earth," the disintegration of pub-

[48] Ibid., p. 165.

[49] See both Williams's account of mental experiments she undertook to see if she could get help for her enslaved great-great-grandmother without the discourse of rights (ibid., pp. 157–58) and her account of the different subject positioning that led her and a white male colleague to have very different attitudes toward formal legal arrangements such as rental contracts (pp. 146–49). See also the essay by Robert Williams, Jr., "Taking Rights Aggressively: The Perils and Promise of Critical Legal Theory for Peoples of Color" (*Law and Inequality: A Journal of Theory and Practice* 5 [1987], pp. 103–34), in which he argues that Critical Legal Studies critiques of rights and those who clamor for them involve a certain condescension, even racism, in their blindness to the privileged position from which they make their arguments.

lic obligations and a political culture of responsibility. It also leaves uninterrogated the relationship between the promise of rights for black
people as "an illusion [that] became real for only a few"[50] and the function of rights in depoliticizing economic power, in privatizing economic
circumstance—in short, in disguising the workings of class.

Williams's defense of rights veers away from these questions and instead
focuses on the historical deprivation of social, sexual, and physical integrity that rightlessness conjured for blacks in the United States. With Robert Williams, she argues that if rights function to individuate, separate,
and defend individuals, if they grant individuals a sphere of bodily integrity and privacy, if they announce our personhood even in abstract fashion and our membership even in an abstract community, then these may
be exactly what is needed and wanted by those denied them in a culture
which marks its "others" through such deprivation.[51] "[W]here one's experience is rooted not just in a sense of illegitimacy but in *being* illegitimate, . . . then the black adherence to a scheme of . . . rights—to the
self, to the sanctity of one's own personal boundaries—makes sense."
Given the history of violent "familiarity" and "informality" with which
blacks have been treated by whites in the United States, some distance,
abstraction, and formal rather than intimate recognition might be an important remedy. "For me," Patricia Williams argues, "stranger-stranger
relations are better than stranger-chattel."[52]

Elaborating this argument, Williams delineates the dilemma of "exposure and hiding" as the constant experience and measure of subjugation
of black women. The choice between humiliating exposure and desperate hiding is the nonchoice that configures the drama of Tawana Brawley,
Anita Hill, Williams's own "exaggerated visibility and invisibility" as
black female law professor, black women as slaves—"teeth and buttocks
bared to interested visitors"—and black women's present positioning in
a racial-sexual economy that routinely marks their sexuality as unbarred
availability.[53]

This unnavigable "choice" between exposure and hiding clearly calls
for redress through social practices that accord black women autonomy
and privacy, agency and respect. But perhaps, heeding a Foucaultian appreciation of subject formation, this violent legacy also takes shape as a
complex form of desire in the subjects it creates, a desire symptomized in
Patricia Williams's deeply personal and quasi-confessional writing. Indeed, how else to explain her production of our *intrusion* into her morn-

[50] Patricia Williams, *Alchemy of Race and Rights*, p. 163.
[51] Robert Williams, "Taking Rights Aggressively."
[52] *Alchemy of Race and Rights*, pp. 154, 148.
[53] Ibid., pp. 18, 92–93, 175–77, 196.

ing toilette—her *exposure* of how with astringent, mascara, and lip glaze she hangs her face in contradictions to "deny pain[,] . . . be a role model[,] . . . pav[e] the way for [her] race"—and in this way restages the scene of invasion, the absence of bodily privacy that is the history of African American women? How else to explain the revelation of bouts of depression, humiliating teaching evaluations, unedited dreams and nightmares, long hours of suffering in her terrycloth bathrobe, and vanity before the mirror? Perhaps this historically produced desire—for the right to expose oneself without injury, and for the right to hide without recrimination—undergirds a certain desire for rights, those implements that promise, as liberalism does more generally, to guard exposed subjects and legitimize hiding. But rights could only fulfill this promise if they could bring into view the complex subject formation consequent to a history of violation, precisely the articulation they thwart in figuring desire as natural, intrinsic, and unhistorical.

Thus, as with the relationship between rights and privatization, it may be that the very condition that designates liberalism's "others"—being condemned to exposure or hiding (here homosexuality also comes to mind)—is both intensified and redressed by rights: the same device that confers legitimate boundary and privacy leaves the individual to struggle alone, in a self-blaming and depoliticized universe, with power that seeps past rights and with desire configured by power prior to rights. It may be that the discourse of rights, Maxine Thomas's stock in trade, is precisely what could not protect her from, and indeed what stole the political language for, the unlivable contradictions that finally made this stunningly accomplished black female judge "split at the seams and return to the womb . . . exploded into fragments of intelligence and scattered wisdom."[54] It may be that the withdrawal that rights offer, the unmarking or destigmatizing they promise, has as its cost the loss of a language to describe the character of domination, violation, or exploitation that configures such needs. Indeed, what if the desire for withdrawal into the buffered and enclosed space of liberal personhood marked by rights is *symptom,* and what if treating the symptom distracts us from and thus covers over its generative source? What if, as Marx put it, the "right of the circumscribed individual, withdrawn into himself" responds to the socially produced condition of exposure or hiding, excessive vulnerability or invisibility, humiliation or death, by codifying that condition as natural and installing it in the law?[55]

There is still another strand to Williams's defense of rights: as the historically and currently existing social form of freedom, they are both con-

---

[54] Ibid., pp. 196–97.
[55] "Jewish Question," p. 42.

cretely available and "magic" in the mouths of black people. Yet, even as Williams insists upon the immediate political efficacy of rights and contrasts this efficacy with the "timeless, formless futurism" held out by rights critics, she also makes a fierce argument for the exploitability of the indeterminacy of rights:

> The task . . . is not to discard rights but to see through or past them so that they reflect a larger definition of privacy and property: so that privacy is turned from exclusion based on self-regard into regard for another's fragile, mysterious autonomy; and so that property regains its ancient connotation of being a reflection of the universal self. The task is to expand private property rights into a conception of civil rights, into the right to expect civility from others. . . . Society must *give* [rights] away . . . to slaves[,] . . . to trees[,] . . . to cows[,] . . . to history[,] . . . to rivers and rocks.[56]

The risk here is that the appreciation of the power and flexibility of the word afforded by recent literary theory may have converged with what Marx identified as liberalism's theological impulses to exaggerate a sense of what can be accomplished with words. How resonant of Bauer's understanding of civic emancipation is Patricia Williams's proclamation that "the problem with rights discourse is not that the discourse itself is constricting but that it exists in a constricted referential universe."[57] In literalizing the promise of rights on the one hand and lifting them from historical and social context on the other, an analysis so dependent upon floating signifiers appears to end up intensifying the idealist tendencies of liberal thought. Indeed, how could extending "to all of society's objects and untouchables the rights of privacy, integrity, and self-assertion"[58] contest the steady commodification of the earth and of public life that Williams also decries? Might words be more mutable, more subject to alchemical fire, than the political histories that generate rights, the political economies in which they operate, and the subjectivities they fashion?

In this sense, what Williams calls the "magic" of rights may pertain less to their transmutational capacities than to the fact that while they formally mark personhood, they cannot confer it; while they promise protection from humiliating exposure, they do not deliver it. (Hence the Benetton incident, which no truckload of rights can ameliorate or redress.) The necessarily abstract and ahistoricizing discourse of rights mystifies the conditions and power that delimit the possibility of achieving personhood, while its decontextualizing force deprives political consciousness of recognition of the histories, relations, and modalities of power that produce and situate us as human.

---

[56] Ibid., pp. 163, 164–65.
[57] Ibid., p. 159.
[58] Ibid., p. 165.

Thus, if the provision of boundary and protection from "bodily and spiritual intrusion"[59] offered by rights are what historically subjugated peoples most need, rights may also be one of the cruelest social objects of desire dangled above those who lack them. For in the very same gesture with which they draw a circle around the individual, in the very same act with which they grant her sovereign selfhood, they turn back upon the individual all responsibility for her failures, her condition, her poverty, her madness—they privatize her situation and mystify the powers that construct, position, and buffet her. In this respect, perhaps they not only failed to save Judge Maxine Thomas—perhaps they also intensified the isolation of her struggle with all the contradictory forces of power and freedom that rights disavow in their occupation of the field of justice. If rights are all that separate Williams from her bought-and-sold, raped-and-abused great-great-grandmother, they are also the device that demeans Clarence Thomas's now infamous sister, that permits him to ratify a larger social presumption that if he could become a Supreme Court justice, then so could they both, and only her laziness, her lack of moral fiber or industriousness, or her corruption by "welfare culture" accounts for the difference. Perhaps Williams's contrast of the concrete, immediate, and available character of rights discourse with the "timeless, formless futurism," the "unrealistic[,] . . . unattainable[,] or other-worldly" characteristic of other emancipatory political projects[60] is, finally, a false contrast dependent on a false concreteness. Under the guise of the concrete, what rights promise may be as elusive, as otherworldly, as unattainable as that offered by any other political myth.

.   .   .

Catharine MacKinnon's effort to rectify the masculinism of the law and redress women's inequality depends upon taking seriously Marx's critique of rights, bending it in a feminist direction, and incorporating it into a form of jurisprudence that Marx never entertained. Unlike Marx, MacKinnon seeks to make visible *within* the law, and particularly within rights discourse, precisely the kind of social power that Marx argued was inherently obscured by bourgeois rights discourse. For MacKinnon, the project of feminist jurisprudence, especially in the domain of sexual harassment and pornography, is to make rights articulate and respond to rather than mask the systematic workings of gender subordination.

In MacKinnon's analysis, gender is the congealed effect of a patriarchal organization of sexuality as male dominance and female submission. A

---

[59] Ibid., p. 164.
[60] Ibid., pp. 163–64.

specific organization of sexuality creates gender as a specific organization of work creates class, and a politics that redresses gender inequality is therefore a politics that makes visible the construction and enforcement of women's subordination through the appropriation, commodification, and violation of female sexuality. Sexual harassment, rape, battery, and pornography in this way appear not simply as violations, but as violations that specifically reduce persons to women, that iterate and reiterate—indeed, perform—the category "women," and that thus constitute a violation of women's civil rights, women's right to civic and political equality. In Althusserian terms, MacKinnon regards these practices not simply as hurting but as *interpellating* women as women, where "woman" is analytically conceived as only and always an effect of male dominance constituted by and operationalized as sexual dominance.

MacKinnon criticizes legal claims to objectivity as inherently masculinist, casting the law's claimed aperspectivalism and universalism as "male" in substance as well as form: "In the liberal state, the rule of law—neutral, abstract, elevated, pervasive—both institutionalizes the power of men over women and institutionalizes power in its male form."[61] In arguing that point-of-viewlessness *is* the law's maleness, she adapts for feminism the Marxist view that universal discourse—the discourse of liberal constitutionalism—in an unequal social order is a ruse of power, presenting as generic what actually privileges the dominant. More specifically, she argues that the universalism of the state masks its masculinist substance through the (masculinist) aperspectival form, a form that covers the law's maleness just as the "universality" of the state both constitutes and legitimizes the state's bourgeois character.

MacKinnon thus seeks to make the law "gender equal" precisely by prying this project loose from one of "gender neutrality," indeed by opposing gender equality to gender neutrality. Arguing that the law is most gender biased where it is most gender blind, she seeks to make the law "gender sighted," in part by bringing to light its gendered perspective. MacKinnon's effort to use the law as a means of *recognition* and *rectification* of gender subordination depends upon forcing the law to recognize and reform its own masculinism. This she aims to achieve by establishing both the partiality and the veracity of women's "perspective," a perspective rooted in women's experience of sexual subordination and violation.

MacKinnon seeks to realize the universal claim of liberal equality not by expanding the law's range of inclusion but by installing within the law the capacity to recognize stratifying social power, which its formal categories ordinarily make invisible and which rights discourse in particular

---

[61] *Toward a Feminist Theory of the State* (Cambridge: Harvard University Press, 1989), p. 238.

depoliticizes. Thus, MacKinnon does not abandon the universal formulation of justice claimed for the present by liberals and anticipated in the future by Marxists; nor, however, does she postpone the realization of true universal equality and liberty to a postliberal, nonstate millennium. Rather, MacKinnon aims to compel the law to fulfill its universalist promise by forcing it to recognize and rectify relations of domination among its subjects—in particular, by making it recognize gender as a relation of domination rather than a benign or natural marker of difference.

If the law can be made to articulate rather than mask social domination, if it can be made to reveal gender as the effect of eroticized male dominance, then perhaps substantive rather than merely formal equality can be won through civil rights law. This is what MacKinnon seeks to achieve through a jurisprudence that equates women's equality with women's rights against the incursions of male sexuality, against what MacKinnon posits as the *material basis* of female subordination. The project is ingenious in the parsimony and radicalism of its basic formula: If sexual subordination defines the category "woman," then sexual subordination—whether through rape or marriage, incest or harassment, abortion restrictions or pornography—must be legally construed as a violation of women's civil rights in an egalitarian legal order, a violation of women's right not to be socially subordinated. In this way, sexual harassment and pornography become issues of gender equality rather than issues of gender "difference," and rather than gender generic issues of obscenity, assault, or labor relations.

In this effort to install an *analysis* of women's sexual subordination *in* the law, MacKinnon attempts to resolve the chief Marxist ambivalence about rights and legal reform, namely, their potential mystification of the "real, material basis" of subordination even as they offer formal protection to marked subjects. MacKinnon resolves this dilemma by refusing it, by installing within legal discourse an analysis of the material basis of women's subordination. Thus, rather than emancipating women abstractly while leaving intact the substantive conditions of their subordination, MacKinnon's legal theory and legislative proposals seek to emancipate women from these conditions by making the conditions themselves illegal, by *politicizing them in the law*. Put the other way around, instead of emancipating us abstractly by denying the relevance of sexuality to gender and gender to personhood, a move that, to paraphrase Marx, emancipates sexuality to act after its own fashion, namely *as* male dominance and female subordination, MacKinnon insists that the emancipation of women *is* the right of women to be free from sexual incursion, violation, appropriation, and subordination. She would thus seem to be doing precisely what Marx thought could not be done: employing rights discourse to expose and redress inequalities that its abstract formulations of personhood and equality are thought to obscure and depoliticize.

With due admiration for the brilliance of MacKinnon's argument, there are a number of political and strategic questions to be posed about this work, many of them now sufficiently familiar (and considered at length in chapter four) to be summarized rather than detailed here.

First, if MacKinnon aims to write "women's experience into law," precisely which "women's experience(s)," drawn from which historical moments, and which culture, racial, and class strata, is MacKinnon writing? Certainly many women have argued that MacKinnon's depiction of pornography as "the graphic sexually explicit subordination of women," which violates women's civil rights, squares with neither their experience of being female, their experience of pornography, nor their ambivalence about the legal regulation of porn. Similarly, many feminists have protested MacKinnon's reduction of gender to sexuality, arguing that motherhood or other gendered practices are at least as constitutive of their subordination through gender.

Second, what does it mean to write historically and culturally circumscribed experience into an ahistorical discourse, the universalist discourse of the law? What happens when "experience" becomes ontology, when "perspective" becomes truth, and when both become unified in the Subject of Woman and encoded in law as women's rights? Moreover, what if the identity of women as keyed to sexual violation is an expressly late-twentieth-century and white middle-class construction of femininity, consequent to a radical deprivatization of sexuality on the one side, and erosion of other elements of compulsory heterosexuality, such as the sexual division of social labor, on the other? What does it mean to install in the universalist discourse of law an analysis of women's subordination that may be quite historically and culturally circumscribed?

Third, does a definition of women *as* sexual subordination, and the encoding of this definition in law, work to liberate women from sexual subordination, or does it, paradoxically, reinscribe femaleness as sexual violability? How might installation of "women's experience" as "sexual violation" in the law reiterate rather than repeal this identity? Foucault (along with certain strains in psychoanalytic thought) reminds us that the law *produces* the subjects it claims to protect or emancipate. How, then, might a formulation of women's civil rights as violated by pornography or sexual harassment produce precisely the figure MacKinnon complains we have been reduced to by sexism, a figure of woman wholly defined by sexual violation, wholly identified with sexual victimization?

Fourth, insofar as MacKinnon's attempt to legally encode "women's experience" interpellates women *as* sexually violable, how does this effectively deny the diversity and complexity of women and women's experience? Might this interpellation be particularly unemancipatory for women whose lived experience is not that of sexual subordination to men but, for example, that of sexual outlaw? How does the encoding of women's civil rights as rights against male sexual violation reaffirm the operations of exclusion enacted by the heterosexually normative category, woman?

Fifth, by returning to the analogy with class that inaugurates MacKinnon's analysis of gender and feminist jurisprudence, we can see from yet another angle how her effort to achieve substantive equality through rights may reiterate rather than resolve the opposition between rights and equality articulated in Marx's critique. MacKinnon's method of installing within rights discourse an analysis of the social power constitutive of gender ought to be applicable to class, that form of social power from which her analysis took its inspiration. But to render class exploitation illegal, to outlaw its conditions as MacKinnon seeks to outlaw the conditions of gender domination, would entail circumscription if not elimination of the right to private property, one of the most fundamental rights of liberal capitalist orders. (As Marx reminds us, real emancipation from private property requires the abolition of private property, not the abolition of political distinctions based upon property ownership.)

Now if substantive economic equality, the abolition of class, is incompatible with private property rights, might it be the case that substantive gender equality as MacKinnon defines it is equally incompatible with rights of free speech? If, as MacKinnon argues, sexual dominance is in part a matter of speech (e.g., sexual harassment) and representation (e.g., pornography), then is it any surprise that MacKinnon's effort to "get equality for women" comes into direct conflict with the First Amendment? Here it would appear that MacKinnon has not so much countered as extended and affirmed Marx's critique of rights as masking power and social inequalities. Her analysis *confirms* rather than resolves the opposition Marx articulates between "the rights of man" on one side (property, freedom of expression, freedom of worship, etc.) and the substantive equality (which she calls the civil rights) of women on the other. Appropriating a discourse of civil rights to procure equality for women, MacKinnon opposes the liberties secured by constitutional universalism and in this sense reaffirms rather than reworks Marx's formulation of the opposition between political emancipation and true human emancipation, between liberal universalism and domination in civil society, between bourgeois liberty and real equality.

On the one hand, MacKinnon seeks to encode the "experience" or "subject position" of a fiction called "women" in the timeless discourse of the law, such that women are produced as the sexually violable creatures the law says we are. On the other, she appears engaged in a critique of rights in the name of women's equality. Together these efforts may reveal the extent to which deployment of a Marxist critique of liberal universalism *as* law, rather than *against* the law, paradoxically breeds a politics of severe unfreedom. Legally codifying a fragment of history as a timeless truth, interpellating women as unified in their victimization, and casting the "free speech" of men as that which subordinates women, MacKinnon not only opposes bourgeois liberty to substantive equality but potentially intensifies the regulation of gender and sexuality through rights discourse, abetting rather than contesting the production of gender identity as sexual. In short, as a regulatory fiction of a particular identity is deployed to displace the hegemonic fiction of universal personhood, we see the discourse of rights converge insidiously with the discourse of disciplinarity to produce a spectacularly potent mode of juridical-disciplinary domination.

Perhaps the warning here concerns the profoundly antidemocratic elements implicit in transferring from the relatively accessible sphere of popular contestation to the highly restricted sphere of juridical authority the project of representing politicized identity and adjudicating its temporal and conflicting demands. MacKinnon's ingenious and failed effort at appropriating Marx's critique for legal reform may also stand as a more general caution against installing identity in the law, where inevitably totalized formulations of identity converge with the individuating effects of rights to produce levels of regulation through juridical individuation not imagined even by Foucault. Her failure may caution too that even as the generic man of the universal "rights of man" is problematic for the social powers it discursively cloaks, the specifications of identity in late-twentieth-century rights discourse may be equally problematic for the social powers they discursively renaturalize. In this regard, Marx's critique of rights may function most effectively in an era of proliferating politicized identities as a warning against confusing the domain of rights with the domain of political contestation: rights must not be confused with equality nor legal recognition with emancipation.

What if the value of rights discourse for a radical democratic project today lies not in its potential affirmation of difference, its guarantees of protection, its circumscriptions of autonomy, or as remedy to social injury, but in the (fictional) egalitarian imaginary this discourse could engender? Might rights campaigns converge most effectively with "prepolitical" struggles for membership or postpolitical dreams of radical equality? Certainly the contemporary right-wing reading of campaigns for equal rights for gays and lesbians suggests that the political disruptiveness, the democratizing dimension of rights discourse, may pertain precisely to the sustained universalist fiction of this discourse, a universalism that the charge of "special rights" attacks. The moment at which, through the discourse of rights, lesbians and gays claim their personhood against all that would disallow it is a radically democratic moment, analogous to those moments in U.S. history when white women and African Americans made similar claims.

If, as Marx argued 150 years ago, the democratizing force of rights discourse inheres in its capacity to figure an ideal of equality among persons qua persons, regardless of socially constructed and enforced particularities, then the political potency of rights lies not in their concreteness, as Patricia Williams argues, but in their idealism, in their ideal configuration of an egalitarian social, an ideal that is contradicted by substantive social inequalities. Such a claim further implies, with Marx, that the democratic *value* of political emancipation lies partly in its revelation of the *limits* of political emancipation. But while Marx counted on a progressive dialectical process for such revelation, it now becomes a project for discursive struggle whose parameters are invented rather than secured in advance and whose outcome is never guaranteed.

If rights figure freedom and incite the desire for it only to the degree that they are void of content, empty signifiers without corresponding entitlements, then paradoxically they may be incitements to freedom only to the extent that they discursively deny the workings of the substantive social power limiting freedom. In their emptiness, they function to encourage possibility through discursive denial of historically layered and institutionally secured bounds, by denying with words the effects of relatively wordless, politically invisible, yet potent material constraints. Still more paradoxically, when these material constraints *are* articulated and specified as part of the content of rights, when they are "brought into discourse," rights are more likely to become sites of the production and regulation of identity as injury than vehicles of emancipation. In entrenching rather than loosening identities' attachments to their current constitutive injuries, rights with strong and specified content may draw upon our least expansive, least public, and hence least democratic sentiments. It is, rather, in their abstraction from the particulars of our lives—and in their figuration of an egalitarian political community—that they may be most valuable in the democratic transformation of these particulars.

CHAPTER SIX

Liberalism's Family Values

> Women represent the interests of the family and of sexual life. The work of civilization has become increasingly the business of men, it confronts them with ever more difficult tasks and compels them to carry out instinctual sublimations of which women are little capable. . . . Thus the woman finds herself forced into the background by the claims of civilization and she adopts a hostile attitude toward it.
> —Sigmund Freud, *Civilization and Its Discontents*

> The family, as person, has its real external existence in property; and it is only when this property takes the form of capital that it becomes the embodiment of the substantial personality of the family. . . .
>
> The family as a legal entity . . . must be represented by the husband as its head. Further, it is his prerogative to go out and work for its living, to attend to its needs, and to control and administer its capital.
> —G. W. F. Hegel, *Philosophy of Right*

> The bourgeoisie has torn away from the family its sentimental veil. . . .   —Karl Marx, *Manifesto of the Communist Party*

AT THE CLOSE of *The Protestant Ethic and the Spirit of Capitalism*, Max Weber unsettles his account with the reflection that capitalism no longer requires the religious asceticism he painstakingly established as indispensable to its formation:

> The Puritan wanted to work in a calling; we are forced to do so. . . . To-day the spirit of religious asceticism . . . has escaped from the cage. But victorious capitalism, since it rests on mechanical foundations, needs its support no longer. The rosy blush of its laughing heir, the Enlightenment, seems also to be irretrievably fading, and the idea of duty in one's calling prowls about in our lives like the ghost of dead religious beliefs.[1]

---

[1] *The Protestant Ethic and the Spirit of Capitalism*, trans. T. Parsons (New York: Charles Scribner's Sons, 1958), pp. 181–82.

On one reading, Weber has characteristically subverted the strength of his endeavor. Marking its anachronistic quality, he casts it—like the figure of the true politician in "Politics as a Vocation"—as something of an impotent *crie de coeur* against the force of rationalization that increasingly orders everything: culture, capitalism, politics. Yet Weber's discernment of capitalism's Protestant roots and character lingers in another register, one not captured by a historiography of causality and a sociology of functional equivalents, which Weber thus cannot himself fully articulate analytically, even as he alludes to it poetically—"prowls about in our lives like the ghost. . . ." If capitalism no longer requires the Protestant ethic, if it now "rests upon mechanical foundations" and therefore appears equally compatible with Chinese post-Confucian post-Maoism and Iranian Islamic fundamentalism, it nonetheless reproduces certain Protestant cultural expressions and figures. In this way, its Protestant "origins" live somewhere in a cultural—as opposed to a substantively economic—modality that capitalism is and generates.

In *The Sexual Contract,* Carole Pateman argues that the sexual subordination of women in marriage is both required by and an effect of the social contract ostensibly generative of liberal political orders. Insisting that the social contract to make civil society and the state *cannot come into being* without a sexual contract that subordinates women in marriage, she also insists that the sexual contract is where patriarchalism *lives* in the political and legal order ordinarily understood as its supersession. While Locke's response to Filmer is conventionally regarded as a critique of patriarchalism (the divine right of fathers and kings), Pateman reads it otherwise—as the reorganization rather than the abolition of patriarchy. Locke's critique of Filmer, she reminds us, depended upon separating political right from paternal right such that "masculine right over women is declared non-political" but is not thereby transcended.[2]

To the contrary, Pateman and many other feminist theorists have argued, the liberal formulation of free and equal men in civil society required that patriarchalism be *relocated* from the political to the private domain. In this relocation, both the conceptual continuity and the homology Filmer ascribed to the relation between the political and the familial suffered permanent rupture: "paternal power" is now sharply differentiated from "political society."[3] Where the family had been conceived by Filmer (and by Hobbes) as a miniature of the state, "a little monarchy," its character is reformulated in liberalism as opposite to that of the state. Where the civil subject was understood by Filmer to reiterate

---

[2] Pateman, *The Sexual Contract* (Stanford: Stanford University Press, 1988), p. 90.

[3] "Paternal power" and "political society" constitute two successive chapters in Locke's *Second Treatise on Government,* and operationalize his critique (in the *First Treatise*) of Filmer's collapse of them.

the familial and religious subject, liberalism reformulates them as complementary such that the civil and familial domains do not constitute a single identity unified within a single subject but produce instead a divided, "naturally" alienated one. This splitting of the subject and stark differentiation between family and civil society is linked, of course, to the growing chasm between the household and society occasioned by the shrinking productive function of the household, the steady removal of production and exchange to the distinctly bounded realm of the economy.

Pateman makes a compelling case for conjugal right as the basis for father right, and the sexual contract as the basis for the social contract. However, Pateman does not query whether or on what level *contemporary* liberalism requires a social contract. She thus elides the question of the relation between the tales of social contract spun by Hobbes, Filmer, Locke, Pufendorf, and Rousseau and the contemporary basis of legitimacy and citizenship in liberal regimes. Put differently, Pateman, like Weber, elegantly crafts the historical case; unlike Weber, she does not adequately inquire into the nature of the legacy of this history, the nature of its bearing on a time in which both liberalism and women's subordination may well be sustained without contract. Instead, Pateman unconvincingly asserts this legacy in her accounts of contemporary sexist practices in the wage economy and in the household.[4] The assertion is unconvincing because while such practices certainly abound, they are neither ubiquitous nor systematic—they do not appear *inherent* within liberal orders. The assertion is also unconvincing because it eclipses the experience of women who function outside the heterosexual division of labor: her argument cannot account for the existence, let alone the occasional prosperity, of lesbians, single women, or single mothers in a liberal order. In short, since Pateman locates the mechanism of women's subordination (as well as that of workers) in contract as such, it is contract toward which she directs the full force of her feminist anger and critique. In Marx's terms, Pateman would thus appear to be "criticizing a fetish." Or, to sustain the comparison with which we began, the oddness of her move becomes apparent when we imagine railing against Protestantism as a contemporary force of capitalist exploitation and alienation.

As women are no longer required to enter a sexual contract—subordination in marriage—for survival or social recognition (although these both continue to be enhanced by heterosexual marriage), liberal political orders no longer need refer to an imaginary social contract for their legitimacy. While contractarian discourse once demarcated the legitimacy of a liberal capitalist order vis-à-vis a feudal monarchical one,

[4] See *Sexual Contract*, chap. 5.

while the formally "free" and "voluntary" characteristics of contract served to anoint and naturalize the "freedom" of both the wage laborer and the citizen of representative government, no longer are monarchs, feudalism, or slavery that against which liberalism arrays itself for definition. If, in previous centuries, contractarian language was required for justifying revolutions, political foundings, and arguments for extensions of the franchise, the language of contract no longer seems essential for these functions. If this language also operated to legitimate, even inspire, colonial and imperial domination by articulating the superiority of Euro-Atlantic political cultures over those subjugated by them, that legitimation is now achieved through the "self-evident" superiority of rights discourse and constitutional government to all other modalities of political order and disorder. Legitimation is procured, at least provisionally, through the absence of viable alternatives. Not the autonomy of the originally willing subject—to which even most contemporary liberal theorists do not subscribe—but the patent unhappiness of the former Soviet or Somali subject is tendered as proof (enough) of the supremacy of liberal regimes. As liberalism has become one with modernity, rather than a position within it, liberal discourse becomes so naturalized that it no longer depends upon the mythologies and legal fictions generated by origin stories attendant upon a regime at odds with its predecessor (feudal monarchy) or with its ideological "opposite" (communism). Indeed, it is no small irony that in the epoch of rampant ontological degrounding, the forthrightly conventional order of liberalism achieves the status of "nature"—as that to which "human nature" always defaults—and is protected from interrogation precisely through those quotation marks.

If not literally or causally, then, how might the "sexual contract" as predicate, corollary, and effect of the liberal social contract inhabit the contemporary terms of liberal discourse? Where does the legacy of women's subordination through the sexual contract live within liberalism when both social and sexual contract fade as constitutive factors and legitimating forces of liberal orders? In what follows, I shall argue that the legacy of gender subordination Pateman identifies as historically installed in the sexual-social contract is to be found not in contemporary contract relations but in the *terms* of liberal discourse that configure and organize liberal jurisprudence, public policy, and popular consciousness. This contention does not so much quarrel with Pateman's claims about history as require that we think differently about the particular ways the history she delineates bears on the present. In rerouting her historical work in the direction of genealogy, the aim is to deliteralize and dematerialize contract in order to examine the operations of a *discourse* premised on a sexual contract even while its perpetuation as a gendered discourse does not depend on that contract nor the naturalized sexual division of labor on which such a contract was premised.

While the ideological naturalization of *the family* achieved by liberalism's "hidden" sexual contract appears to be falling asunder in the late modern epoch (hence the hyperbolic assertion of "family values" intended to mark feminism and homosexuality as unnatural and themselves a sign of the unraveling of a sound moral-political order), the status of the liberal *civil* subject has never been more secure. This reminds us that while the familial and civil dimensions of liberalism's split subject are interconstitutive and their histories are correlated, these histories are not identical, nor even fully deducible from one another. (Capitalism conditions the production of the familial order but does not exhaust the discourses constitutive of it.) Thus, even as the familial subject naturalized by the classical liberals is patently in crisis today, the possessive individualism of the liberal civil subject is being affirmed from Beijing to Budapest. And insofar as Pateman's account of the structurally inherent quality of women's subordination in liberalism depends upon the express *sexual* subordination of women, what it cannot explain or even articulate is the masculinism of liberal discourse that supersedes such express subordination, that is contained in the masculinism of the civil subject cut loose from the family, that constructs and positions women and men in socially male terms in civil society and the state absent a sexual contract involving the family.

Pateman, of course, is only one of many feminist theorists who have worked to articulate the gendered character of liberal political theory and institutions. Susan Moller Okin has criticized liberal theorists' failure to recognize the mutually reinforcing subordination of women in the spheres of family and economy and their concomitant failure to extend their interest in democratizing public institutions to democratizing the family, childrearing, and housework.[5] Lorenne Clark and Lynda Lange, following C. B. MacPherson's critique of classical liberalism's bourgeois premises, have examined the ways in which assumptions about reproductive work and especially its (presumed negative) bearing on rationality undergird classical liberal theories of membership.[6] Linda Nicholson argues that liberal theory naturalizes a particular version of the family and reifies a distinctly modern and ideological division between family, civil society, and state.[7] Valerie Hartouni reveals the gender of

---

[5] *Justice, Gender, and the Family* (New York: Basic Books, 1989).

[6] *The Sexism of Social and Political Theory*, ed. Lorenne Clark and Lynda Lange (Toronto: University of Toronto Press, 1979).

[7] *Gender and History: The Limits of Social Theory in the Age of the Family* (New York: Columbia University Press, 1986).

liberal personhood in the discourses of contemporary debate about abortion and other reproductive technologies.[8] Essays in Carole Pateman and Elizabeth Grosz's volume on feminist interventions in social and political theory link liberal conceptions of equality, political rationality, desire, and consent to the political exclusion and social subordination of women.[9] Nancy Hirschman exposes liberal theories of obligation as gendered; Joan Tronto criticizes liberalism for privatizing and feminizing the virtue of caring; Nancy Hartsock allies liberalism's abstract formulations with "abstract masculinity."[10] And Catharine MacKinnon has sought to establish the masculinist character of the ideological aperspectivalism of the liberal state, as well as the fundamental contradiction between liberal formulations of equality as sameness and gender as difference.[11] If, as MacKinnon argues, liberal equality is premised upon sameness, yet sex always connotes difference, then liberal equality itself is gendered insofar as it turns on a standard that both denies and precludes the possibility of women's equality with men. Moreover, this is the gendering that liberal discourse obscures every time it deploys gender-neutral language; hence MacKinnon's insistence that the state is most gender biased where it is most gender blind.

Consider, in this regard, the analysis of abortion proffered by liberal legal and political theorist Bruce Ackerman, an analysis that does not once mention gender, women, or the constitution of gender through regimes of sexuality and reproductive work:

> I can think of four reasons a person may wish to abort a fetus; two are plainly legitimate; one, illegitimate, one, troubling.
>
> [1] The first rationale proceeds from the fact that we do not possess a perfect technology of justice that guarantees the right of contraception. As a result, unwanted embryos are conceived; [2] more subtly, but no less wrongly, embryos are conceived before the parents have had time to decide whether they really want to be parents. . . .
>
> [3] Suppose, however, that . . . the parents . . . want to abort the *particular*

---

[8] "Containing Women," in *Technocultures*, ed. Andrew Ross and Constance Penley (New York: Routledge, 1992), and "*Brave New World* in the Discourses of Reproductive and Genetic Technologies," in *In the Nature of Things: Language, Politics, and the Environment*, ed. Jane Bennett and William Chaloupka (Minneapolis: University of Minnesota Press, 1993).

[9] *Feminist Challenges: Social and Political Theory*, ed. Carole Pateman and Elizabeth Grosz (Boston: Northeastern University Press, 1986).

[10] Hirschman, *Rethinking Obligation* (Ithaca: Cornell University Press, 1992); Tronto, *Moral Boundaries* (New York: Routledge, 1993); Hartsock, *Money, Sex, and Power: Toward a Feminist Historical Materialism* (New York: Longman, 1983).

[11] *Toward a Feminist Theory of the State* (Cambridge: Harvard University Press, 1989).

child on the basis of genetic information provided by their doctors. Are "therapeutic" abortions always legitimate?

[4] This leaves a final, terrible case. Suppose a couple simply *enjoy* abortions so much that they conceive embryos simply to kill them a few months later. Cannot the state intervene to stop such brutality?[12]

Striking in Ackerman's analysis is not only the bizarre, improbable character of the final case but its grammar: "Suppose *a couple* simply *enjoy abortions* so much that *they conceive embryos* simply *to kill* them" suppresses the fact that it is women who have abortions, that conception and abortions occur at the site of women's bodies, and that this site is the effect of the very social powers (of women's subordination) making abortion a political issue in the first place. In this suppression, of course, male anxieties about women's control over fetal life (life with which we may presume at least some men intensely identify) are also obscured. In short, the "gender neutrality" of Ackerman's language reinscribes and renaturalizes—by rendering invisible—both the gender subordination enacted in women's lack of control over the terms and conditions of sexuality and reproduction and the distinctive masculinist psychic stakes in the abortion dilemma. The project of this chapter is in part to discern what makes a formulation such as Ackerman's possible in our time: Why and how do the terms of liberal discourse promulgate such abundant confusion about gender, gender neutrality, and gender justice? How does a liberal discourse of generic personhood reinscribe rather than emancipate us from male dominance? Where does male dominance live in the very terms of liberal discourse?

.   .   .

Liberalism is a nonsystematic and porous doctrine subject to historical change and local variation. However, insofar as liberalism takes its definitional shape from an ensemble of relatively abstract ontological and political claims, it is also possible to speak of liberalism in a generic fashion, unnuanced by time or cultural inflection. Indeed, my argument transpires at a level of historical and intellectual generalization with which no single liberal culture or epoch, and no single liberal thinker, could be aligned. It proceeds without distinguishing among the liberalisms of Locke, Tocqueville, Bentham, Constant, or Rawls, between liberalism in France or in the United States, or between liberal political claims in 1848 and 1988. Rather, taking a leaf from liberal thinking itself to theor-

---

[12] *Social Justice in the Liberal State* (New Haven: Yale University Press, 1980), pp. 127–28.

ize about politics in a mythological and ahistorical space and time, the argument proceeds by assuming liberalism to be a contemporary cultural text we inhabit, a discourse whose terms are "ordinary" to a very contemporary "us."

Liberalism will appear here as both a set of stories and a set of practices, as ideology *and* as discourse, as an obfuscating narrative *about* a particular social order as well as a narrative *constitutive of* this social order and its subjects. These two apparently antagonistic formulations—the former associated with a Marxist theory of ideology and the latter with Foucault's critical replacement of that theory with the notion of discourse—are both important to apprehending the operation of gender in liberalism.[13]

I want to argue, first, that liberalism is premised on and perpetuates a sexual division of labor, the actual powers of which are obscured by the terms of liberal discourse. Yet I also want to argue that liberal discourse produces subjects without regard to their "social positioning" by other discourses of gender, class, and race. In this regard, liberalism both produces and positions gendered subjects whose production and positioning it disavows through naturalization (an ideological moment) *and* produces abstract, genderless, colorless sovereign subjects (a more discursive moment), whose sovereignty and abstract equality contend uneasily with the discourses marking relative will-lessness and inferiority according to socially marked attributes. Thus while acknowledging that discourses other than those of the liberalism are constitutive of the subject "women," including those conscious and unconscious discourses of gen-

---

[13] To my knowledge, no one has yet satisfactorily articulated a relationship between discourse and ideology as terms of critical theory, and a footnote is certainly not the place for such an articulation. However, a few notes in this direction may be appropriate.

What does each term "do" that implicates or requires the other? In Foucault's formulation of power in and as a regime of truth, the ideological element of discourse appears not in opposition to materiality but in relation to the effects of power that it naturalizes or ontologizes. Thus, the discursive production of the subject can be conceived as ideological not in relation to some "real" subject or nondiscursive account of the subject, but insofar as this discourse naturalizes itself and thereby renders effects of power—subjects—as objects in the prediscursive world. (To some extent, Marx grasped this process through the terms "reification" and "commodification," but limited their scope to capitalist relations.)

In Marx's formulation of ideology as a function of class inequality, and in particular as consequent to the camera obscura issuing from the social division between manual and mental labor (see *The German Ideology*), ideology is that which obscures the terms of its own making along with the power that makes the world. But this claim, designed to describe the relationship of ideology to power, reveals yet does not account for the extraordinary power of ideology itself. In other words, what Marx did not explain, and what Althusser formulated the interpellative dimension of ideology to address, was the extent to which ideology does not simply (mis)represent the world but is itself productive of the world, and particularly of the subject.

der in the heterosexual nuclear family articulated by psychoanalysis, I reject the thesis that women "escape" the discourse of liberal individualism by virtue of a "different voice," orientation toward "relationality," or "maternal thinking."[14] If there are nonliberal discourses of gender cohabiting with liberalism that foment the kind of subject formation these designations seek to capture, women do not thereby elude formation by liberal discourse as well. In short, while liberalism is not the only discourse constitutive of gender, it is inevitably one of the discourses producing and positioning the gendered subject.

Within liberal discourse itself, there is both an expressly gendered and a generic strain, the former often subterranean and surfacing only at points at which the family, heterosexuality, maternity, or sexual violence is explicitly at issue. Yet the generic or gender-neutral strain, while wielding substantial force, overlooks the extent to which subjects are interpellated and positioned as gender, and it is in this regard that liberalism "misdescribes" or ideologically obscures the extent to which its subjects are shaped and positioned by a sexual division of labor and a sex difference that liberal discourse presumes to transcend. The gendered ideological moments of liberalism, then, pertain on the one hand to essentializing gender as difference; on the other, to glossing the social power of gender formation with generic or neutral language.

This analysis pays little attention to the great variety in liberalism(s) present even at the doctrine's inceptive moments in seventeenth-century Europe, emphasizing instead liberalism's historical emergence out of the breakup of feudal economic and monarchical political arrangements. New forms of property, modes of production, and attendant subject formation generated a need for new political institutions that permitted the free circulation of capital and property, secured a mass of free laborers, and articulated the formal liberty and equality of relatively abstract human beings in incipient mass society.[15] In this sense, liberalism emerges out of both a specific "social" (class) division of labor and a "sexual" (gendered) one and is also part of the economic and social transition to capitalism, marking continuity as well as change in these divisions of labor.[16]

[14] For contributions to such theses (although these authors do not themselves necessarily make the argument that women "escape" liberal discourse), see Nancy Chodorow, *The Reproduction of Mothering* (Berkeley: University of California Press, 1978); Carol Gilligan, *In a Different Voice* (Cambridge: Harvard University Press, 1982); Seyla Benhabib, *Situating the Self* (New York: Routledge, 1992); and Sara Ruddick, *Maternal Thinking* (Boston: Beacon, 1989).

[15] See Karl Polanyi, *The Great Transformation* (Boston: Beacon, 1944).

[16] No more lyrical summary of this process can be found than Marx's account in *The Manifesto of the Communist Party* (in *The Marx-Engels Reader*, 2d ed., ed. R. C. Tucker [New York: Norton, 1978]): "The bourgeoisie . . . has put an end to all feudal, patriarchal, idyllic

Within a general sexual division of labor—female labor within and male labor outside the household—two roughly contradictory tendencies unfold in the course of capitalism's development. On one side, as household production shrinks and (increasingly industrialized) socialized production takes its place, women's varied tasks associated with the double-sided reproduction of labor—generating the new, replenishing what exists—are increasingly privatized and confined to the household, while men's work is increasingly socialized and removed from the home. The steady widening of the spatial separation between "home" and "work" has significant indirect effects: women's work in the home becomes less visible as work, and the constitutive values of the realm of civil society are distinguished from the order of the family. As a "separate sphere," the family thus becomes available for sentimentalism, for reification as a naturalized haven in a heartless world. However, on the other side, the steady movement of "women's work" into the market (production of food and clothing, education and socialization of children, service work of every variety) increasingly reduces women's work in the home to service functions and also erodes the separation between home and market, rendering the membrane between them highly permeable in both directions. This tendency articulates the "housewife" as a historically specific—fleeting, rather than permanent—feature of liberal capitalist arrangements, subjects "the family" to new and ultimately untenable pressures, and generally undermines the spatially organized sexual division of labor on which liberalism is premised. Feminism is one historical effect of these eroded arrangements.

Prior to further consideration of the feminism spawned by these conflicting forces, a schema of liberalism itself may be helpful. What follows aims to be a nontendentious narrative of liberalism's constitutive elements:

(1) *A tripartite social order.* Consequent to the social divisions achieved by capitalism and sketched above, liberalism addresses a social ontology imagined to be divided naturally into state, economy (civil society), and family. While these realms are obviously interconstitutive and without distinct boundaries, they are analytically separated in ordinary discourse, in the domain of law, and in a range of other institutional and academic discourses from welfare policy to family psychology.[17]

---

relations. It has pitilessly torn asunder the motley feudal ties that bound man to his 'natural superiors' and has left remaining no other nexus between man and man than naked self-interest, than callous 'cash payment' " (p. 475).

[17] Largely consequent to the forces of twentieth-century capitalism, the distinctions among them are less sustainable than at any previous time in liberalism's history, as is made clear on one side by the extensive civil functions of the state and on the other by the increasing number of individuals living outside the aegis of the heterosexual nuclear family.

(2) *Unit of political analysis.* The basic unit of political analysis in liberalism is both the individual and the family, a paradox already mentioned and to which we will return shortly. For the moment, what is significant is the contrast between liberalism and those political orders in which the basic unit of political analysis is the state, tribe, estate, *polis,* city, village, kingdom, empire, class, ethnic group, or other site of collective identity.

(3) *The political.* The legitimate domain of the political in liberalism is the state. The state is also conceived as the sole domain in which political power is at play; civil society, to the extent that it is acknowledged as a domain of power, is understood as a field of *natural* power and natural social relations. (We thus speak of political intervention *in* the economy in order to describe state economic policy.) The family is cast as even more natural than civil society, or as divinely ordained and ordered, as outside history and thus fully outside convention.

(4) *The subject.* The liberal subject is the individual, a paradoxical creature whose isolation renders it quite vulnerable to "socialization" by family and society, although, as the language of socialization indicates, it has a precultural essential and transcendent nature. This nature is the foundation of the subject's presumed sovereignty. In Locke's account, "Man being born . . . with a Title to perfect Freedom . . . hath by Nature a Power to preserve[,] . . . to judge . . . and punish. . . . "[18] Liberal individuals are conceived as bundles of power, as origins of power, rather than as effects of power; socialized, rather than as socially constructed; divided by reason (objectivity) and passion (subjectivity), rather than as interpellated or subjected by discourses of "truth."[19]

(5) *Rights and liberties.* Individuals within liberalism are accorded rights and liberties by the state. These rights and liberties are exercised by individuals against each other in civil society (civil rights) and against excess arrogation of power by the state (political rights).

(6) *The state.* The state's primary and consistently legitimate function is to protect its members from dangers without and to secure citizen's rights and liberties within. The state has no higher purpose, and although it may undertake other tasks, such undertakings always cast into question state neutrality, thereby politicizing the state in ways that may result in crises of legitimation.[20]

(7) *Equality.* Civil equality consists of all citizens being subject to the same laws, and it corresponds to a presumed natural equality rooted in

[18] *Two Treatises of Government,* ed. P. Laslett (Cambridge: Cambridge University Press, 1960), pp. 366–67.

[19] I have put the matter this way to emphasize the extent to which Foucault's critique of the subject is a critique of liberal discourses of the subject.

[20] See Jurgen Habermas, *Legitimation Crisis,* trans. T. McCarthy (New York: Beacon, 1975).

our mutual subjection to nature and in our mutual endowment with the capacity to threaten or destroy one another.[21] Liberal equality thus constitutes liberal subjects as equally subjected to and by the law. "Equality before the law" means being treated *as if* we were equal, regardless of differences in our circumstances, social markings, and locations in (unavowed) relations of social powers.

(8) *Liberty.* Liberal liberty consists of acting according to one's desires where the law does not limit or proscribe them. In Hobbes's terms, "Liberty, or freedom, signifieth . . . the absence of Opposition; (by Opposition, I mean externall Impediments of motion;) and may be applyed no lesse to Irrationall, and Inanimate creatures, than to Rationall."[22] Liberties converge with rights insofar as they are individual, instrumental, and articulate boundaries between individuals.

(9) *The Good.* Values and goals are presumed to be individually discerned and pursued, neither determined nor enforced by political institutions. Debates about what values the state shall promote or proscribe, especially in the moral domain, thus constitute a distinctly illiberal discourse. Locke's *Letter Concerning Toleration* marks the privatization of values consistent with liberal political doctrine; Mill's *On Liberty* marks self-direction as an ethical imperative:

> He who lets the world, or his own portion of it, choose his plan of life for him has no need of any other faculty than the ape-like one of imitation. . . . Human nature is not a machine to be built after a model, and set to do exactly the work prescribed for it, but a tree, which requires to grow and develop itself on all sides, according to the tendency of the inward forces which make it a living thing.[23]

Michael Sandel contemporizes this formulation in his critical account of deontological liberalism: "society, being composed of a plurality of persons, each with his own aims, interests, and conceptions of the good, is best arranged when it is governed by principles that do not *themselves* presuppose any conception of the good."[24]

In brief, in this account of liberalism: The *state* is fully *conventional;* it is the domain for reconciliation of civil differences, hence a domain of *universality;* and it is the domain of "real political life" for liberals. *Civil Society* or *the economy* is *natural to man;* it is the domain where rights are

---

[21] Hobbes, *Leviathan,* ed. C. B. MacPherson (Harmondsworth, Middlesex: Penguin, 1968), p. 183; Locke, *Two Treatises,* p. 309.

[22] *Leviathan,* p. 261.

[23] John Locke, *Letter Concerning Toleration* (1689); John Stuart Mill, *On Liberty,* ed. E. Rapaport (Indianapolis: Hackett, 1978), pp. 56–57.

[24] *Liberalism and the Limits of Justice* (Cambridge: Cambridge University Press, 1982), p. 1.

exercised and individuality is expressed, hence a domain of *particularity;* and the stratifications within it constitute the domain of "real political life" for Marxists. The *family* or *personal life* is *natural to woman* and in some formulations *divinely ordained;* it is a domain governed by needs and affective ties, hence a domain of *collectivity;* and the hierarchy within it also constitutes the domain of "real political life" for feminists.

If civil society in liberal doctrine is the place where man's acquisitive, accumulative, self-interested, or "trucking and bartering" nature expresses itself, it also is defined by abutting the domain of the (unnatural) political on one side and the (hypernatural) familial on the other. While the state is conceived as forthrightly conventional, erected for the purposes of arbitrating collectively what our natural individualism will not permit, the family is something of an anchor for man in civil society, tethering what is otherwise in a kind of perpetual agitation, and civilizing and temporizing an otherwise ruthless social ethos. Hence the insistence, relatively continuous from Jean-Jacques Rousseau and John Stuart Mill to Phyllis Schlafly, that women in the family are the seat of moral restraint in an immoral world.

What is the relationship between the "naturalness" of civil society and the "naturalness" of the family in liberal doctrine? Evidently each is gendered such that the nature of man is expressed in the former while the nature of woman is realized in the latter; it could also be said that the family is natural without being fully expressive of man's nature. This suggests a certain persistence of Aristotelianism in modernity, in which the naturalness of the household grounds man but does not articulate his telos precisely because it is not a fully human domain. Consider, in this regard, Hegel's formulation of the family as necessary but insufficient to man's ethical life in civil society and freedom in the state: "Man therefore has his actual substantial life in the state, in learning, etc. and otherwise in work and struggle with the external world and with himself. . . . Woman, however, has her substantial vocation in the family, and her ethical disposition consists in this piety."[25]

There is a second dimension to the naturalness of civil society in liberalism. Conceived in terms of temporal (mythohistorical) rather than spatial relations, as a modulated and regulated version of its mythical antecedent (the state of nature), civil society may be understood as nature civilized but not transcended. Civil society is bounded with power, lined with limits, and above all disarmed, but it does not thereby lose its wildness. Put differently, for man in civil society, the state is the lid and the family is the anchor: without the hedge afforded by each, man is destruc-

---

[25] *Philosophy of Right,* ed. and trans. T. M. Knox (Oxford: Oxford University Press, 1957), paragraph 166, p. 114.

tive of both self and other; by nature he is neither internally nor socially harmonious. Yet neither the state nor the family constitutes an adequate domain for the expression of man's nature or fulfillment of his desires. In Hegel's formulation, "the disposition [appropriate to the family] is to have self-consciousness of one's individuality *within this unity* as essentiality which has being in and for itself, so that one is present in it not as an independent person but as a *member*."[26]

Many feminist critics of liberalism have commented upon the apparent contradiction between classical liberalism's representation of the state of nature as a domain of unrelieved individualism and the positing of families or mother-child bonds there. Hobbes confronts this problem directly, arguing that "the naturall inclination of the Sexes, one to another, and to their children" is not enough to bind individuals in the state of nature, and that mother and child enter instead into something of a prepolitical contract.[27] However, as Pateman points out, the terms of this contract, in which a child "obeys him by whom it is preserved," are quite inconsistent with Hobbes's formulation of contract and covenant elsewhere in *Leviathan*.[28] Locke, interestingly, deals with the problem in a more explicitly Hobbesian fashion than Hobbes. For Locke, the combination of dependency created through childrearing and woman's inferior strength creates the conditions for her attachment and subordination to men. This overdetermined argument for natural subordination contrasts sharply with Locke's assumption of the independence and equality of men among men in the state of nature and begins to reveal the gendered ontology underlying the Lockean social contract.

What Locke etches lightly, I shall argue, stands as the most coherent reconciliation of naturalized familial bonds with ontological individualism in liberalism. In brief, the unchecked individualism of the state of nature does not extend to all persons: while men are regarded as autarkic and obligated to nothing, women are regarded as always already attached to men and obligated to children. This attachment and this obligation calling forth the presence of proto-families in the state of nature in turn enable the easy naturalization of family in civil society. Conversely, this presence illuminates something of the gender of the generic person figured by liberalism: the naturalization of families means that women simply cannot be the possessive individualists men are. In this regard, the formulation of man contained in the "Rights of Man" is clearly more literal—a more meaningful and explicit omission of women—than many liberals today want to believe. This omission, as Patricia Williams argues

---

[26] *Philosophy of Right*, paragraph 158, p. 110.
[27] *Leviathan*, p. 253.
[28] Ibid., p. 254; Pateman, *Sexual Contract*, pp. 44–50.

in a different context, constitutes "a form of expression, . . . a literal part of original intent[,] . . . [an] omission that has been incorporated into a theory of neutrality."[29]

Critics of liberalism ranging from C. B. MacPherson to Roberto Unger to Michael Sandel have insisted that its implicit or explicit theories of justice, morality, psychology, and economics are predicated upon a particular kind of person that it simultaneously reflects, engenders, and distorts. But not only, as C. B. MacPherson argues, is this figure a rational calculator, driven by passionate self-interest, and expressive of the possessive individualism perfectly tailored to bourgeois acquisitiveness and accumulation:[30] he also bears an array of character attributes that confer his specifically masculine status. Fiercely autonomous and diffident, he is unencumbered by anyone or anything, independent in both senses of the term (free of dependents and dependency in civil society). He is not oriented toward relationships and persons but toward self and things. If he is "at home" anywhere, it is in the sphere of civil society insofar as his nature is expressed there and he performs all of his significant activities there. The political is an instrument to his happiness (in Marx's terms, political life in the liberal state is reduced to "a mere means"), while the household is a place to retreat *to* and emerge *from* rather than a place to *be;* it is a "man's castle" in an oddly instrumental, compensatory, and transitional sense. Household property, including women, launches rather than confers what Kant calls "civil personality": it is prerequisite to rather than constitutive of that personality.

In short, the central terms of liberal discourse assume that men circulate in civil society while women are stationed in the family—this notwithstanding the fact of women working in the wage economy (a fact that the class and gender character of classical liberal man tacitly obscures). Within liberalism, the familial haven in a heartless world, while critical for the hereditary transmission of property accumulated in civil society and as the inert anchor of man's individualistic energies, functions neither as the unit of analysis in politics nor as a unit of activity in civil society. But this is not to reiterate the conventional point that the individual, rather than any form of association, is the fallacy upon which liberal doctrine is built and to whose interests it is devoted. Rather, it is to explain how the systematic (rather than contingent) subordination of women reconciles what otherwise constitutes a persistent legal and political tension between the individual and the family in liberalism. Only by assuming women's natural subordination, by assuming woman as sup-

---

[29] *The Alchemy of Race and Rights* (Cambridge: Harvard University Press, 1991), p. 121.

[30] C. B. MacPherson, *The Political Theory of Possessive Individualism: Hobbes to Locke* (London: Oxford University Press, 1962).

plement to man, can the apparent tension between liberal individualism and liberal familialism be reconciled; only at the site of this assumption can one discern liberalism's family values.

We may arrive at the same point by reflecting on the relationship between the condition of perpetual insecurity and mortal danger in the "state of nature" and the warm safety and protectiveness held out by the liberal version of the family. If the family, like the state of nature, is a "natural condition" and as such is ordinarily beyond the purview of the state and the eyes of the law, why isn't there war of all against all here? The answer lies not in affinity or affection, which no liberal takes to be a determinant part of human nature, but in the naturalized lack of equality and competition in the family. The liberal conception of the natural cohesiveness and peacefulness of the family thus depends upon its lacking the fundamental condition of the state of nature—equality of desire and equality of ability to enact desire. Not only is brute equality prerequisite to the state of war in the state of nature, but sufficient rationality of that state's inhabitants is presumed by all state of nature theorists to argue that it is as irrational to attack as to trust when one is certain to lose. This suggests that the "natural peace" of the family is consequent to the naturalized subordination of women and children to men, revealing liberal ontology to be fundamentally rather than contingently gendered as male dominance and female submission.

The gendered character of the tension between the family and the individual as the basic unit of analysis in liberalism is discernible in an infamous passage from Blackstone's *Commentaries on the Laws of England:* "the husband and wife are one person in the law; that is, the very being, or legal existence of the woman is suspended during the marriage, or at least is incorporated and consolidated into that of the husband."[31] It is also manifest in the conventional marriage ceremony's nonparallel nominatives, "man and wife." And it is apparent as well in the persistent difficulty of establishing marital rape as rape in law and the courtroom. While many feminists attribute this resistance to sexist conventions—women's "presumed consent" to (all) sex in marriage, or women conceived as the sexual property or chattel of men in marriage—the foregoing suggests that the difficulty may inhere in the presumed nonviolence of masculine dominance in the family, a nonviolence itself made possible through institutionalized inequality. (Liberal state-of-nature theory presumes that violence inheres among equals, not between dominant and subordinate persons. Liberalism, presuming rational men, has no theory of violence practiced for reasons—psychic, erotic, etc.—independent of material gain.) Indeed, the articulation of women's personhood over the last cen-

[31] Cited in Pateman, *Sexual Contract,* p. 91.

tury reveals the extent to which female subordination is required for the sustenance of family bonds: what claims to female personhood bring to light are both the extent to which the modern family *does* resonate with the state of nature—replete with sexual and physical abuse—and the extent to which women's individuality in a world governed by the values of capital is incompatible with the maintenance of the family form.[32]

If the family naturalized by liberal doctrine is at the same time configured by liberal doctrine, the family is not ontologically *outside* of nor *prior* to civil society, but is, in the transition from feudal patriarchalism to liberal capitalism, rendered *opposite and subordinate* to civil society. From this perspective, the family (and not the state that brokers civil conflict) is civil society's "other." Within a feudal monarchical regime, the household as a productive unit stood in opposition to the state and was subjected by it; in liberalism's reconfiguration, state and civil society stand in opposition to the family—its values, concerns, activities, and putative ethos. Thus it would not appear to be the case, as Susan Okin suggests, that contemporary liberal political theorists have omitted the family from their concerns with justice—the family is not simply "left out" of liberal political thought.[33] Rather, liberalism emerges with the rise of civil society, specifies civil society as the domain proper to justice, and in doing so opposes civil society to the household or family, thus entailing a very specific theorization of the family. (Locke's argument for liberalism's legitimacy, it will be recalled, proceeds precisely by opposing political to paternal power: by defining citizens against fathers.) In this regard, those arguments put forth by putative critics of contemporary liberal theory— such as Michael Sandel and Allan Bloom—that the family is outside the purview of liberal standards of justice conform more accurately to liberalism's project of justice and its formulation of the family than do the arguments to extend liberal tenets to the family awkwardly advanced by Michael Walzer, John Rawls, or Susan Okin.[34]

[32] And at the same time, as Sheila Rowbotham pointed out years ago, emotional demands on the family intensify rather than diminish with the development of capitalism. In *Woman's Consciousness, Man's World* (Harmondsworth, Middlesex: Penguin, 1973), she writes: "The family under capitalism carries an intolerable weight: all the rags and bones and bits of old iron the capitalist commodity system can't use. Within the family women are carrying the preposterous contradiction of love in a loveless world. They are providing capitalism with the human relations it cannot maintain" (p. 77).

[33] *Justice, Gender, and the Family,* chap. 2.

[34] Sandel, *Liberalism and the Limits of Justice;* Allan Bloom, *The Closing of the American Mind: How Higher Education Has Failed Democracy and Impoverished the Souls of Today's Students* (New York: Simon and Schuster, 1987); Michael Walzer, *Spheres of Justice: A Defense of Pluralism and Equality* (New York: Basic Books, 1983); John Rawls, *A Theory of Justice* (Cambridge: Harvard University Press, Belknap Press, 1971); and Okin, *Justice, Gender, and the Family.*

. . .

If the social order presumed by liberalism is itself pervasively gendered, representing both a gendered division of labor and a gendered division of the sensibilities and activities of subjects, we should expect to find this gendering as well in the terms defining the interests, activities, and political freedom of the subject in civil society, the political subject of liberalism. The remainder of this essay outlines the ways in which the constitutive terms of liberal political discourse depend upon their implicit opposition to a subject and set of activities marked "feminine," and at the same time obscure both this dependence and this opposition.[35] The discussion proceeds by identifying constitutive dualisms in liberal discourse and then discerning how the power of the dominant term in the dualism is achieved through its constitution by, dependence upon, and disavowal of the subordinate term. Tracking how the second term is pushed out of the first in the latter's claim to primacy and power permits an understanding of how these dualisms are operations not merely of division or distinction but dominance—male dominance—at the heart of liberal discourse.

The constitutive dualisms of liberalism under consideration are

equality	difference
liberty	necessity/encumbrance
autonomy	dependence/dependents
rights	needs/relations/duties
individual	family
self-interest	selflessness
public	private
contract	consent

Perhaps with the exception of the final pair, the association of most of these antinomies with gender is not new; a range of feminist thinkers have explored them for quite diverse critical and normative purposes. My concern, however, is to establish them as specifically bound to the production and reproduction of a masculinist liberal subject, a subject premised upon a sexual division of labor and activities, a subject that persists even as this division unravels and even as it is detached from physiological correlates. What follows will also seek to establish the ways in which these gendered dualisms constitute not merely a discourse of sexual difference within liberal discourse but reveal liberalism *as* a discourse *of* male dominance.

[35] Feminine here has no transcendent or essential referent but rather refers solely to the sexual division of labor that converts itself into a gendered ontology.

Equality—Difference.   In liberalism, equality is defined as a condition of sameness, a condition in which humans share the same nature, the same rights, and the same terms of regard by state institutions. Individuals are guaranteed equality—the right to be treated the same as everyone else—because we are regarded as having a civil, and hence political, sameness. This sameness is the token of our economic and political interchangeability. However, as MacKinnon and others have made clear, while equality is cast as a matter of sameness, gender in liberalism consistently emerges as a problem of difference, or simply *as* difference: there is *human* equality on the one hand, and *gender* difference on the other. Here it is important to note that liberal equality's conceptual opposite is not inequality but difference: while inequality is the problem to which equality as sameness is the solution, difference is the problem to which equality as sameness does not apply. In liberalism, injustice occurs when those considered the same are treated differently; but ontological difference is a problem outside the purview of justice.

The consequences for gender justice of a formulation of equality as sameness and gender as difference are significant: If difference (gender) is the conceptual opposite of universal human sameness (liberal humanism), then gender difference—that is, female sexual difference—is the conceptual opposite of the liberal human being, and equality as sameness is the conceptual opposite of gender as difference. Consider that for the last decade, feminist theory classes, feminist legal theorists, and popular science journals have obsessed relentlessly over a single question: "How do women differ from men?" This question arises not because it is intrinsically an interesting or good question but because our discourse of equality is sameness and our anxiety about gender equality pertains to gender difference. Put the other way around, equality as sameness is the term that maintains difference as a problem for women (and other "others" of liberal humanism). Equality as sameness is a gendered formulation of equality, because it secures gender privilege through naming women as different and men as the neutral standard of the same.

Why can't women be included in a formulation of equality as sameness? This is to ask whether and in what respects women can be the same as men, a question that comes in many versions: Who and what is stopping them from being so? Is the "sex difference" relevant to the terms of political sameness? Which has greater *political* relevance, human sameness or sexual difference? However these questions are answered, none of them interrogates an ontology of masculine sameness, an ontology that produces a formally masculinist standard insofar as it is premised upon its *differentiation from women.* The sameness of men requires the difference that is women, just as whiteness requires people of color, heterosexuality requires homosexuality, and so forth. Put another way, differences among men are named "woman," displaced from men onto women, whose status as "difference" is then cast as intrinsic, even while it is a construction that functions less as a description of women than as the premise of men's sameness. Thus the liberal formulation of equality does not merely serve to mask privilege and social inequality insofar as it confounds formal equality before the law with substantive social equality. Rather, liberal equality is masculinist *because* its terms are sameness and difference, terms that both allegorize gender and establish gender's place within liberal discourse.

Liberty—Necessity.   Liberty, which denotes the sovereignty of the liberal subject, marks the freedom to *do* what one *desires,* the freedom to discover and pursue one's interests where the law does not interfere. Insofar as liberalism premises our liberty on a relatively unencumbered will—the possibility of choosing—and a domain of free movement—the possibility of acting—liberty signifies our sovereignty in both a subjective and a worldly sense. We are considered to have liberty when we have choices and when we have the capacity to exercise our deliberative faculty. The opposite of liberty is therefore not slavery but will-lessness and/or constraint. Just as equality is premised upon overcoming inequality but is not its opposite, liberty is what liberates us from the condition of slavery or political subjection but is not its opposite. Liberal liberty's opposite is encumbrance, constraint by necessity: barriers to deliberating, choosing, or acting. If we are free when we have free will, when the will desires and is free to act on its own behalf, we are unfree when we are without desire or aim on the one hand, and weighed down, constrained by necessity, and lacking choice or freedom of movement on the other.

Within almost any sexual division of labor in history, women have been encumbered by the bonds of necessity and the stigma of ontological immanence. Bound over time to relationships they are born to honor and tend, confined spatially to caretaking and labor in the household, women are also bound symbolically to the work their bodies are said to signify; in this sense, they are without the mark of subjective sovereignty, the capacity to desire or choose. This is what Simone de Beauvoir names "the worst curse that was laid upon woman . . . biologically destined for the repetition of Life."[36] Indeed, the "pro-choice" language of reproductive politics aims at giving women the status of choosing rather than immanent beings; in seeking to emancipate us from both semiotic and physical constraints of the female body, it asserts our right to share the voluntarist premises of liberal freedom with men. And much of the polit-

[36] *The Second Sex,* trans. H. M. Parshley (New York: Random House, 1952), p. 72.

ical language opposing abortion aims to deny women precisely this right, insisting either that a woman should not have such liberty in the first place, or that she necessarily loses this liberty when her body's "natural processes" take over, when she is *taken over* by her nature, by nature, by necessity, by another.[37] A similar rehearsal of women's relative consignment to her body transpires in political and legal arguments about rape and sexual harassment, where the question of women's own desire and self-determination remains a question so long as "consent" and "incitement" are the terms through which the sexual (non)agency of women is brokered. The character of argument in both domains reveals the gendered characteristics of liberal freedom, the extent to which the sexual and reproductive liberty of men is premised upon an immanent and constrained other.

A formulation of liberty that has as its opposite immanence, necessity, encumbrance, and external nature is not, of course, the only possible formulation of human freedom.[38] It is, rather, a notoriously bourgeois but now also evidently gendered formulation, and a formulation that depends upon and enforces a gendered division of labor in which women are encumbered while men are free, in which encumbrance and subjection by the body function as the permanent constraint on freedom. This

[37] Here, of course, familiar associations appear between nature-necessity-woman on one side and human-liberty-man on the other. What also appears is an interesting paradox of human liberty: signified by mind, actualized by body, it can be confounded by either.

[38] Some will discern a convergence between my account of liberal freedom and existential formulations of freedom. And I do mean to suggest that they share masculinist, even misogynist premises—precisely those for which de Beauvoir's *Second Sex* has often been criticized. Here is de Beauvoir:

> Every time transcendence falls back into immanence, stagnation, there is a degradation of existence into the "*en-soi*"—the brutish life of subjection to given conditions—and of liberty into constraint and contingence. This downfall represents a moral fault if the subject consents to it; if it is inflicted upon him, it spells frustration and oppression. In both cases it is an absolute evil. Every individual concerned to justify his existence feels that his existence involves an undefined need to transcend himself, to engage in freely chosen projects.
>
> Now, what peculiarly signalizes the situation of woman is that she—a free and autonomous being like all human creatures—nevertheless finds herself living in a world where men compel her to assume the status of the Other. They propose to stabilize her as object and to doom her to immanence since her transcendence is to be overshadowed and forever transcended by another ego (*conscience*) which is essential and sovereign. (pp. xxxiii–xxxiv)

De Beauvoir's argument does not question the terms of liberty from which woman as Other has been excluded; in particular, it does not identify the masculinism of a formulation of liberty that ontologically positions woman as its antithesis. Rather, her argument calls for woman's recognition as "a free and autonomous being like all other human creatures" such that she can be assimilated to this formulation of liberty, a call that falters at the site of the body.

formulation of liberty, and the identification of the liberal subject with it, requires that someone somewhere be fully bound by necessity, while others eschew this responsibility, thereby institutionally securing the un-free nature of such responsibility. In liberal discourse, of course, the do-main of avowed and naturalized encumbrance is the private, familial, sexual, and reproductive domain(s), the domains through and within which women are marked and positioned as women. The sphere of lib-erty, the sphere of civil society, is defined historically against feudal ties of encumbrance and relationality, ties that persist, as the Filmer-Locke quarrel reminds us, in the familial domain, the domain of patriarchalism now divested of political standing.

The liberal formulation of liberty is thus not merely opposed to but premised upon encumbrance; it is achieved by displacing the embodied, encumbered, and limited nature of existence onto women, a displace-ment that occurs discursively and practically through a set of assigned activities, responsibilities, and emotional attributes. Insofar as this for-mulation of liberty *requires* the existence of encumbered beings, the social activity of those without liberty, it can never be fully universalized. A liberty whose conceptual and practical opposite is encumbrance cannot, by necessity, exist without it; liberated beings defined as unencumbered depend for their existence on encumbered beings, whom their liberty in turn encumbers. In this regard, liberalism would seem to tacitly sustain rather than break with the explicit belief of the ancient citizens of Athens: some must be slaves so that others might be free.[39]

Autonomy—Dependency/Dependents.   The autonomous self and psyche of the liberal subject, whose liberty we have just considered, also derives from and inscribes a gendered sexual division of labor. The autonomy of the liberal subject has three aspects.

First, this subject, which is expressly civil rather than familial, moves about freely in civil society. He is not encumbered by conflicting respon-sibilities or demands elsewhere; he does not have dependents attached to him in civil society, making claims on him, surviving directly by his hand. This dimension of autonomy refers to the absence of immediate constraints on one's entry into and movement within civil society, and it contrasts directly with women's encumbrance by familial responsibilities that limit her movement into and within civil society.

Second, the liberal subject is autonomous in the sense that he is pre-sumed capable of providing for himself; he is not conceived as dependent

---

[39] Recall that Hannah Arendt lamented modernity's inability to sustain what she took to be "the Greeks'" appreciation of this truism. See *The Human Condition* (Chicago: Univer-sity of Chicago Press, 1958), pp. 50–73.

on others for survival or protection. Ontologically naturalized, this dimension of autonomy is facilitated by the state in its provision of collective protection and its establishment of an individual's rights not to be infringed upon by others. This dimension of autonomy also contrasts with the condition of women when they are engaged in child raising, with a culture of naturalized and legitimate violence against women, and with the construction of women as inherently emotionally dependent or needy.

The third feature of the liberal subject's autonomy pertains to a presumed self-interest and self-orientation. The subject of liberalism drawn for us by Hobbes and Locke as well as contemporary liberals and bourgeois economists is presumed to have an identity and bearing of diffident, acquisitive self-regard. Needless to say, this figure of self-interest and self-orientation is quite at odds historically with what men have wanted women to be, with what women were allowed to be, with what families have required of women, and with what women have been socially constructed to be.

These three aspects of the autonomy of the liberal subject correspond to three ways in which that subject is gendered masculine. That subject is, first, drawn in opposition to women's activity, responsibility, character, experience, and the expectations placed upon her. Indeed, the autonomous woman—the childless, unmarried, or lesbian woman—is within liberalism a sign of disordered society or nature gone awry on the one hand, or of individual failure to "adapt to femininity" on the other. Second, the autonomous subject of liberalism requires a large population of nonautonomous subjects, a population that generates, tends, and avows the bonds, relations, dependencies and connections that sustain and nourish human life. Indeed, as Adam Smith himself knew, and worried about at length in *The Theory of Moral Sentiments,* a world of unrelieved autonomous individuals is an unlivable world: it offers no bases for association and connection other than utilitarian or instrumental ones. As Durkheim and later Habermas added, such a culture is not simply undesirable but is, rather, impossible to the extent that it lacks an internal principle of cohesion. In Durkheim's formulation, market contracts require precontractual sensibilities and relations (truth telling and honor) for their viability; in Habermas's account, mass participation in a capitalist workforce depends on motivations induced by precapitalist social formations—religious, cultural, and familial—all of which capitalism weakens in the rationalizing course of its development. Finally, the putative autonomy of the liberal subject partakes of a myth of masculinity requiring the disavowal of dependency, the disavowal of the relations that nourish and sustain this subject. Male autonomy constituted in opposition to dependency and immediate responsibility for dependents is achieved by displacing both onto women, thus sustaining the fantasy of a creature who is self-sufficient and self-made from birth to death.

Put another way, the autonomous liberal subject is a fantastic figure, born into and existing wholly in the realm of civil society, who disavows the relations, activities, and subjects that sustain him in civil society from their sequestered place in the family. This creature is not only fantastic, however, but ultimately dependent: the "autonomous" subject depends on the subjection of the "dependent" ones for emotional and physical sustenance. Consequently, efforts by women to assume such autonomy are often maligned as selfish, irresponsible, or, more to the point, simply "unfeminine." If liberal autonomy were universalized, the supports upon which it rests would dissolve.

Insofar as it operates within these terms, liberal feminism finds itself in the position either of arguing for women's right to autonomous personhood, thereby joining men in the disavowals and repudiating the relations, dependents, and dependency for which women have been made responsible, or arguing for female "difference," thereby reifying the effects of this economy. Neither approach challenges the gendered division between public and private that locates civic autonomy in opposition to the family, sexuality, and reproduction. Neither approach challenges the liberal antinomy between autonomy and dependence/dependents by articulating a formulation of autonomy in the context of connection or by replacing permanent hierarchies of dependence with mutual, partial, or contingent dependencies.

Rights—Needs.   Operating as both articulations and custodians of our autonomy, rights within liberal discourse (though not necessarily in other contexts) are the political face of the sovereign subject in civil society. Even when we have rights *to* and not only against something—for example, the right to free speech—rights assertion is inevitably a propellant movement. The motion of rights is to push away or push away from—*against* others, *against* the state, *against* incursions, limitations, or encroachments upon our autonomy. Insofar as rights operate to distance and demarcate, they are a means of socially organizing us by separating us, using the fiction of our autonomy and independence to produce a social order reflecting it.[40]

---

[40] In *Alchemy of Race and Rights,* Patricia Williams makes this point from the perspective of those who have been rightless historically:

> Unlike [a white male colleague], I am still engaged in a struggle to set up transactions at arm's length, as legitimately commercial, and to portray myself as a bargainer of separate worth, distinct power, sufficient *rights* to manipulate commerce. (p. 148)

> For the historically disempowered, the conferring of rights is symbolic of all the denied aspects of their humanity: rights imply a respect that places one in the referential range of self and others, that elevates one's status from human body to social being. (p. 153)

This mode of organizing relationships in civil society contrasts sharply with the need-based familial order. It is a commonplace of liberalism that rights pertain to civil society while needs govern the family. Hence the protracted difficulties of establishing reproductive rights, rights against sexual and physical violence for family subordinates (sanctions against marital rape and battery as well as child abuse), and economic rights in the family. When women try to inject rights (and hence their autonomy and personhood) into the family, they are often reproached for infusing the family with market values, for corrupting the domain of love, need, and reciprocity with the language of contract and right. This reproach, of course, elides the potent critique of the family implicit in the feminist argument for the appropriateness of rights discourse there: to the extent that the demand for rights by subordinated subjects signifies both the presence of an oppressive or threatening power and a desire for protection from such power, such a demand challenges the myth of the family as a nonviolent sanctuary mutually cherished by all of its inhabitants. In short, the desire for rights on the part of women or children disrupts the myth of paternalism and protectionism that governs familial patriarchalism.[41]

The opposition between rights claims and needs claims corresponds not only to the opposition between civil society and the family, but to that between liberty—which rights actualize—and encumbrance—of which needs are the presumed effect. Moreover, rights relationships presume conditions of formal equality, while needs relations permit legitimate inequalities based upon "differences": for example, those between children and parents, women and men, the mentally disabled and the mentally competent. Rights relations presume autonomy and independence while relations of need presume intimacy and dependence.

However, the opposition between rights and needs is not a relation of simple mutuality or complementarity. Rather, rights and needs are constitutive and productive of each other in liberalism. The domain of rights produces a domain of need in a literal sense (as property rights produce a class of tenants and of the homeless); moreover, rights are presumed independent of need *and* are invoked to triumph over need claims ("I have a right to that whether or not you need it"). Yet rights are only viable as

---

"[W]ithout boundary" for blacks has meant not untrammeled vistas of possibility but the crushing weight of total—bodily and spiritual—*intrusion*. (p. 164)

[41] Interestingly, paternal right—a right secured in the domain of civil society and backed by law *outside* the family—is routinely invoked in both pre- and postfeminist eras to bid for a variety of male privileges, from corporal punishment of children to preventing women from aborting a man's progeny. This invocation partakes of that function of rights radically opposite to mitigating the vulnerability of the powerless insofar as it extends and legitimizes the power of the dominant.

political, social, and economic currency to the extent that needs are provided for in a rightless domain, to the extent that there is an order of need not governed by right, where life-sustaining relationships cannot be severed by the invocation of rights. As even the most adamant rights theorists will concede, a world of unrelieved rights-bearing individuals, a world ordered wholly by rights, is an unlivable world, a world without basis for connection or bonding, and a world without security for the needy and dependent. If granting women the status of full rights-bearing and rights-invoking creatures is to sanction them to act without regard for the needs of others, it is to literally unglue the social bond, a bond that now appears to be profoundly gendered. Moreover, granting women this status intensifies the disavowals entailed in liberal rights formation. As the order of rights is dependent upon a separate realm of need-satisfaction—a dependence it disavows—the rights-bearing individual disavows the provision for his needs on which his rights are premised and the order of need itself produced by his invocation of rights. Thus, while the enfranchisement of women as rights-bearing individuals formally de-links gender from definition by right and need, it does not disrupt the interconstitutive and hierarchical relationship of right and need, nor the capacity of this relationship to construe subject positions that "happen to be gendered."

Individual—Family (Self-interest—Selflessness). The concept of the individual in liberalism, while popularly contrasted with the social or the communal (as in "the individual versus society"), actually has its discursive opposite in the family. As the family dissolves individuals, individualism dissolves the family, and as woman's right to be an individual is curtailed by her identification with the family, man's relationship to the family is limited by his status as an individual.

We can see the discursive relationship between the individual and the family in liberalism more clearly by returning to the question of how liberalism claims both the individual and the family as a basic unit of analysis. Why is there ambiguity if not outright confusion in most liberal theory about the status of the family and the individual in the state of nature and in civil society? Or, why does Kant refer to women as being "without civil personality"?[42]

In liberal discourse, the individual is presumed to have roots in the family, but the family is something other than a composite of individuals. As a haven in a heartless world, it functions discursively as the background of the socially male individual. While the individual is

---

[42] *The Metaphysics of Morals,* excerpted in *Political Writings,* ed. H. Reiss (Cambridge: Cambridge University Press, 1970), p. 139.

understood to be made possible through the family—harbored, grounded, and nourished there—all cannot be individuals or there would be no family, no "it" that harbors, grounds, and nourishes. Thus, according to Hegel, while "man . . . has his actual substantial life in the state, in learning[,] . . . in work[,] . . . so that it is only through his division that he fights his way to self-sufficient unity with himself[,] . . . woman has her substantial vocation in the family."[43]

The gendered antinomy between individual and family emerges as well in the terms expressing the respective ethos of civil society and the family: "self-interest" on one hand and "selflessness" on the other. In civil society, individuals are said to exist only for themselves and the appropriate ethos is thus selfishness. In the family, (adult) individuals are expected to exist for the family, to be selfless in relation to the good of the whole. Clearly, if every individual bore a self-interested character, there could be no realm of selflessness, and if all were selfless, there would be no individuals. There are two ways of solving this problem: by splitting the subject into two, diametrically opposed psychic orientations, or by establishing a (gendered) division of psychic orientation among subjects, a division legitimated by gender ideology. Most theorists of liberalism, critical and otherwise, simply assume the latter solution; in doing so, they tacitly rather than explicitly naturalize the family and women's role within it. An interesting exception is Rousseau, who, while no admirer of liberalism, nonetheless struggles within the social formations that structure it. In *Émile,* Rousseau so meticulously crafts masculine and feminine orientations toward the self that many have accused him of contradicting his naturalistic ontologies in the production of Sophie's selfless femininity. Rousseau makes clear that Sophie's total lack of *amour de soi-meme* is required to prevent Émile's sense of self from becoming *amour propre,* that dangerous variety of self-love that is at bottom a nest of vanity and insecurity, breeding decadent and corrupting social and political behavior. In this regard, Rousseau makes clear that feminine selflessness is a *socially necessary* prop for a healthy variety of masculine selfhood; it is not simply valuable for family management but is an indispensable element of the delicate psychic economy prerequisite to civic virtue in modernity. Rousseau is thus quite explicit about a matter that his liberal kinsmen handle more indirectly: it takes two (female and male) to make one (citizen).

The antinomy between civil self-interestedness and familial selflessness suggests that liberalism is all or nothing about selves: one group surrenders selfhood so that another group can have it. This formulation, captured in the "hostile" relation between family and civil society theorized

---

[43] *Philosophy of Right,* paragraph 166, p. 114.

as a universal axiom in Freud's *Civilization and Its Discontents,* also reveals the extent to which the self-interested individual is premised upon a selfless one, indeed, draws the material and sustenance of its "self" from the selflessness of another. As the "individual" is made possible through the family it claims both to represent and support, as labor in civil society is made possible through the invisible labor of the household, so the self-interested subject of liberalism both requires and disavows its relationship to the selfless subject of the household, typically gendered female. Again, it is a commonplace that women who assert themselves as self-interested individuals confront the reproach of "selfishness," itself a metonymy for failed femininity. Accused of organizing themselves around a self they are not supposed to have, they are figured as monstrous in their departure from a (selfless) nurturant nature.[44] Conversely, if men become too selfless, even in the household, their masculinity is called into question: this is the discomforting figure of the househusband or the perverse one of the nellie queen.

Contract-Consent. Social contract theory is conventionally understood to rely mechanically, and for legitimacy, on a combination of tacit and express forms of consent. Contracts as such consist of consent to the terms of the contract by eligible parties, an eligibility determined by markers of rationality, maturity, and freedom from duress. As critics of contract theory have often pointed out, however, contract presumes individuals abstracted from relations of power or equal within those relations; ability to contract is thus equated with equality in contract. In this vein, Marxists and feminists have challenged, respectively, the validity of the measures by which workers are said to "consent" to wage work in wage contracts, or women can be said to "consent" to sex in marriage contracts or other inegalitarian settings. Both have questioned what social relations of power and inequality must be disguised in order to present those subordinated by such relations as freely consenting to choices offered them.

While concurring generally with the critiques of contract and social contract theory that these challenges proffer, I want to consider the problem of consent from a different angle, one that emphasizes the gendered relation between contract and consent. Within liberalism, contract is a civil act abstracted from relations of power: it is expressive of, and performs, formal equality and relations of distance. Consent is a more intimate act implicating relations of power; it marks the presence of power, arrangements, and actions that one does not oneself create but to which

---

[44] One only need reach back to the 1992 presidential campaign for a recent instance of such female monstrousness. Recall Republican Party and media hysteria over Hillary Clinton's disinclination to take her husband's name or "stay home and bake cookies."

one submits. (The *Oxford English Dictionary* gives one meaning of consent as "voluntary agreement to or acquiescence in what another proposes or desires; compliance, concurrence, permission.")[45] Insofar as consent involves agreeing to something the terms of which one does not determine, consent marks the subordinate status of the consenting party. Consent in this way functions as a sign of legitimate subordination.

Statutes concerning rape provide an excellent example of this. If, in rape law, men are seen to *do* sex while women *consent* to it, if the measure of rape is not whether a woman sought or desired sex but whether she acceded to it or refused it when it was pressed upon her, then consent operates both as a sign of subordination and a means of its legitimation. Consent is thus a response to power—it adds or withdraws legitimacy—but is not a mode of enacting or sharing in power. Moreover, since consent is obtained or registered rather than enacted, consent is always mediated by authority—whether in a second or third person—and is thus both constitutive of that authority and legitimated by it.[46] In these two respects, consent would appear to be profoundly at odds with radical democratic forms of equality and autonomy.

What, in this context, is the standing of the social contract as that to which we consent, tacitly or expressly, in order to acquire *civil* society? Consent here too is a mark of subordination, in this case subordination by subjects to the state they "authorize" as sovereign, as the legitimate "monopoly of violence," or as that entity invested with the powers of legislating, executing, and enforcing law. The story of the move from state of nature to civil society, whether told by Hobbes, Locke, Freud, or Rousseau, is a story of transition from ontologically imposed subjection by nature to deliberately chosen (self-imposed) subjection by the state. But this subjection, through which subjects of the state (citizens) are brought into being, is neither the whole nor the conclusion of the story. Rather, it would appear that as men collectively consent to the social contract by which they are subjected, with the aim of becoming beings

---

[45] *Oxford English Dictionary,* 2d ed., s.v. "Consent."

[46] Since "consent" is such a critical term in debates about sexuality and pornography among feminists, I want to clarify that while I am suggesting that where consent really matters, it matters because it marks relations of subordination. It is nevertheless often used—infelicitously in my view—to legitimate activities in relatively egalitarian settings. Thus, for example, feminist justifications of sadomasochism that rely on the "consensual" nature of the activity defensively address the anxiety that the manifest appearance of sexual domination or inequality might obscure the mutual desire for the activity. But this defense, rather than quelling the anxiety, probably activates it precisely by raising a subterranean specter of inequality in the language of consent. Why not say "this is her desire" rather than "she consented to what may appear as her violation"? Why is consent the only language we have for mutual agreement that is not contract, and what is revealed by the failure of language here?

individually contracting with one another, they institutionalize a condition in which women become beings consenting to individual men.[47]

. . .

If the attributes and activities of citizenship and personhood within liberalism produce, require, and at the same time disavow their feminized opposites, then the liberal subject emerges as pervasively masculinist not only in its founding exclusions and stratifications but in its contemporary discursive life. To the extent that the attributes of liberal personhood and liberal justice are established by excluding certain beings and certain domains of activity from their purview, liberalism cannot fulfill its universalist vision but persistently reproduces the exclusions of humanist Man.

The hollowness of liberalism's universalist promise, then, inheres not only in its depoliticization of invidious social powers, not only in its often cruel celebration of fictional sovereignty, but in its emergence out of and sustenance of female difference and subordination. Feminism operating with unreconstructed liberal discourse is therefore trapped. It is not just a matter of choosing between becoming persons in the generic (male) sense or struggling for recognition as women, as a difference that cannot be equality, a difference that is an ideologically ontologized division of labor. Rather, the trap consists in working with formulations of personhood, citizenship, and politics that themselves contain women's subordination, that can indeed be extended to women, or to activities inside "the family," but are not thereby emancipated from their masculinism by virtue of such extension. Moreover, to the extent that many elements of women's subordination are tied to a division of labor that does not require all biological women to occupy the position assigned their gender, the emancipation of particular women can be "purchased" through the subordination of substitutes. Put differently, the gendered terms of liberal discourse solicit the production of a bourgeois feminism that emancipates certain women to participate in the terms of masculinist justice without emancipating gender as such from those terms. In short, gender and class converge here, as every middle- and upper-class woman

---

[47] In revisiting the question of women's subjection through and by the founding of the state, a question exceeding liberal formations but reiterated within them, we are placed at the threshold of themes and thinkers beyond the scope of this chapter. These would include the fall, betrayal, or subjection of women attendant upon political foundings narrated in different registers by thinkers as diverse as Aeschylus, Machiavelli, Rousseau, Engels, and Freud. They have been analyzed with particular acuity by Norman O. Brown in *Love's Body* (Wesleyan: Wesleyan University Press, 1959), and by Melissa Matthes in "Sexual Difference, *Virtu*, and Theatricality: The Rape of Lucretia and the Founding of Republics" (Ph.D. diss., University of California, Santa Cruz, 1994).

knows who has purchased her liberty, personhood, and equality through child care and "household help" provided by women earning a fraction of their boss's wage.

One question often posed within feminist political and legal theory is whether justice for women should be sought in the masculinist terms of liberal "sameness" or in the terms of some feminist version of "difference." But if the masculinist terms of liberal discourse contain within and thereby construct a feminized other, and if "difference" is how that other is named, this ostensible dilemma would appear to be largely internal to liberalism, not disruptive of it. It is not a dilemma *between* liberalism and alternative discourses of political life, but a dilemma whose terms emerge from and reiterate liberal masculinism and thus contain few possibilities for subversive resolution.

Let us therefore pose a different question. Since it is certain that under the banner of feminism women will continue to struggle for equality within liberal regimes, are contemporary social forces such that reproduction, sexuality, and emotional work are likely to become more commodified and the social order more fractured and individualistic—in short, more masculinist for women and men alike? Are the lives of men as well as women likely to be more pervasively regulated by the unreconstructed discourses of rights, autonomy, formal equality, and liberty, not only in the domains of civil and entrepreneurial life but in the domains of childrearing, health, sexuality, and so forth? Or are the social forces such that the sovereign, rights-bearing subject of liberalism is likely to be increasingly challenged both as an empirical fiction and a normative ideal, a challenge that could signify the breakdown of historically masculinist norms governing political life? Are the political discourses of rights and autonomy being decentered by discourses of need or mutual dependency in crucial domains of public life? And do these latter discourses subvert or reiterate liberal conventions of feminine positioning and concerns? If, as seems likely, both tendencies are currently at work, both reaffirming and decentering masculinist liberal discourse, what hybrid liberal political culture is figured by their entwining? And what new cast of democratic possibility might be forged from such a culture?

CHAPTER SEVEN

Finding the Man in the State

> Every man I meet wants to protect me. Can't figure out what
> from.
> —Mae West

> State is the name of the coldest of all cold monsters.
> —Friederich Nietzsche, *Thus Spoke Zarathustra*

A MATURING feminist epistemological intelligence and late modern reflections upon the socially constructed "self" combine to obstruct easy determinations about what, other than primary and secondary sex characteristics (themselves not immune to ambiguity and tractability), may be identified with confidence as female or male, feminine or masculine, woman or man. All such determinations, whether derived from feminist readings of history, biology, philosophy, anthropology, or psychoanalysis, have foundered on the shoals of fictional essentialism, false universals, and untenable unities. In addition to these theoretical interrogations, political challenges to feminisms that are white, heterosexual, and middle class by women who are otherwise have made strikingly clear that "woman" is a dangerous and depoliticizing metonymy: no individual woman harbors the variety of modes of subjection, power, desire, danger, and resourcefulness experienced by women living inside particular skins, classes, epochs, or cultures. "All that is solid melts into air"—the sanguine "we" uttered in feminist theory and practice only two decades ago is gone for good.

Feminist theory rooted in female identity may be irreconcilable with the diverse and multiple vectors of power constructing and diversifying identity; however, feminist claims about masculine domination do not thereby disintegrate. The workings of power-producing subjects are recorded in different stories and require different tools of storytelling than the phenomenon of hegemonic or ubiquitous formations of power. Just as we can decipher the course(s) of capital even if we cannot deduce every important feature of capitalist society from this course, so we can articulate some of the mechanisms of pervasive if unsystematic male domination even if we cannot deduce the precise identity of particular women and men from such articulation. Put differently, while gender *identities* may be diverse, fluid, and ultimately impossible to generalize, particular modes of gender *power* may be named and traced with some precision at a

relatively general level. While these modes of power are themselves protean, porous, and culturally and historically specific, they are far more
circumscribable than their particular agents, vehicles, and objects. It is in
a similar vein that Foucault traces great variety in the effects of disciplinary power while grouping all these effects under the aegis of one kind of
power.[1]

For purposes of developing a feminist critical theory of the contemporary liberal, capitalist, bureaucratic state, this means that the elements of
the state identifiable as masculinist correspond not to some property contained within men but to the conventions of power and privilege *constitutive* of gender within an order of male dominance. Put another way, the
masculinism of the state refers to those features of the state that signify,
enact, sustain, and represent masculine power as a form of dominance.
This dominance expresses itself as the power to describe and run the
world *and* the power of access to women; it entails both a general claim to
territory and claims to, about, and against specific "others." Bourgeois,
white, heterosexual, colonial, monotheistic, and other forms of domination all contain these two moments—this is what distinguishes them
from other kinds of power. The two moments are interwoven, of course,
since control of vast portions of social territory—whether geographic or
semiotic—carries with it techniques of marginalization and subordination. Thus, for example, dominant discourses render their others silent
or freakish in speech by inscribing point-of-viewlessness in their terms of
analysis and adjudications of value. The powerful are in this way discursively normalized, naturalized, while the dominated appear as mutants,
disabled. In this light, Aristotle's characterization of women as "deformed males" makes perfect sense.[2]

Amid late modern circumspection about grand theory, the absence of a
comprehensive account of the masculinist powers of the state is an admit-
tedly ambiguous lack.[3] However, two overlapping sets of political devel-

---

[1] *Discipline and Punish: The Birth of the Prison*, trans. A. Sheridan (New York: Random
House, 1977).

[2] "The female is as it were a deformed male; and the menstrual discharge is semen,
though in an impure condition; i.e., it lacks one constituent, and one only, the principle of
soul" (*Generation of Animals* 737a25).

[3] A sampling of recent feminist literature on the state would include Kathy Ferguson,
The Feminist Case against Bureaucracy (Philadelphia: Temple University Press, 1984); Catharine MacKinnon, "Feminism, Marxism, Method, and the State: Toward a Feminist Jurisprudence," *Signs* 8 (1983), pp. 635–58, *Feminism Unmodified: Discourses on Life and Law*
(Cambridge: Harvard University Press, 1987), and *Toward a Feminist Theory of the State*
(Cambridge: Harvard University Press, 1989); Zillah Eisenstein, *Feminism and Sexual Equality* (New York: Monthly Review, 1984); Michèle Barrett, *Women's Oppression Today: Problems in Marxist Feminist Analysis* (London: New Left Books, 1980); Varda Burstyn,
"Masculine Dominance and the State," *The Socialist Register,* ed. Ralph Miliband and John

opments in the United States suggest the need for as full and complex a reading of the state powers that purvey and mediate male dominance as feminist theorists can achieve. First, the state figures prominently in a number of issues currently occupying and often dividing North American feminists, including campaigns for state regulation of pornography and reproductive technologies, contradictory agendas for reforms in labor, insurance, and parental leave legislation (the "difference-equality" debate in the public policy domain), and appeals to the state, at times cross-cut by appeals to the private sector, for pay equity, child support, and day care funding. Second, an unprecedented and growing number of women in the United States are today directly dependent upon the state for survival. Through the dramatic increase in impoverished "mother-headed households" produced by the socially fragmenting and dislocating forces of late-twentieth-century capitalism, and through the proliferation and vacillation in state policies addressing the effects of these forces, the state has acquired a historically unparalleled prominence— political and economic, social and cultural—in millions of women's lives.

State-centered feminist politics, and feminist debates about such politics, are hardly new. Nineteenth-century feminist appeals to the state included campaigns for suffrage, protective labor legislation, temperance, birth control, and marriage law reform. In the twentieth century, the list expanded to campaigns for equal opportunity, equal pay, equal rights, and comparable worth; reproductive rights and public day care; reform of rape, abuse, marriage, and harassment laws; and in the last decade, labor legislation concerned with maternity, as well as state

---

Saville (London: Merlin Press, 1983); Mary McIntosh, "The State and the Oppression of Women," in *Feminism and Materialism,* ed. Annette Kuhn and AnnMarie Wolpe (London: Routledge, 1978); Rosalind Petchesky, *Abortion and Women's Choice: The State, Sexuality, and Reproductive Freedom* (New York: Longman, 1984); Eileen Boris and Peter Bardaglio, "The Transformation of Patriarchy: The Historic Role of the State," in *Families, Politics and Public Policy: A Feminist Dialogue on Women and the State,* ed. Irene Diamond (New York: Longman, 1983); Carol Brown, "Mothers, Fathers, and Children: From Private to Public Patriarchy," in *Women and Revolution,* ed. Lydia Sargent (Boston: South End, 1980); Linda Nicholson, *Gender and History: The Limits of Social Theory in the Age of the Family* (New York: Columbia University Press, 1986); Eli Zaretsky, "The Place of the Family in the Origins of the Welfare State," in *Rethinking the Family: Some Feminist Questions,* ed. Barrie Thorne (New York: Longman, 1982); Rachel Harrison and Frank Mort, "Patriarchal Aspects of Nineteenth-Century State Formation" in *Capitalism, State Formation, and Marxist Theory: Historical Investigations,* ed. Phillip Corrigan (London: Quartet Books, 1980); Nancy Fraser, *Unruly Practices: Power, Discourse, and Gender in Contemporary Social Theory* (Minneapolis: University of Minnesota Press, 1989), chaps. 7, 8; Mimi Abramovitz, *Regulating Women* (Boston: South End, 1988); Jennifer Dale and Peggy Foster, *Feminists and State Welfare* (London: Routledge, 1986); *Women, the State, and Welfare,* ed. Linda Gordon (Madison: University of Wisconsin Press, 1990); and *Playing the State: Australian Feminist Interventions,* ed. Sophie Watson (London: Verso, 1990).

regulation of pornography, surrogacy, and new reproductive technologies. In North American feminism's more militant recent past, argument about the appropriateness of turning to the state with such appeals frequently focused on the value of "reform politics"—a left skepticism—or on the appropriateness of state "intervention" in familial and sexual issues—a liberal nervousness. Less often raised is the question I want to pose centrally here: whether the state is a specifically problematic instrument or arena of *feminist* political change. If the institutions, practices, and discourses of the state are as inextricably, however differently, bound up with the prerogatives of manhood in a male dominant society as they are with capital and class in a capitalist society and with white supremacy in a racist society, what are the implications for feminist politics?

A subset of this question about feminist appeals to the state concerns the politics of protection and regulation, the inescapable politics of most state-centered social policy. While minimal levels of protection may be an essential prerequisite to freedom, freedom in the barest sense of participating in the conditions and choices shaping a life, let alone in a richer sense of shaping a common world with others, is also in profound tension with externally provided protection. Whether one is dealing with the state, the Mafia, parents, pimps, police, or husbands, the heavy price of institutionalized protection is always a measure of dependence and agreement to abide by the protector's rules. As Rousseau's elegant critique of "civil slavery" made so clear, institutionalized political protection necessarily entails surrendering individual and collective power to legislate and adjudicate for ourselves in exchange for external guarantees of physical security, including security in one's property.[4] Indeed, within liberalism, paternalism and institutionalized protection are interdependent parts of the heritage of social contract theory, as "natural liberty" is exchanged for the individual and collective security ostensibly guaranteed by the state.[5]

If those attached to the political value of freedom as self-legislation or direct democracy thus have reason to be wary of the politics of protection, women have particular cause for greeting such politics with caution. Historically, the argument that women require protection by and from men has been critical in legitimating women's exclusion from some

[4] See Rousseau's "Discourse on the Origin and Foundations of Inequality among Men," in *Jean-Jacques Rousseau: The First and Second Discourses*, ed. R. Masters (New York: St. Martin's, 1964), part 2, and *The Social Contract*, book 1, chap. 4.

[5] The classic formulation of these arrangements are contained in Hobbes's *Leviathan* and Locke's *Second Treatise On Government;* the classic critic is Jean-Jacques Rousseau. For feminist commentary see Carole Pateman, *The Sexual Contract* (Stanford: Stanford University Press, 1988), and the essays in part 2 of *Feminist Challenges: Social and Political Theory,* ed. Carole Pateman and Elizabeth Grosz (Boston: Northeastern University Press, 1986).

spheres of human endeavor and confinement within others. Operating simultaneously to link "femininity" to privileged races and classes, protection codes are also markers and vehicles of such divisions among women, distinguishing those women constructed as violable and hence protectable from other women who *are* their own violation, who are logically inviolable because marked *as* sexual availability without sexual agency.[6] Protection codes are thus key technologies in regulating privileged women as well as in intensifying the vulnerability and degradation of those on the unprotected side of the constructed divide between light and dark, wives and prostitutes, good girls and bad ones.[7] Finally, if the politics of protection are generically problematic for women and for feminism, still more so are the specific politics of sexual protection, such as those inherent in feminist antipornography legislation and criminalization of prostitution. Legally codifying and thereby ontologizing a cultural construction of male sexual rapaciousness and female powerlessness, such appeals for protection both desexualize and subordinate women in assigning responsibility to the state for women's fate as objects of sexist sexual construction. Moreover, if, as I will argue, state powers are no more gender neutral than they are neutral with regard to class and race, such appeals involve seeking protection *from* masculinist institutions *against* men, a move more in keeping with the politics of feudalism than freedom. Indeed, to be "protected" by the same power whose violation one fears perpetuates the very modality of dependence and powerlessness marking much of women's experience across widely diverse cultures and epochs.

As potentially deleterious but more subtle in operation than the politics of *protection* inherent in state-centered feminist reforms are the politics of *regulation* entailed by many such reforms. Foucault, and before him Weber and Marcuse, mapped in meticulous detail "the increasing organization of *everything* as the central issue of our time" and illuminated the evisceration of human depths and connection, as well as the violent structures of discipline and normalization achieved by this process.[8] Yet with

---

[6] See Hortense J. Spillers, "Interstices: A Small Drama of Words" in *Pleasure and Danger: Exploring Female Sexuality,* ed. Carol Vance (Boston: Routledge, 1984), for what remains one of the most complex explorations of this element in the construction of African American women.

[7] See Jacqueline Dowd Hall, "The Mind That Burns in Each Body," in Vance, *Pleasure and Danger; Good Girls, Bad Girls: Feminists and Sex Trade Workers Face to Face,* ed. Laurie Bell (Toronto: Seal, 1987); and MacKinnon, *Feminism Unmodified.*

[8] Herbert Dreyfus and Paul Rabinow, *Michel Foucault: Beyond Structuralism and Hermeneutics* (Chicago: University of Chicago Press, 1982), p. xxii. See also Sheldon Wolin, *Politics and Vision: Continuity and Innovation in Western Political Thought* (Boston: Little, Brown, 1960), chap. 10. Recently, several political economists and cultural theorists have argued that this tendency—a tendency specific to modernity and especially *organized* capitalism—is

few exceptions, feminist political thinkers and activists eschew this assessment, pursuing various political reforms without apparent concern for the intensification of regulation—the pervasively disciplining and dominating effects—attendant upon them. Comparable worth policy, for example, involves extraordinary levels of rationalization of labor and the workplace: the techniques and instruments of job measurement, classification, and job description required for its implementation make Taylorism look like child's play. Similarly, state-assisted child support guarantees, including but not only those utilizing wage attachments, invite extensive state surveillance of women's and men's daily lives, work activities, and sexual and parental practices, as well as rationalization of their relationships and expectations. Given a choice between rationalized, procedural unfreedom on one hand, and arbitrary deprivation, discrimination, and violence on the other, some, perhaps even most, women might opt to inhabit a bureaucratized order over a "state of nature" suffused with male dominance. So also would most of us choose wage work over slavery, but such choices offer nowhere a vital politics of freedom.

The second historical development calling for a feminist theory of the state—the dramatic increase in impoverished, woman-supported households over the last two decades—raises a related set of issues about dependence and autonomy, domination and freedom. The statistics are familiar: today, approximately one-fifth of all women are poor and two out of three poor adults are women; women literally replaced men on state poverty rolls over the last twenty years. The poverty rate for children under six is approximately 25 percent—and is closer to 50 percent for African American and Hispanic children. Nearly one-fifth of U.S. families are officially "headed by women," but this fifth accounts for half of all poor families and harbors almost one-third of all children between three and thirteen.[9] Approximately half of poor "female-headed" households are on welfare; over 10 percent of all U.S. families thus fit the profile of being headed by women, impoverished, and directly dependent on the state for survival.[10] These data do not capture the growing

---

in decline, indeed that the hallmark of postmodernity is *disorganization*. See Scott Lash and John Urry, *The End of Organized Capitalism* (Madison: University of Wisconsin, 1987), and Claus Offe, *Disorganized Capitalism* (Cambridge: MIT Press, 1985).

[9] Ruth Sidel, *Women and Children Last: The Plight of Poor Women in Affluent America* (New York: Penguin, 1986), pp. 3, 16, 24; and Hilda Scott, *Working Your Way to the Bottom: The Feminization of Poverty* (London: Pandora, 1984), p. 19. Figures drawn from these volumes were updated with Census Bureau and Bureau of Labor Statistics data from the 1990s.

[10] "Dependence" is, of course, the terminology chosen by neoconservatives to indict the growth of the welfare state for producing a "welfare-dependent" population, a formulation that can be criticized on a number of grounds. Empirically, a small fraction of those on the welfare rolls at any one time are "chronic," i.e., are on the welfare rolls for more than two

urban homeless population, male and female, whose poverty is neither registered nor attenuated by the state.

An appreciation of the gendered characteristics of the institutions now figuring so largely in the lives of millions of U.S. poor women and children is surely critical to formulating intelligent feminist strategies for dealing with the state.[11] Indeed, quietly paralleling the controversial feminist advocacy of state regulation of pornography is an equally questionable but less hotly debated feminist insistence upon state solutions to female poverty. While Linda Gordon, Mimi Abramovitz, and a handful of other feminist welfare state critics do work to problematize this insistence, the dominant position in feminist political discourse is typified by Barbara Ehrenreich and Frances Fox Piven, who began arguing in the early 1980s that left and radical feminists must overcome their "categorical antipathy to the state."[12] In Ehrenreich and Piven's view, such indiscriminate (and implicitly unfounded) mistrust of authority and institutions obscures how potentially empowering for the women's movement is the considerable and growing involvement of women with the state—mostly as clients and workers but also as constituents and politicians. Largely on the basis of hypothetical alliances (between middle-class women in the welfare state infrastructure and their clients) and imagined

---

years. According to Fred Block and John Noakes, "welfare dependent adults" comprise fewer than one in sixteen of all adults in poverty, including those with medical and emotional problems ("The Politics of the New-Style Workfare," *Socialist Review* 18, no. 3, [1988], p. 54). Moreover, as Ehrenreich and others have pointed out, the discourse of welfare "dependence" constructs welfare clients in the degrading idiom of addiction or the condescending idiom of childhood, and it also intends to contrast the supposedly independent condition of wage workers and the dependent straits of welfare clients. What, ask socialist feminist critics of this language, is so independent about the life of a woman bound to a low-paying job for survival? (See, for example, Barbara Ehrenreich, "The New Right Attack on Social Welfare," in *The Mean Season: The Attack on the Welfare State,* ed. Fred Block et al. [New York: Pantheon, 1987], pp. 187–88.) While I am in complete accord with this critique, it also begs a critical question: insofar as the discourse of neoconservatives reflects rather than contests the discourse of the welfare state, how and in what ways does the state, through such discursive practices, *produce* dependent state subjects? If dependence on the state for survival is no "worse"—morally or economically—than dependence on the local MacDonald's franchise for survival, it is also not any less a site of production of women's lives and consciousnesses. Thus, critique of reactionary discourse *about* the welfare state opens rather than concludes a discussion of how the state constructs the women it processes.

[11] See Wendy Brown, "Deregulating Women: The Trials of Freedom under a Thousand Points of Light," *sub/versions* 1 (1991), pp. 1–8.

[12] Frances Fox Piven, "Ideology and the State: Women, Power, and the Welfare State," in Gordon, *Women, the State, and Welfare,* p. 250; and Barbara Ehrenreich and Frances Fox Piven, "Women and the Welfare State," in *Alternatives: Proposals for America from the Democratic Left,* ed. Irving Howe (New York: Pantheon, 1983).

possibilities for militant collective action (in the vein of welfare rights actions of the 1960s), Piven and Ehrenreich argue that the welfare state is not merely a necessary holding action for millions of women but constitutes the base for a progressive mass movement: "The emergence of women as active political subjects on a mass scale is due to the new consciousness and new capacities yielded women by their expanding relationships to state institutions."[13]

Ehrenreich and Piven are sanguine about precisely what I want to place in question, that U.S. women's "expanding relationships to state institutions" unambiguously open and enrich the domain of feminist political possibilities. Do these expanding relationships produce only active *political* subjects, or do they also produce regulated, subordinated, and disciplined *state* subjects? Does the late-twentieth-century configuration of the welfare state help to emancipate women from compulsory motherhood or also help to administer it? Are state programs eroding or intensifying the isolation of women in reproductive work and the ghettoization of women in service work? Do female staff and clients of state bureaucracies—a critical population in Ehrenreich and Piven's vision of a militant worker-client coalition—transform the masculinism of bureaucracy or reiterate it, becoming servants disciplined and produced by it? Considering these questions in a more ecumenical register, in what ways might women's deepening involvement with the state entail exchanging dependence upon individual men for regulation by contemporary institutionalized processes of male domination? And how might the abstractness, the ostensible neutrality, and the lack of a body and face in the latter help to disguise these processes, inhibiting women's consciousness of their situation qua women, and thereby circumscribing the impetus for substantive feminist political change?

In the interest of addressing—developing more than answering—these questions, this essay offers a contour sketch of the specifically masculinist *powers* of the late modern U.S. state. Although it does not build toward policy recommendations or a specific political program, it issues from and develops two political hunches: First, domination, dependence, discipline, and protection, the terms marking the itinerary of women's subordination in vastly different cultures and epochs, are also characteristic effects of state power and therefore cast state-centered feminist politics under extreme suspicion for possibly reiterating rather than reworking the condition and construction of women. Second, insofar as state power is, *inter alia,* a historical product and expression of male predominance in public life and male dominance generally, state power itself is surely and

[13] Piven, "Ideology and the State," p. 251; see also pp. 258–59, and Ehrenreich and Piven, "Women and the Welfare State," p. 38.

problematically gendered; as such, it gives a specifically masculinist spin to the generic problematic of the high tension and possible incompatibility between prospects for radical democracy and the growing, albeit diffused, powers of the state in the late twentieth century.

.   .   .

Discerning the socially masculine dimensions of the state requires coming to terms with the theoretical problematic of the state itself, specifically the paradox that what we call the state is at once an incoherent, multifaceted ensemble of power relations and a vehicle of massive domination. The contemporary U.S. state is both modern and postmodern, highly concrete and an elaborate fiction, powerful and intangible, rigid and protean, potent and without boundaries, decentered and centralizing, without agency, yet capable of tremendous economic, political, and ecological effects. Despite the almost unavoidable tendency to speak of the state as an "it," the domain we call the state is not a thing, system, or subject, but a significantly unbounded terrain of powers and techniques, an ensemble of discourses, rules, and practices, cohabiting in limited, tension-ridden, often contradictory relation with one another.[14] The seemingly paradoxical dimension of a nonentity exercising this degree of power and control over a population may be best captured by Foucault's account in *The History of Sexuality:*

> *Power relations are both intentional and nonsubjective.* If in fact they are intelligible, this is not because they are the effect of another instance that "explains" them, but rather because they are imbued, through and through, with calculation:

---

[14] Other feminist scholars concerned with the state have sought to grasp this feature of it. In Harrison and Mort's account, "the State should be seen not as a monolithic and unified 'subject,' but as a differentiated set of practices and institutions which at specific historical moments may stand in contradiction or opposition" ("Patriarchal Aspects of Nineteenth-Century State Formation," p. 82). According to Burstyn, "the term, 'state,' like the term 'mode of production' . . . is a generalization and abstraction. It sums up and schematises a system of relations, structures, institutions and forces which, in industrialized society, are vast, complex, differentiated and as an inevitable result, contradictory at times as well" ("Masculine Dominance and the State," p. 46). While the emphasis upon "contradiction" in each of these descriptions is meant to mark something like what I am calling the incoherence of the state, it actually does the opposite. Contradiction, as it is employed in the Marxist tradition with which Harrison, Mort, and Burstyn identify, implies a coherent system containing a basic internal logic and set of conflicts. While I do not want to deny the presence of substantive internal conflicts in state power and processes—e.g., the state's simultaneous tendency toward bureaucratic rigidity and its need for flexibility, or its steadily increasing interventionism and its dependency upon neutrality for legitimacy—I am seeking to break with an understanding of state power as systematic or even adherent to a linear political logic.

there is no power that is exercised without a series of aims and objectives. But this does not mean that it results from the choice or decision of an individual subject; let us not look for the headquarters that presides over its rationality. . . . [T]he logic is perfectly clear, the aims decipherable, and yet it is often the case that no one is there to have invented them.[15]

Insofar as "the state" is not an entity or a unity, it does not harbor and deploy only one kind of political power; to start the story a bit earlier, political power does not come in only one variety. Any attempt to reduce or define power as such, and political thinkers from Machiavelli to Morgenthau to MacKinnon have regularly made such attempts, obscures that, for example, social workers, the Pentagon, and the police are not simply different faces of the state in an indigent woman's life but different *kinds* of power. Each works differently as power, produces different effects, engenders different kinds of possible resistance, and requires a different analytical frame; at the same time, each emerges and operates in specific historical, political, and economic relation with the others, and thus also demands an analysis that can nonreductively capture this relation.

In what follows, four distinct modalities of contemporary U.S. state power are considered. These four are not exhaustive of the state's powers but each carries a feature of the state's masculinism and each has been articulated in traditional as well as feminist political thought. The *juridical-legislative* or *liberal* dimension of the state encompasses the state's formal, constitutional aspects. It is the dimension Marx, in his early writings, criticized as bourgeois, it is central to Catharine MacKinnon's and Carole Pateman's theorization of the state's masculinism, and it is the focus of the recently established field of feminist jurisprudence.[16] The

[15] *The History of Sexuality*, vol. 1, *An Introduction*, trans. R. Hurley (New York: Vintage, 1980), pp. 94–95, emphasis added.

[16] MacKinnon, *Toward a Feminist Theory of the State*, and *Feminism Unmodified*; Pateman, *Sexual Contract*. Introductions to the prolific domain of feminist jurisprudence include Christina Brooks Whitman, "Feminist Jurisprudence," *Feminist Studies* 17 (1991), pp. 493–507; Christine Littleton, "In Search of a Feminist Jurisprudence," *Harvard Women's Law Journal* 10 (1987), pp. 1–7; Heather Ruth Wishik, "To Question Everything: The Inquiries of Feminist Jurisprudence," *Berkeley Women's Law Journal* 1 (1985), pp. 64–75; Ann Scales, "Towards a Feminist Jurisprudence," *Indiana Law Journal* 56 (1981), pp. 375–444, and "The Emergence of Feminist Jurisprudence," *Yale Law Journal* 95 (1986), pp. 1373–1403; Marie Ashe, "Mind's Opportunity: Birthing a Poststructuralist Feminist Jurisprudence," *Syracuse Law Review* 38 (1987), pp. 1129–73; and Ellen C. DuBois, Mary C. Dunlap, Carol J. Gilligan, Catharine A. MacKinnon and Carrie J. Menkel-Meadow, "Feminist Discourse, Moral Values, and the Law—A Conversation," *Buffalo Law Review* 34, no. 1 (1985), pp. 11–87. Other sample literature in this genre includes Patricia Williams, *The Alchemy of Race and Rights* (Cambridge: Harvard University Press, 1991); *Feminist Legal Theory: Foundations*, ed. D. Kelly Weisberg (Philadelphia: Temple University Press, 1993); Mary Joe

capitalist dimension of the state includes provision of capitalism's moorings in private property rights as well as active involvement in capitalist production, distribution, consumption, and legitimation.[17] This dimension of the state has been sketched by Marx in his later writings and exhaustively theorized by twentieth-century neo-Marxist scholars,[18] and a number of European and North American Marxist-feminists have analyzed aspects of masculine privilege inscribed in it.[19] The *prerogative* dimension of the state pertains to that which marks the state as a state: legitimate arbitrary power in policy making and legitimate monopolies of internal and external violence in the police and military. As the overt power-political dimension of the state, prerogative includes expressions of national purpose and national security as well as the whole range of legitimate arbitrary state action, from fiscal regulation to incarceration procedures. Machiavelli and Hobbes are prerogative power's classic theorists; the analyses of war and militarism undertaken by Judith Steihm, Carol Cohn, Jean Bethke Elshtain, Nancy Hartsock, and Cynthia Enloe, as well as by nonacademic cultural and eco-feminists, have opened the terrain of prerogative state power to feminist theoretical critique.[20] The

---

Frug, *Postmodern Legal Feminism* (New York: Routledge, 1992); Martha Minnow, *Making All the Difference: Inclusion, Exclusion, and American Law* (Ithaca: Cornell University Press, 1990); and *At the Boundaries of Law: Feminism and Legal Theory*, ed. Martha Fineman and Nancy Thomadsen (New York: Routledge, 1991).

[17] The most succinct accounts of the state's involvement with "organized capitalism" are those of James O'Connor, *Fiscal Crisis of the State* (New York: St. Martin's, 1973), and *Accumulation Crisis* (London: Blackwell, 1986); Jurgen Habermas, *Legitimation Crisis*, trans. T. McCarthy (Boston: Beacon, 1975); and Claus Offe, *Contradictions of the Welfare State*, ed. J. Keane (Cambridge: MIT Press, 1984). On the postmodern state and postindustrial capitalism, see Lash and Urry, *End of Organized Capitalism*, and Offe, *Disorganized Capitalism*.

[18] In addition to the works cited in the previous note, a short list of neo-Marxist accounts of the capitalist state would include Louis Althusser, *Lenin and Philosophy* (London: New Left Books, 1971); *State and Capital: A Marxist Debate* ed. John Holloway and Simon Picciotto (London: Arnold, 1978); Fred Block, "The Ruling Class Does Not Rule: Notes on the Marxist Theory of the State," *Socialist Revolution* 7 (1977), reprinted in *Revising State Theory: Essays in Politics and Postindustrialism* (Philadelphia: Temple University Press, 1987); Ralph Miliband, *The State in Capitalist Society* (New York: Basic Books, 1969); and Nicos Poulantzas, *Political Power and Social Classes*, trans. T. O'Hagen (London: New Left Books, 1973). Surveys and analyses of these debates can be found in Martin Carnoy, *The State and Political Theory* (Princeton: Princeton University Press, 1984); David Gold et al., "Recent Developments in Marxist Theories of the Capitalist State," *Monthly Review* 27, no. 5 (1975), pp. 29–43; no. 6 (1975), pp. 36–51; and Bob Jessop, "Recent Theories of the Capitalist State," *Cambridge Journal of Economics* 1, no. 4 (1977), pp. 553–73, and *The Capitalist State: Marxist Theories and Methods* (New York: New York University Press, 1982).

[19] See Barrett, *Women's Oppression Today;* Burstyn, "Masculine Dominance and the State"; Eisenstein, *Feminism and Sexual Equality;* McIntosh, "State and the Oppression of Women"; and Zaretsky, "Place of the Family in the Origins of the Welfare State."

[20] Judith Steihm, ed., *Women and Men's Wars* (Oxford: Pergamon, 1983), and *Women's Views of the Political Worlds of Men* (Dobbs Ferry, N.Y.: Transnational, 1984); Nancy Hart-

bureaucratic dimension of the state, like the others, is expressed in tangible institutions as well as discourse: bureaucracy's hierarchicalism, proceduralism, and cult of expertise constitute one of several state "voices" and the organizational structure of state processes and activities. Classically theorized by Max Weber, cast in a narrower frame by Michel Foucault as the problematic of "disciplinary" power, this dimension of state power has been subjected to feminist critique by Kathy Ferguson.[21]

Before elaborating each of these dimensions of state power, three prefatory notes about male dominance and state power are in order. First, the argument I am here advancing is that all dimensions of state power, and not merely some overtly "patriarchal" aspects, figure in the gendering of the state. The state can be masculinist without intentionally or overtly pursuing the "interests" of men precisely because the multiple dimensions of socially constructed masculinity have historically shaped the multiple modes of power circulating through the domain called the state—this is what it means to talk about masculinist power rather than the power of men. On the other hand, while all state power is marked with gender, the same aspects of masculinism do not appear in each modality of state power. Thus, a feminist theory of the state requires simultaneously articulating, deconstructing, and relating the multiple strands of power composing both masculinity and the state. The fact that neither state power nor male dominance is unitary or systematic means that a feminist theory of the state will be less a linear argument than the mapping of an intricate grid of overlapping and conflicting strategies, technologies, and discourses of power.

A second significant feature of state and male domination and the quality of their interpenetration pertains to the homology in their characteristics—their similarly multiple, diverse, and unsystematic composition and dynamics. Apprehending and exploiting this homology entail recognizing that male dominance is not rooted, as domination by capital is, in a single mechanism that makes possible a large and complex system of social relations. What links together the diverse forms or "stages" of the economic order called capitalism—the liberal or competitive form, the monopoly or organized form, the postindustrial or disorganized form—is its linchpin of profit-oriented ownership and control of the means of production. Thus, however deeply and variously involved the state may be with capitalist accumulation and legitimation, the state's capitalist *basis* remains its guarantee of private ownership as private prop-

---

sock, *Money, Sex, and Power: Toward a Feminist Historical Materialism* (New York: Longman, 1983); Jean Bethke Elshtain, *Women and War* (New York: Basic Books, 1987); Cynthia Enloe, *Does Khaki Become You? The Militarization of Women's Lives* (Boston: South End, 1983); and *Radical America* 20, no. 1 (1986), an issue devoted to "Women and War."

[21] *The Feminist Case against Bureaucracy.*

erty rights. There is no parallel way in which the state is "male" because male dominance does not devolve upon a single or essential principle, which is why it is so hard to circumscribe and inappropriate to systematize. [22] In most cultures, male dominance includes the regularized production of men's access to women as unpaid servants, reproducers, sex, and cheap labor, as well as the production of men's monopolies of intellectual, political, cultural, and economic power. But the masculinity and hence the power of men is developed and expressed differently as fathers, as political rulers or members of a political brotherhood, as owners and controllers in the economy, as sexual subjects, as producers of particular kinds of knowledges and rationality, and as relative nonparticipants in reproductive work and other activities widely designated as women's purview. The diversity and diffuseness of masculinist power result in parallel diversity across women's experience inside the family and out, as mothers and prostitutes, scholars and secretaries, janitors and fashion models. These differences cannot be reduced to the intersection of gender with class, race, and sexuality; they pertain as well to the different effects of the multiple dimensions and domains of male power and female subordination. [23]

A related feature of the homology between masculinist and state power pertains to their ubiquitous quality. State and masculine domination both work through this ubiquitousness rather than through tight, coherent

[22] Many feminists have strained toward such systemization; none more fiercely, however, than Catharine MacKinnon. For more extended critique of this effort on MacKinnon's part, see my reviews of *Feminism Unmodified* in *Political Theory* 17 (1989), pp. 489–92, and of *Toward a Feminist Theory of the State* in *The Nation*, 8–15 January 1990, pp. 61–64.

[23] This point may be sharpened by recalling the difficulties of analyzing gender relations utilizing unreconstructed tools of Marxism. Marx and Engels posit historical constructions of the family as a function of the sexual division of labor specified by a particular mode of production. But neither the sexual division of labor nor the more general structure of power within the family are simply produced by relations of production (as Engels implies without ever really establishing). Rather, it is politically procured privileges granted to men by men that make possible the sexual division of labor as such. Political power, buttressed and conditioned by but still distinguishable from economic power, confers privileges upon men that extend beyond the privileges conferred by the sexual division of labor in any particular epoch.

Political power may be used to secure privileges other than purely economic ones. Marx elided this because his focus was class, the economic moment of society and the place where political power most closely reiterates or simply mirrors economic power. Dominant economic interests must be very nearly directly served by a capitalist state, although this may include managing contradictions and dealing with legitimacy problems. But why is the dominant class male? And why, then, are women not all one class? It is the gap between these two phenomena—the pervasiveness of male dominance and the impossibility of persuasively formulating women as a class—that makes clear the extent to which political privilege is not so closely hinged to economic dominance in the case of men as in the case of the bourgeoisie.

strategies. Neither has a single source or terrain of power; for both, the power producing and controlling its subjects is unsystematic, multidimensional, generally "unconscious," and without a center. Male power, like state power, is real but largely intangible except for the occasions when it is expressed as violence, physical coercion, or outright discrimination—all of which are important but not essential features of either kind of domination, especially in their late modern incarnations. The hegemonic effect of both modes of dominance lies in the combination of strategies and arenas in which power is exercised. Concretely, if men do not maintain some control over relations of reproduction, they cannot as easily control women's labor, and if they do not monopolize the norms and discourse of political life, they exercise much less effective sexual and economic control over women. But these strategies buttress and at times even contradict each other; they are not indissolubly linked to one another.[24] Women's subordination is the wide effect of all these modes of control, which is why no single feminist reform—in pay equity, reproductive rights, institutional access, child care arrangements, or sexual freedom—even theoretically topples the whole arrangement. The same is true of the state: its multiple dimensions make state power difficult to circumscribe and difficult to injure. There is no single thread that, when snapped, unravels the whole of state or masculine dominance.

One final prefatory note on discerning gender in the state: In the U.S. context, as well as that of other historically colonial or slave-based political economies, state power is inevitably racialized as well as gendered and bourgeois. But the white supremacist nature of contemporary state power—the specific mores and mechanisms through which state power is systematically rather than incidentally racist—are only beginning to be theorized by scholars investigating the inscription of race and race supremacy in political power, and these speculations are not further developed here.[25] What can be argued with some certainty is that while the

[24] Although drawn from outside the United States and focusing on different kinds of states than those I am analyzing here, two fascinating accounts of conflicting strands of male dominance negotiated through state policy and jurisprudence can be found in M. Jacqui Alexander, "Redrafting Morality: The Postcolonial State and the Sexual Offences Bill of Trinidad and Tobago," in *Third World Women and the Politics of Feminism*, ed. Chandra Mohanty et al. (Bloomington: Indiana University Press, 1991), and in Zakia Pathak and Rajeswari Sunder Rajan, " 'Shahbano,' " in *Feminists Theorize the Political*, ed. Judith Butler and Joan W. Scott (New York: Routledge, 1992).

[25] A sampling from this developing literature, particularly strong in Britain, would include *The Bounds of Race*, ed. Henry L. Gates, Jr., and Dominick LaCapra (Ithaca: Cornell University Press, 1990); Paul Gilroy, *There Ain't No Black in the Union Jack* (London: Hutchinson, 1987), and *The Black Atlantic: Modernity and Double Consciousness* (Cambridge: Harvard University Press, 1993); *Anatomy of Racism*, ed. David Goldberg (Minneapolis: University of Minnesota Press, 1990); Stuart Hall, *Race Articulation and Societies Structured in*

racialized, gendered, and class elements of state power are mutually constitutive as well as contradictory, the specific ways in which the state is
racialized are distinctive, just as the gendered aspects of state power are
analytically isolatable from those of class, even while they mingle with
them historically and culturally. In other words, however these various
modes of social, political, and economic domination intersect in the daily
constitution and regulation of subjects, as modes of political power they
require initially separate genealogical study. To do otherwise is to reiterate the totalizing, reductionistic moves of Marxist theories of power and
society, in which analysis of one kind of social power, class, frames all
modes of domination.

. . .

Let us now fill out the four modalities of masculinist state power sketched
above.

1. The Liberal Dimension.   Liberal ideology, legislation, and adjudication is predicated upon a division of the polity into the ostensibly autonomous spheres of family, civil society (economy), and state. In classical as
well as much contemporary liberal discourse, the family is cast as the
"natural" or divinely given—thus prepolitical and ahistorical—part of
the human world. Civil society is also formulated as "natural" in the
sense of arising out of "human nature," although the civility of civil society is acknowledged by liberal theorists to be politically "achieved" and it
is also within civil society that the rights guaranteed by the (nonnatural)
state are exercised. In the classic liberal account, the state is the one conventional and hence fully malleable part of this tripartite arrangement; it
is constructed both to protect citizens from external danger and to guarantee the rights necessary for commodious commerce with one another.
  The problem with this discourse for women has been rehearsed extensively by feminist political theorists such as Carole Pateman, Catharine

---

Dominance (Paris: UNESCO, 1980); Manning Marable, *Race, Reform, and Rebellion: The
Second Reconstruction in Black America, 1945–1982* (London: Macmillan, 1984); Martha Min-
now, *Making All the Difference;* Michael Omi and Howard Winant, *Racial Formation in the
United States: From the 1960s to the 1980s* (London: Routledge, 1986); Peter Scranton, *The
State of the Police* (London: Pluto, 1985); Cornel West, *A Genealogy of Racism* (London:
Routledge, 1990); Wahneema Lubiano, "Like Being Mugged By a Metaphor: The World-
ing of Political Subjects," in *Multiculturalism?* ed. Avery Gordon and Christopher Newfield
(Minneapolis: University of Minnesota Press, 1994); and Kimberle Crenshaw, "De-
marginalizing the Intersection of Race and Sex: A Black Feminist Critique of Anti-
discrimination Doctrine, Feminist Theory, and Antiracist Politics," *The University of
Chicago Legal Forum* 139 (1989), pp. 139–52.

MacKinnon, and Lorenne Clark. First, since the family is cast as natural and prepolitical, so also is woman, the primary worker within and crucial signifier of the family, constructed in these terms. In this discourse, women are "naturally" suited for the family, the reproductive work women do is "natural," and the family is a "natural" entity. Everywhere nature greets nature and the historical constructedness and plasticity of both women and the family is nowhere in sight. As the family is depoliticized, so is women's situation and women's work within it; recognized neither politically nor economically as labor, this work has a discursively shadowy, invisible character.[26] Second, since much of women's work and life transpires in the "private" or familial realm, women's involvement with the place where rights are conferred and exercised—civil society—is substantially limited by comparison with men. Thus, even when women acquire civil rights, they acquire something that is at best partially relevant to their daily lives and the main domain of their unfreedom. Third, historically the "private sphere" is not actually a realm of privacy for women to the extent that it is a place of unfettered access to a woman by her husband and children. "Privacy is everything women . . . have never been allowed to have; at the same time the private is everything women have been equated with and defined in terms of men's ability to have."[27] Insofar as it arises as a realm of privacy from other men for men, the private sphere may be the last place on earth women experience either privacy or safety—hence the feminist longing for a "room of one's own" within men's "haven in a heartless world." In classical formulations of liberalism, rights do not apply in this sphere; rather this realm is constructed as governed by norms of duty, love, and custom in addition to nature, and until quite recently it has been largely shielded from the reach of law. Indeed, the difficulties of establishing marital rape as rape, wife battering as battery, or child abuse as abuse derive, *inter alia,* from liberal resistance to recognizing personhood inside the household; in the liberal formulation, persons are rights-bearing individuals pursuing their interests in civil society.[28] Thus Tyrell

---

[26] See Sheila Rowbotham, *Woman's Consciousness, Man's World* (Harmondsworth, Middlesex: Penguin, 1973), chap. 4.

[27] MacKinnon, "Feminism, Marxism, Method, and the State," p. 656.

[28] The "right to privacy," tenuously established by the Supreme Court in *Griswold v. Connecticut,* generally deplored by conservatives and defensively clung to by liberals, perfectly expresses this difficulty with recognizing personhood in the household. In the sphere of the family, the Court recognizes household privacy in lieu of rights attendant upon civil persons. For critiques of the right to privacy along these lines, see Catharine MacKinnon, "The Male Ideology of Privacy: A Feminist Perspective on the Right to Abortion," *Radical America* 17, no. 4 (1983), pp. 23–35, and Wendy Brown, "Reproductive Freedom and the 'Right to Privacy': A Paradox for Feminists," in Diamond, *Families, Politics, and Public Policy.*

in the eighteenth century, and Kant and Blackstone in the nineteenth, argued that it was reasonable for women to be politically represented by their husbands because "women have no civil personality"—they exist only as members of households, while personhood is achieved in civil society.[29] Within liberalism, the nonpersonhood of women, the extra-legal status of household relations, and the ontological association of both with nature are all mutually reinforcing.

According to the very origins myths of liberalism, men come out of the "state of nature" to procure rights for themselves *in* society; they do not establish the state to protect or empower individuals inside families.[30] The relevance of this for contemporary analysis lies in its revelation of the masculinism at the heart of the liberal formulation of political and civil subjects and rights: the liberal subject is a man who moves freely between family and civil society, bearing prerogative in the former and rights in the latter. This person is male rather than generic because his enjoyment of his civil rights is buttressed rather than limited by his relations in the private sphere, while the opposite is the case for women: within the standard sexual division of labor, women's access to civil society and its liberties is limited by household labor and responsibilities. Liberalism's discursive construction of the private sphere as neither a realm of work nor of power but of nature, comfort, and regeneration is inherently bound to a socially male position within it; it parallels the privileging of class entailed in bourgeois characterizations of civil society as a place of universal freedom and equality.

One problem with liberal state power for women, then, is that those recognized and granted rights by the state are walking freely about civil society, not contained in the family. Women doing primary labor and achieving primary identity inside the family are thus inherently constrained in their prospects for recognition as persons insofar as they lack the stuff of liberal personhood—legal, economic, or civil personality. They are derivative of their households and husbands, subsumed in identity to their maternal activity, and sequestered from the place where rights are exercised, wages are earned, and political power is wielded. Moreover, because the liberal state does not recognize the family as a political entity or reproduction as a social relation, women's situation as unpaid workers within the family is depoliticized. Finally, while women

---

[29] From Blackstone's *Commentaries on the Laws of England:* "By marriage, the husband and wife are one person in law; . . . the very being or legal existence of the woman is suspended" (cited in Carole Pateman, "Women and Consent," *Political Theory* 8 [1980], pp. 152, 155).

[30] Hobbes, *Leviathan,* ed. C. B. MacPherson (Harmondsworth, Middlesex: Penguin, 1968), pp. 223–28; Locke, *Two Treatises of Government,* ed. P. Laslett (Cambridge: Cambridge University Press, 1960), pp. 361–77.

have now been granted roughly the same panoply of civil and political rights accorded men, these rights are of more limited use to women bound to the household and have different substantive meaning in women's lives. It is as gratuitous to dwell upon an impoverished single mother's freedom to pursue her own individual interests in society as it is to carry on about the property rights of the homeless.

This last point raises a final consideration about the liberal state's maleness, one suggested by the work of thinkers as different from each other as Luce Irigaray and Carol Gilligan.[31] The liberal subject—the abstract individual constituted and addressed by liberal political and legal codes—may be masculine not only because his primary domain of operations is civil society rather than the family, but because he is presumed to be morally if not ontologically oriented toward autonomy, autarky, and individual power. Gilligan's work suggests that social constructions of gender in this culture produce women who do not think or act like liberal subjects, that is, in terms of abstract rights and duties. For Gilligan, insofar as women develop much of their thinking and codes of action within and for the comparatively nonliberal domain of the family, relationships and needs rather than self-interest and rights provide the basis for female identity formation and decision-making processes. While Irigaray moves in the domain of philosophy and psychoanalysis rather than empirical social science, her insistence that "the subject is always masculine" is predicated upon a convergent account of the repudiation of dependency entailed in the psychic construction of the male subject.

By incorporating selected insights from these thinkers, I do not mean to suggest that there is something *essentially* masculine about the liberal subject or state. Supplementing either the theoretical or empirical accounts with historical, cultural, and political-economic components, one could plausibly argue that liberal discourse and practices are the basis for the social construction of bourgeois masculinity rather than the other way around. But causation is a poor analytical modality for appreciating the genealogical relationship between masculinity and liberalism, a relationship that is complexly interconstitutive. One effect of this genealogy is that the liberal state not only adjudicates for subjects whose primary activities transpire in civil society rather than the family, but does so in a discourse featuring and buttressing the interests of individualistic men against the *mandatory* relational situation of women in sequestered domains of caretaking. Similarly, not only does the liberal state grant men access to women in the private sphere by marking the private sphere as a

---

[31] Carol Gilligan, *In a Different Voice* (Cambridge: Harvard University Press, 1982); Luce Irigaray, "The Subject Is Always Masculine," in *This Sex Which Is Not One*, trans. C. Porter (Ithaca: Cornell University Press, 1985). See also Nancy Hartsock's formulation of "abstract masculinity" in *Money, Sex, and Power*.

natural and need-ordered realm largely beyond the state's purview, it requires that women enter civil society on socially male terms. Recognition as liberal subjects requires that women abstract from their daily lives in the household and repudiate or transcend the social construction of femaleness consequent to this dailiness, requirements that in addition to being normatively problematic are—as every working woman knows— never fully realizable. Thus, not merely the structure and discourse but the ethos of the liberal state appears to be socially masculine: its discursive currencies are rights rather than needs, individuals rather than relations, autogenesis rather than interdependence, interests rather than shared circumstances.

2. The Capitalist Dimension.   The masculinism of the capitalist dimension of the state, like that of the liberal dimension, is also moored in a public/private division, albeit one that moves along a somewhat different axis. In this division, men do paid "productive" work and keep women in exchange for women's unpaid work of reproducing the male laborers (housework), the species (child care), and caring for the elderly or infirm. The sexual division of labor historically developed by capitalism is one in which almost all women do unpaid reproductive work, almost all men do wage work, and the majority of women do both.

A large portion of the welfare state is rooted in capitalist development's erosion of the household aspect of this division of labor, in the collapse of the exchange between wage work in the economy and unpaid work in the family and the provision of household care for children, old, and disabled people that this exchange secured. But as feminist scholars of the welfare state Mimi Abramovitz, Nancy Fraser, and Linda Gordon make clear, the fact that the familial exchange process has broken down does not mean that capitalism and the capitalist state are no longer structured along gender lines.[32] First, these arrangements, on which the "family wage" and unequal pay systems were based, leave their legacy in women's sixty-four-cents-on-the-dollar earning capacity and ghettoization in low-paying jobs. Second, unpaid reproductive work continues, and continues being performed primarily by women, even though this work is increasingly (under)supported by the welfare state rather than by a male wage. Consequently, ever-larger numbers of working- and middle-class women are doing all of life's work—wage work, child care, domestic labor, sustenance and repair of community ties—within an economy that remains organizationally and normatively structured for

[32] Abramovitz, *Regulating Women;* Gordon, introduction to *Women, the State and Welfare;* Fraser, "Struggle over Needs" and "Women, Welfare, and the Politics of Need Interpretation," in *Unruly Practices.*

male wage earning and privilege insofar as it assumes unpaid female labor, and especially child care, in the home.

In *Capital,* Marx speaks ironically of the double sense in which the worker within capitalism is "free": he is free to dispose of his own labor as a commodity and he is free from any other means of sustaining himself (i.e., property). Women, of course, do not bear the first kind of "freedom" when they are engaged in reproductive work—they cannot "freely" dispose of their labor as a commodity or "freely" compete in the labor market. This is one of the mechanisms by which capitalism is fundamentally rather than incidentally gendered. Indeed, as long as significant parts of domestic labor remain outside the wage economy and women bear primary responsibility for this work, women will be economically dependent on someone or something other than their own income-earning capacities when engaged in it.

The social transformation we are currently witnessing is one in which, on the one hand, for increasing numbers of women, this dependence is on the state rather than individual men; on the other hand, the state and economy, rather than individual men, are accorded the service work of women. While much work historically undertaken in the household is now available for purchase in the market, women follow this work out into the economy—the labor force of the service sector is overwhelmingly female.[33] Thus, as capitalism has irreversibly commodified most elements of the private sphere, the domain and character of "exchange" in the sexual division of labor has been transported from the private and individualized to the public and socialized. The twin consequences are that much of what used to be women's work in the home is now women's work in the economy and that the state and economy, rather than husbands, now sustain many women at minimal levels when they are bearing and caring for children.

In sum, the capitalist dimension of the state entails women's subordination on two levels. First, women supply unremunerated reproductive labor, and because it is both unremunerated and sequestered from wage work, most women are dependent upon men or the state for survival when they are engaged in it. Second, women serve as a reserve army of low-wage labor and are easily retained as such because of the reproductive work that interrupts their prospects for a more competitive status in the labor force.[34] The state's role in these arrangements lies in

---

[33] Sidel, *Women and Children Last,* pp. 61–62.

[34] There is no better testimony to this than the "workfare" clauses of welfare enacted by the 1988 Family Support Act, stipulations that will do little to break "the cycle of poverty" or "the feminization of poverty" but will supply millions of cheap, docile female workers to the economy during a predicted shortfall of low-wage labor in the coming decade. Not ten years earlier, Reagan publicly named women in the workforce as a prime cause of high male

securing, through private property rights, capitalist relations of production in the first place; buttressing and mediating—through production subsidies, contracts, bailouts, and fiscal regulation—these relations of production; maintaining—through legal and political regulation of marriage, sexuality, contraception, and abortion—control of women's reproductive work; and perpetuating, through a gendered welfare and unemployment benefits system and the absence of quality public day care, the specifically capitalist sexual division of labor.[35]

3. *The Prerogative Dimension.*   Prerogative power, the state's "legitimate" arbitrary aspect, is easily recognized in the domain of international state action. Here, as Hegel reminds us, "the Idea of the state is actualized"—the state expresses itself as a state and is recognized as such by other states.[36] For Locke, the occasional imperative of maximum efficiency and flexibility of state action in both the domestic and international arena justifies the cultivation and deployment of prerogative power.[37] Among political theory's canonical figures, however, it is neither Hegel nor Locke but Machiavelli who treats most extensively the dynamics and configurations of prerogative power—its heavily extralegal, adventurous, violent, and sexual characteristics. Machiavelli theorizes political power in a register in which violence, sexuality, and political purpose are thoroughly entwined, precisely the entwining that signals the presence of prerogative power.[38]

That an early-sixteenth-century Florentine could illuminate this feature of the late modern U.S. state suggests that unlike liberal, capitalist, and bureaucratic modalities of state power, prerogative power is not specific to modernity. Indeed, for liberals, prerogative power is the liberal state's expressly nonliberal dimension. Classical liberal thought depicts princely prerogative as precisely what liberalism promises to diminish if not can-

---

unemployment rates. Reagan was not alone: very few politicians advocated workfare for female welfare clients in 1980.

[35] See Barbara Nelson, "The Origins of the Two-Channel Welfare State: Workmen's Compensation and Mother's Aid," and Nancy Fraser, "Struggle Over Needs," in Gordon, *Women, the State, and Welfare.* See also Abramovitz, *Regulating Women.*

[36] *Philosophy of Right,* trans. T. M. Knox (Oxford: Oxford University Press, 1957), p. 209.

[37] *Two Treatises,* pp. 421–27. See also Sheldon Wolin, "Democracy and the Welfare State: The Political and Theoretical Connections between *Staatsräson* and *Wohlfahrtsstaatsräson,*" in *The Presence of the Past: Essays on the State and the Constitution* (Baltimore: Johns Hopkins University Press, 1989).

[38] In addition to Machiavelli's *oeuvre,* see Hanna Pitkin, *Fortune Is a Woman* (Berkeley: University of California Press, 1984); Wendy Brown, *Manhood and Politics: A Feminist Reading in Political Theory* (Totowa, N.J.: Rowman and Littlefield, 1988); and Wolin, "Democracy and the Welfare State."

cel: historically, monarchical power is dethroned, and mythically, the state of nature (in which everyone has unlimited prerogative power) is suppressed. In this regard, the emergence of liberalism is conventionally conceived as the advent of an epoch in which political organization bound to the privileges of the few is usurped by the needs of the many, in which *raison d'état* shifts from power to welfare, in which the night watchman replaces the prince. But there is another way of reading the origins of the liberal state, in which the arbitrary and concentrated powers of monarchy are not demolished. Rather, princely power is dissimulated and redeployed by liberalism as state prerogative that extends from war making to budget making. In this reading, the violence of the state of nature is not overcome but reorganized and resituated in, on the one hand, the state itself as the police and the military, and, on the other, the zone marked "private" where the state may not tread and where a good deal of women's subordination and violation is accomplished.

Max Weber's tale of origins about the state is quite suggestive for mapping the connections between the overt masculinism of international state action (the posturing, dominating, conquering motif in such action) and the internal values and structure of state-ruled societies. According to Weber, the state has a double set of origins. In one set, organized political institutions are prefigured in the formation of bands of marauding warriors, "men's leagues," who live off, without being integrated into, a particular territorial population and who randomly terrorize their own as well as neighboring populations. In the other, institutionalized political authority is prefigured in the earliest household formations, where male or "patrimonial" authority is rooted in a physical capacity to defend the household against the pillaging warrior leagues.[39]

The first set of origins, which features a combination of predatory sexuality, territoriality, violence, and brotherhood in warrior league activity, certainly adduces a familiar face of prerogative power—egregious in the ways of street gangs, rationalized and legitimized in most international state activity. In this vein, what Charles Tilly calls "war making and state making as organized crime" Ortega y Gasset conjures as the

---

[39] *Economy and Society*, ed. G. Roth and C. Wittich (Berkeley: University of California Press, 1978), pp. 357–59. Other theorists have suggested that these fraternal organizations reveal the extent to which what we call politics is rooted in "male juvenile delinquency" insofar as the warriors raped and pillaged not out of necessity, as a Marxist reading would have it, but for sport, fun, and prestige. Underscoring the intensely homosocial nature of the leagues and the quintessential expression of their power in the abduction and gang rape of young women from neighboring tribes, these authors posit a gendered and sexual rather than economic underpinning to all political power and political formations. See Norman O. Brown, *Love's Body* (Wesleyan: Wesleyan University Press, 1959), and José Ortega y Gasset, "The Sportive Origin of the State," in *History as a System and Other Essays toward a Philosophy of History* (New York: Norton, 1961).

"sportive origins of the state," and Norman O. Brown anoints "the origins of politics in juvenile delinquency[:] . . . politics as gang rape." All posit, *contra* Marx, a gendered and sexual rather than economic underpinning to the political formations prefiguring states.[40] But if we add to this picture the second strain of Weber's origins story, that concerned with the foundations of male household authority, it becomes clear how contemporary prerogative power constructs and reinforces male dominance across the social order, and not only through overtly masculinist displays of power by the Pentagon or the police.

In Weber's account, while warrior leagues are initially consociated "beyond and above the everyday round of life," they are eventually "fitted into a territorial community," at which point a recognizable "political association is formed."[41] This association presumably retains many of the characteristics it had as a more mobile enterprise, especially its foundation in organized violence, which, for Weber, is *the* identifying characteristic of the state. During this transition, the social structure of the territorial population shifts from one of mother-children groups to father-headed households. The authority of the adult male, Weber suggests, derives not from his place in the division of labor but from his physical capacity to dominate and defend his household, a capacity significant only because of the omnipresent threat to household security posed by the warrior leagues.[42] Thus, male household authority would appear to be rooted in its provision of protection from institutionalized male violence. In other words, the patriarchal household and its legitimate structure of authority arise not merely as an economic unit but as a barrier between vulnerable individuals and the sometimes brutal demands or incursions of the state's prefigurative associations. This arrangement is codified and entrenched through asymmetrical legal privileges and an asymmetrical sexual division of labor: household patriarchs "protect" dependent and rightless women from the violence of male political organization. In this respect, the state is an insignia of the extent to which politics between men are always already the politics of exchanging, violating, protecting, and regulating women; the one constitutes the imperatives of the other.

Widely disparate Western political origins stories, from those of the Greek tragedians to Freud to modern social contract theorists, resonate with Weber's. In each, a single event or process heralds the disempowering and privatizing of women on the one hand and the emergence of

[40] Charles Tilly, "War Making and State Making as Organized Crime," in *Bringing the State Back In,* ed. P. Evans et al. (Cambridge: Cambridge University Press, 1985); Ortega y Gasset, "The Sportive Origin of the State," pp. 26–32; Brown, *Love's Body,* p. 13.

[41] *Economy and Society,* p. 906.

[42] Ibid., p. 359.

formal political institutions on the other. According to these stories, the birth and consolidation of organized political power *entails* women's loss of power and public status. Moreover, once the women are conquered and the men are organized, the supreme political organ of society guarantees individual men access to individual women and protects each man's claim to his woman against infringement by other men. Thus, the basic narrative is always a version of Freud's contract among the brothers after they have killed the father: to prevent the situation that necessitated the patricide, they erect the state and through it convenant to keep their hands off each other's women, thereby relaxing the tension that an absent father introduces into a brotherhood. From this perspective, the "private" sphere appears to be necessary for this deal to work: it is the place of access to women by men, a place outside the eyes or reach of law and other men, where every man is "king in his own castle." The threshold of the home is where the state's purview ends and individual man's begins. Not surprisingly, this threshold—what it marks, prohibits, and contains—is among the boundaries most actively contested and politicized by contemporary feminist jurisprudence concerned with marital rape, battery, property rights, reproductive rights, and other issues relevant to woman's achievement of personhood or "civil personality."

These stories articulate a basic political deal about women, a deal arranged by men and executed by the state, comprising two parts: one between men and the other between the state and each male citizen. In the first, the state guarantees each man exclusive rights to his woman; hence the familiar feminist charge that rape and adultery laws historically represent less a concern with violations of women's personhood than with individual men's propriety over the bodies of individual women. In the second, the state agrees not to interfere in a man's family (de facto, a woman's life) as long as he is presiding over it (de facto, her).[43]

According to Weber's version of these arrangements, the character of political power concerned with security, protection, or welfare is shaped by the ultimate "power purposes" of a political organization. This suggests that the gendered structure of liberalism is partly determined by the gendered character of prerogative power, in which women are cast as

[43] In short, the state's purview begins where man's ends, and there lies the rub for millions of poor women today, since these arrangements contain only two possibilities for women who cannot singlehandedly provide for themselves and their families. Either the state guarantees the rights of the man in their lives or the state *is* the man in their lives. The state stays outside the household door unless there is no man presiding over the home; at that point, if the state assumes the provider role, it also assumes as much about its access rights to a woman's space as any man could ever display. The infamous AFDC "man in the house" rule was the concrete expression of this: Two men—the state and a woman's boyfriend or husband—could not be in the woman's home at the same time, but each was guaranteed access to her and her home in the absence of the other's claim.

requiring protection from the world of male violence while the superior status of men is secured by their supposed ability to offer such protection. For Weber, the modern legacy of the warrior leagues lies in the state's telos of domination, realized through territorial monopoly of physical violence and resulting in a "legitimate authority" predicated upon this domination. This reading of state origins also leads Weber to formulate politics and the state as appropriately concerned not with the well-being of the population but with what he terms the "prestige of domination."[44] The legitimacy of prerogative power is rooted in the state's pursuit of self-affirmation through displays of power and prestige, and not in protection or sustenance of human life.

The problem here is one most feminists can recite in their sleep. Historically, women have been culturally constructed and positioned as the creatures to whom this pursuit of power and glory for its own sake stand in contrast: women preserve life while men risk it; women tend the mundane and the necessary while men and the state pursue larger-than-life concerns; men seek immortality while women look after mundane affairs; men discount or threaten the realm of everyday life while women nurture and protect it. Simone de Beauvoir casts this not as an ideology or discourse of gender, but as indeed the factual history of gender's origin:

> The warrior put his life in jeopardy to elevate the prestige of the horde, the clan to which he belonged. And in this he proved dramatically that life is not the supreme value for man, but on the contrary that it should be made to serve ends more important than itself. The worst curse that was laid upon woman was that she should be excluded from these warlike forays. For it is not in giving life but in risking life that man is raised above the animal; that is why superiority has been accorded in humanity not to the sex that brings forth but to that which kills.[45]

The problem then, lies not in women's exclusion from the domain of prerogative state power but in its gendered character. The distinction between daily existence preserved by women and the male pursuit of power or prestige through organized violence simultaneously gives a predatory, rapacious, conquering ethos to prerogative power and disenfranchises women from this kind of power. Conventional constructions of masculine sexuality (as opposed to masculine rationality, interests, or privileges) are heavily featured in this domain because this dimension of state power is more immediately visceral and corporeal than, for exam-

[44] *Economy and Society,* pp. 910–11; Arthur Mitzman, *The Iron Cage: An Historical Interpretation of Max Weber* (New York: Knopf, 1970), p. 82.

[45] *The Second Sex,* trans. H. M. Parshley (New York: Random House, 1952), p. 72.

ple, bureaucratic or juridical power, both of which tend to organize and work on bodies without touching them so directly.

The masculinism of state prerogative power inheres in both its violent and its transcendent (i.e., above life) features, as well as in their relation: women are the "other" of both these moments of prerogative power as well as the conduit between them. Yet because prerogative power appears to its subjects as not just the power to violate but also the power to protect—quintessentially the power of the police—it is quite difficult to challenge from a feminist perspective. The prerogative of the state, whether expressed as the armed force of the police or as vacillating criteria for obtaining welfare benefits, is often all that stands between women and rape, women and starvation, women and dependence upon brutal mates—in short, women and unattenuated male prerogative.[46]

4. The Bureaucratic Dimension.   Max Weber and Michel Foucault formulate bureaucratization and its normalizing, disciplining effects as *the* distinct and ubiquitous domination of our age.[47] Neither limits this mode of domination to the state; to the contrary, each regards the modern filtration of bureaucracy or disciplinary institutions across the social order as precisely what permits a decrease in the overt exercise of (prerogative) state power without a corresponding decline in political and social control.[48] Indeed, one of the most significant aspects of bureaucratization is its blurring of a clear line between state and civil society. Consider the proliferating social services bureaucracies, regulative bureaucracies, and military-(post)industrial complexes: the purview of each involves institutionalized penetration and fusion of formerly honored boundaries between the domain of political power, the household, and private enterprise.

In *The Feminist Case against Bureaucracy,* Kathy Ferguson employs the insights of Foucault and Weber to explore two different moments of masculinism in bureaucratic power. She argues first that bureaucratic power "feminizes" bureaucratic staff and clientele by rendering them dependent and submissive and by forcing them into strategies of impres-

[46] For an unequivocal expression of the view that the state insulates women from more brutal victimization by sexism, see Frances Fox Piven and Richard A. Cloward, "The Contemporary Relief Debate," in Block et al., *The Mean Season:* "[J]ust as the availability of income supports helps people cope with the vagaries of the labor market, so does it reduce the helplessness of women and children in the face of the weakening of the traditional family" (p. 97).

[47] *Economy and Society,* pp. 223, 987, 1393–94; and "Politics as a Vocation," in *From Max Weber,* ed. H. H. Gerth and C. W. Mills (New York: Oxford University Press, 1946), p. 82; Foucault, *Discipline and Punish.*

[48] In Weber's understanding this is the triumph of rational legal authority; in Foucault's, it is the supplanting of sovereign or juridical power with disciplinary power.

sion managing that "protect them from the worst aspects of domination while simultaneously perpetuating that domination." Second, she insists that bureaucratic discourse is masculinist insofar as it bears what Carol Gilligan, Nancy Chodorow, Nancy Hartsock, and others identify as socially male values of abstract rationality, formal proceduralism, rights orientation, and hierarchy, while opposing or colonizing socially female values of substantive rationality, need-based decision making, relationality, and responsibility.[49] For Ferguson, the masculinism of bureaucratic discourse thus lies in a dual production: it creates *feminized* subjects while it excludes or colonizes *female* subjects.

Ferguson's distinction between "femininity" and "femaleness" is drawn from the complexity of women's experience as subordinates (the site of production of "femininity") *and* as caregivers (the site of production of "femaleness"). However, insofar as these are not separate sites of activity and women do not actually have these experiences separately, the distinction would appear to be rooted in a false essentializing of femaleness as caregiving.[50] Moreover, if bureaucracy's creation of subordinates *is* the process of feminization, then bureaucratic domination and male domination each lose their singularity; in assimilating them to each other, gender and bureaucracy both disappear as specifiable kinds of power. Domination in Ferguson's analysis thus begins to appear flatly generic, notwithstanding her effort to distill distinctly feminized modes of coping with subordination.

More persuasive than Ferguson's argument about bureaucracy's feminization of subjects is her account of the way the structures and values of bureaucracy—hierarchy, separation, abstract right, proceduralism—stand in relation to what she posits as women's socially constructed experience as caregivers. When measured by the norms of bureaucratic discourse, the values of a caregiving milieu appear immature or irrational: this is the political face of Gilligan's critique of the norms of Kohlberg's development psychology. Not only does bureaucratic discourse perpetuate the devaluation of practices oriented toward need and care, it carries the state's masculinism in agencies and agents dealing with women as caregivers insofar as it both judges its female clients in masculine terms and constructs them as feminized dependents.

[49] *Feminist Case against Bureaucracy*, pp. 92, 158–69.

[50] Ferguson certainly seeks to avoid such essentialism by identifying as a *political struggle* the "complex process of calling out that which is valuable in each gender and carefully disentangling it from that which is riddled with the effects of power" (*Feminist Case against Bureaucracy*, p. 170). However, in this formulation—which distinguishes what is "riddled with power" from what is not—and in her identification of "women's experience" as "*distorted* by oppression," there does seem to persist a notion of a female experience, if not subjectivity, that is unconstructed or undistorted by power and hence essential to a particular set of beings or activities.

Ferguson's critique of bureaucracy by no means exhausts the possible range of bureaucratic power's masculinist features. I have argued elsewhere that the instrumental rationality constituting both the foundation of bureaucratic order and the process of bureaucratic rationalization is grounded in the social valorization of maximized power through maximized technocratic control.[51] This particular expression of a will to power—domination through regimes of predictability, calculability, and control—appears to be socially masculine in the West insofar as the ultimate value is control, and the uncontrollable as well as that which is to be controlled—external nature or the body politic—are typically gendered female in these discourse. Finally, bureaucratic power quite obviously "serves" male dominant interests through its disciplinary function: state agencies of every variety create disciplined, obedient, rule-abiding subjects. This aspect of bureaucracy's involvement with masculine dominance does not require that bureaucratic power itself be masculinist, only that it be an effective instrument of domination and that the policies it executes are gendered, whether they be enacted through HUD, the IRS, or military regulations. In this mode, bureaucracy's regulatory and disciplining capacities enable and mask male dominant interests external to bureaucracy, much as Foucault casts the disciplinary organization of schools and hospitals as auxiliaries of a generalized aim of social control. The fact that bureaucracy as discipline is both an *end* and an *instrument,* and thereby operates *as power* as well as *in the service of other powers,* all the while presenting itself as extrinsic to or neutral with regard to power, makes it especially potent in shaping the lives of female clients of the state.

. . .

As the sites and registers of women's relationships to the state expand in late modernity, both the characteristics and the meaning of the state's maleness transmogrify. Ceasing to be primarily a domain of masculinist powers and an instrument of male privilege and hegemony, albeit maintaining these functions, the state increasingly takes over and transforms the project of male dominance. However, as it moves in this direction, the state's masculinism becomes more diffuse and subtle even as it becomes more potent and pervasive in women's lives. Indeed, while the state replaces the man for many women, its jurisprudential and legislative powers, its welfare apparatus, and even its police powers often appear as leading agents of sex equality or female protection. In this regard, the late modern state bears an eerie resemblance to the "new man" of pseudo-

[51] *Manhood and Politics,* chap. 8.

feminist infamy. Beneath a thin exterior of transformed/reformed gender identity and concern for women, the state bears all the familiar elements of male dominance. Through its police and military, the state monopolizes the institutionalized *physical* power of society. Through its welfare function, the state wields *economic* power over indigent women, arbitrarily sets the terms of their economic survival, and keeps them dangling and submissive by providing neither dependable, adequate income level nor quality public day care.[52] Through age-of-consent laws on contraception, regulation of abortion and other reproductive technologies, and stipulating that mothers be heterosexual and free of substance abuse, the state controls and regulates the *sexual* and *reproductive* construction and condition of women. Through its monopoly of political authority and discourse, the state mediates the *discursive, semiotic,* and *spatial* terms of women's political practices. Thus, while the state is neither hegemonic nor monolithic, it mediates or deploys almost all the powers shaping women's lives—physical, economic, sexual, reproductive, and political—powers wielded in previous epochs directly by men.

In short, in precise contrast to Foucault's argument about the declining importance of the state in the disciplinary age, *male* social power and the production of female subjects appears to be increasingly concentrated in the state. Yet like the so-called new man, the late modern state also represents itself as pervasively hamstrung, quasi-impotent, unable to come through on many of its commitments, because it is decentralizing (decentering) itself, because "it is no longer the solution to social problems," because it is "but one player on a global chessboard," or because it has forgone much of its power in order to become "kinder, gentler." The central paradox of the late modern state thus resembles a central paradox of late modern masculinity: its power and privilege operate increasingly through disavowal of potency, repudiation of responsibility, and diffusion of sites and operations of control.

We may now return to Piven and Ehrenreich's claim, rehearsed earlier, about the ostensibly radical potential inherent in women's growing involvement with the state. Such an argument depends upon a Marxist conviction about the inevitably radicalizing effects of collectivizing subjects previously isolated and dispersed in their oppression.[53] This conviction in turn presumes a transcendental subject, a subject who simply *moves* from isolated to collectivized conditions, as opposed to a subject who *is produced* or engendered by these respective conditions. In this regard, Piven and Ehrenreich's analysis is impervious to how the discursive

[52] Wolin, "Democracy and the Welfare State," pp. 160–63.

[53] "The welfare state brings together millions of poor women who depend on welfare state programs. These constituencies are not . . . simply atomized and therefore helpless people. Rather the structure of the welfare state itself has helped to create new solidarities" (Piven, "Ideology and the State," p. 260).

and spatial disciplinary strategies of the late modern workplace and state affect workers or state clients. Just as microelectronics assembly plants in Third World Free Trade Zones do not simply employ women workers but produce them—their bodies, social relations, sexualities, life conditions, genders, psyches, consciousnesses[54]—the state does not simply handle clients or employ staff but produces state subjects, as bureaucratized, dependent, disciplined, and gendered. Put another way, capitalism's steady erosion of the liberal boundary between public and private, its late-twentieth-century disruption of the boundary between household and economy, and the politicization of heretofore private activities such as reproduction and sexuality achieved by these developments do not automatically generate political consciousness or struggles for freedom any more than the state's increasing entanglement with the economy automatically generates working-class consciousness or militance.[55] Again, this is because the state does not simply address private needs or issues but configures, administers, and produces them. While Piven speaks of women as "partly liberated from the overweening power of men by the 'breakdown' of the family,"[56] what is "liberated" from the private sphere may then be colonized and administered by one or more dimensions of masculinist state power. Indeed, the state may even assist in separating individuals and issues from the "private" sphere in order to effectively administer them. This is certainly one way of reading the workings of birth control legislation in the nineteenth century, and surrogacy legislation and "squeal laws" requiring parental notification in the late twentieth.[57] It is also an important caution to feminists evaluating current

[54] On the production of a new culture of female workers in Free Trade Zones, see the excellent pamphlet by Annette Fuentes and Barbara Ehrenreich, *Women in the Global Factory* (Boston: South End, 1983).

[55] In *Legitimation Crisis*, Habermas argued that the "recoupling" of the economic and political spheres effected by "advanced capitalism" would inherently repoliticize the economy and thereby intensify the state's legitimation problems (see pp. 46–48, 68–70). While this move from market capitalism (and its attendant ideology of inequality produced by natural forces) to state-administered and thereby politicized capitalism has certainly occurred, Habermas underestimated North Americans' tolerance for state-administered economic inequality.

[56] "Ideology and the State," p. 259.

[57] In the United States, nineteenth-century recognition of women in the household as separate legal personalities barely preceded state regulation of contraception, abortion, and female labor—state recognition of women as persons thus facilitated state regulation of women's sexuality and of reproductive and productive work (see Boris and Bardaglio, "The Transformation of Patriarchy," pp. 73–74). State recognition of women as persons becomes a means of control, for anything must be separated out from a mass, individuated, to be efficiently and effectively controlled. As Foucault reminds us, the key mechanisms of disciplinary power are precisely those of individuation and isolation. "Discipline is a political anatomy of detail[.] . . . disciplinary space tends to be divided into as many sections as there are bodies or elements to be distributed" (*Discipline and Punish*, pp. 139, 143).

proposals by the Clinton administration to "end welfare as we know it," whose chief strategy appears to be workfare administered individually to women by "personal social workers." Here, not only intensified regulation of poor women at the individual level but greater levels of integration between invasive bureaucratic state power and the low-wage economy are the specters haunting the future of poor women's lives.

However important "the family" remains—particularly in its absence—in constructing the gendered unconscious, it is decreasingly the daily superintendent of masculine dominance in late modern life. Today, women's struggles for social, political, and economic freedom in the United States more often transpire in or near the domain of the state, whether these concern issues of poverty, welfare benefits and regulations, in vitro fertilization, abortion, day care, surrogacy, teenage reproductive rights, sexual freedom (including the rights and claims of sex workers), affirmative action, education, or employment. From what I have argued about the historical legacies and contemporary reworkings of masculinism in state powers, it is clear that there are dangers in surrendering control over the codification of these issues to the state, as well as in looking to the state as provider, equalizer, protector, or liberator. Yet like male dominance itself, masculinist state power, consequent to its multiple and unsystematic composition, is something feminists can both exploit and subvert, but only by deeply comprehending in order to strategically outmaneuver its contemporary masculinist ruses.

Index

David
Nugent   257-283